C000215473

HEIRS TO TIBET

ANDREW POWELL

Heirs to Tibet

Travels Among the Exiles in India

HEINEMANN : LONDON

William Heinemann Ltd
Michelin House, 81 Fulham Road, London SW3 6RB
LONDON MELBOURNE AUCKLAND

First published 1992

A CIP catalogue record for this book
is held by the British Library
ISBN 0 434 59932 8

Phototypeset by Wilmaset Ltd, Birkenhead, Wirral
Printed in Great Britain
by Clays Ltd, St. Ives plc

For Jennifer, who had to stay at home

'. . . all agree in describing the Tibetans as kind, gentle, honest, open and cheerful. They are humorous, able to enjoy leisure, intelligent, and self-reliant; and they accord a high position to women. They have inborn good manners. . . . The good treatment . . . of their domestic animals has impressed many travellers.'

Tibet and its History, Hugh Richardson

CONTENTS

ACKNOWLEDGEMENTS

Writers who travel must surely incur the heaviest debts of gratitude. Adequate recognition of the kindness shown to me would inevitably run to a dozen pages.

In brief then, my profound thanks must go first to my friend and companion, Tenzin, for his good nature, patience and infinite courtesy. Certainly this book could not have been written in its present form without him. Nor would it be easy to overstate the contribution of his wife, Lisa, who provided unflagging support and helped to arrange many of the tedious logistics of our travels together.

Among the hundreds of Tibetans who generously gave their time and hospitality, I would particularly like to thank Geshe Tenzin Tethong, Private Secretary to HH the Dalai Lama, for his good-humoured help and advice, and Rapten and Khando Chazotsang for delicious meals and zestful conversation at their home in Dharamsala.

In England I am particularly indebted to Graham Harrison and Rebecca Willis for their constant encouragement; to my literary agent, Lisa Eveleigh, for her soothing voice and ego-support; to Tom Weldon and

Emma Rhind-Tutt at Heinemann for their professional skill and saintly forbearance and above all to Jennifer Sharp, who put up with writer's block and writer's gloom with consistent and heroic fortitude. Finally I would like to remember my faithful companion during long hours at the word-processor: Lucy, a black cat of elegant appearance, affectionate nature, and unexampled literary taste.

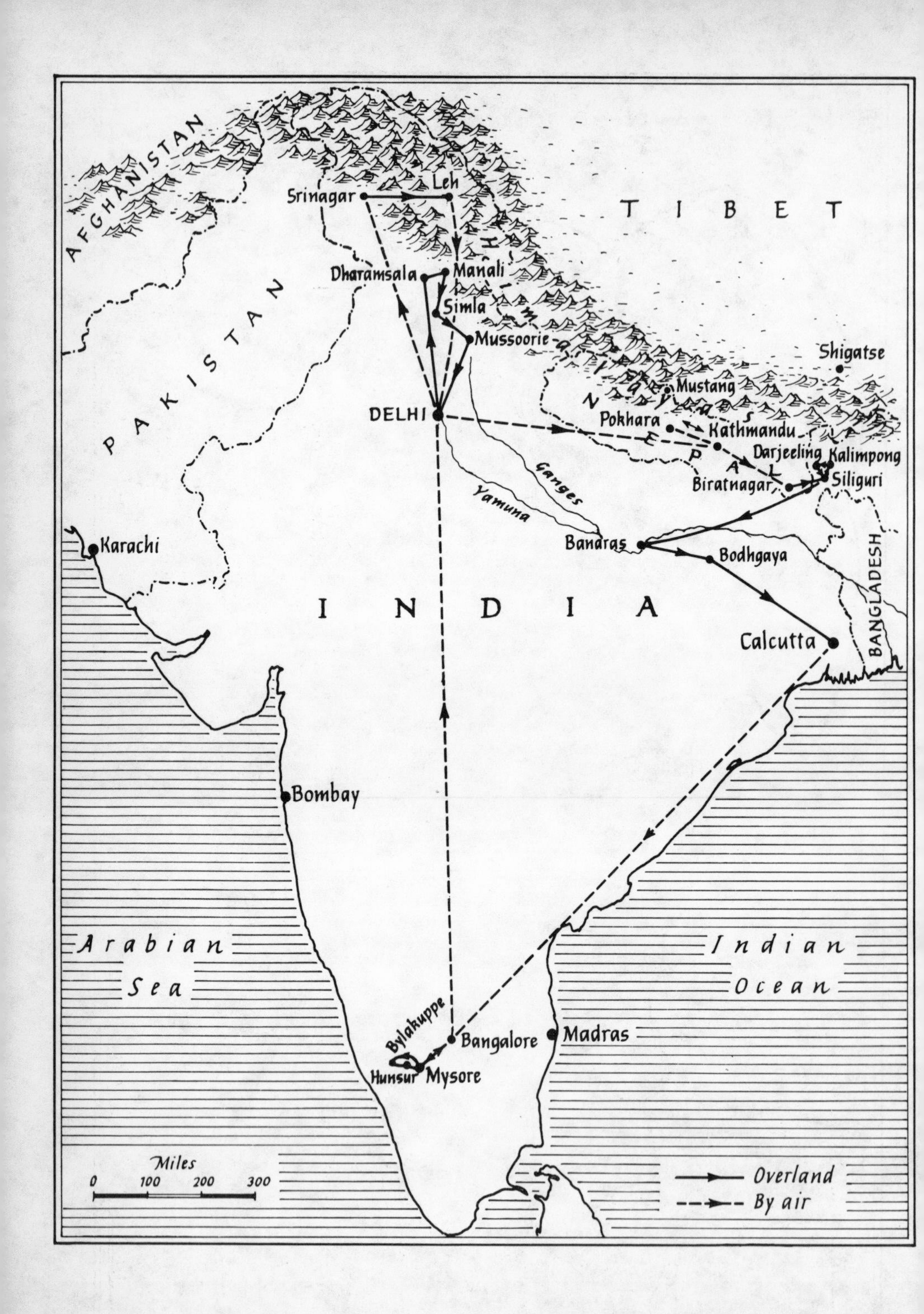

AFGHANISTAN
PAKISTAN
TIBET
INDIA
NEPAL
BANGLADESH
Himalayas
Srinagar
Leh
Dharamsala
Manali
Simla
Mussoorie
DELHI
Shigatse
Mustang
Pokhara
Kathmandu
Darjeeling
Kalimpong
Biratnagar
Siliguri
Ganges
Yamuna
Banaras
Bodhgaya
Calcutta
Karachi
Bombay
Arabian Sea
Indian Ocean
Bylakuppe
Bangalore
Madras
Hunsur
Mysore
Miles
0 100 200 300
Overland
By air

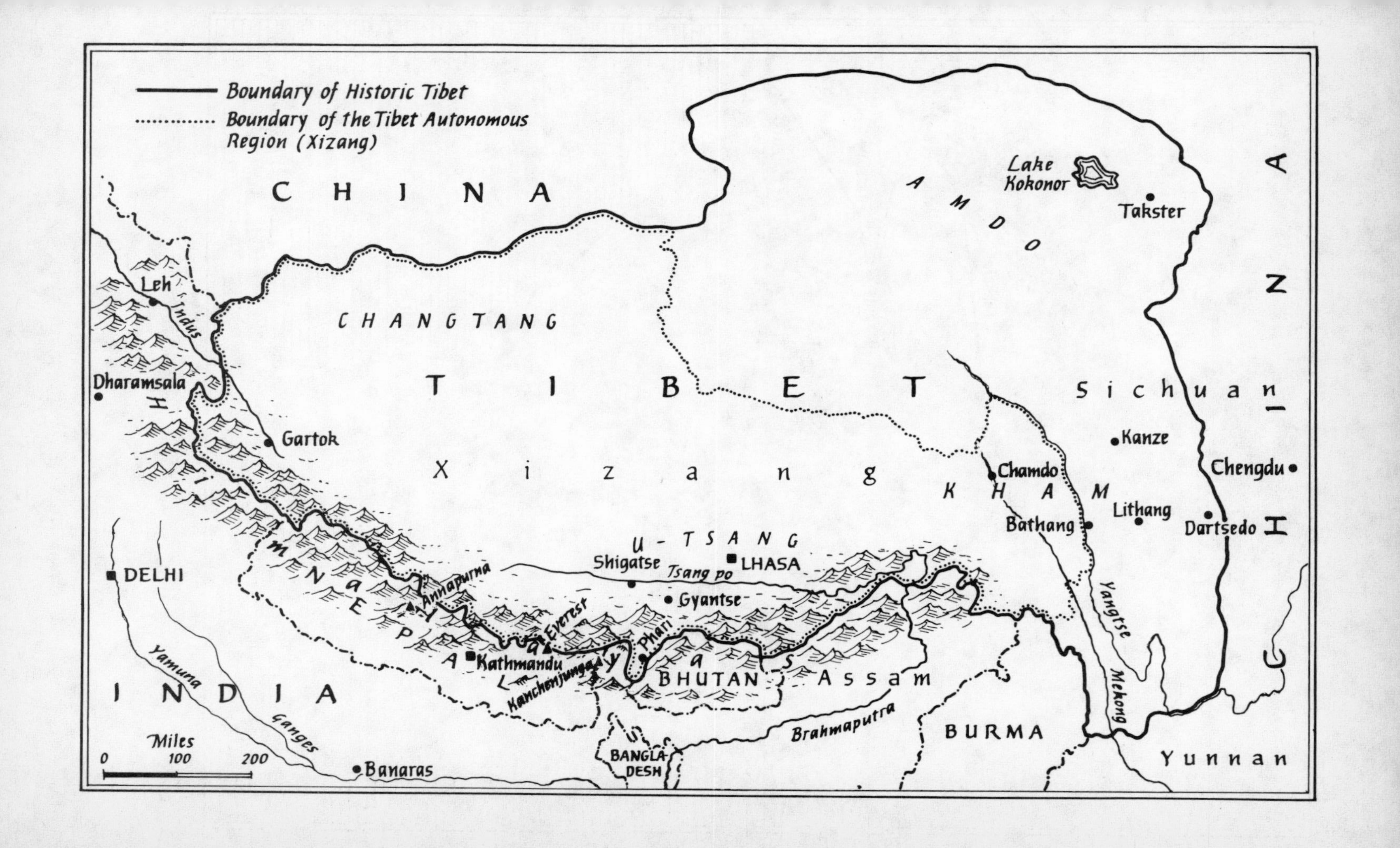

Boundary of Historic Tibet
Boundary of the Tibet Autonomous Region (Xizang)
CHINA
CHANGTANG
TIBET
Xizang
AMDO
KHAM
U-TSANG
Lake Kokonor
Takster
Sichuan
Kanze
Chengdu
Chamdo
Lithang
Bathang
Dartsedo
Yangtse
Mekong
Yunnan
Leh
Indus
Dharamsala
Gartok
HIMALAYA
Shigatse
Tsang po
LHASA
Gyantse
Annapurna
Everest
Kathmandu
Kanchenjunga
Phari
NEPAL
BHUTAN
Assam
Brahmaputra
BURMA
BANGLA DESH
DELHI
INDIA
Yamuna
Ganges
Banaras
Miles
0
100
200

Prologue

LHASA – 1987

Ten o'clock on a sunny April morning, the sky a serene and flawless blue. Not just a flat blue ceiling, but a shining, translucent blue that draws the eye further and further out into empty space and infinity. A Tibetan sky.

Spring was clearly on its way as many of the trees on the path up to Sera were bright with blossom, their winter branches decked out with exuberant tufts of boudoir pink. The summits of the bare hills that surround the Lhasa Valley had been dusted overnight with snow, but in general the atmosphere was blithe and genial.

Parking my bike in the deep, chilly shadow of a mud-brick wall, I slogged up the hill. The ground was sticky: not from rain, but from thawing frost. To the left of the track fifteen or twenty people, an even mixture of men and women, were hard at work on a building site. The men were swinging picks, or digging, while the women carried away baskets of earth and stones. One man was planing down what looked like roof timbers. Yellow curls of wood lay around him in the mud like fallen petals.

It was April 1987 and a thaw in China's foreign

relations was fully underway. Deng Xiaoping was still a friend of the West, a man who had lifted the bamboo curtain, undergone a Pauline conversion to market economics, and declared himself pleased to take a softer line on China's so-called 'minority peoples'.

A full two years had yet to elapse for this dapper figure to become 'the Butcher of Tiananmen Square', for his neat grey, collarless suit to be caked – metaphorically speaking – in the blood of his people, and for his Stalinist alter ego to announce itself unashamed of the slaughter. Anyway, what slaughter? What massacre?

Which is why on that sunny spring morning I was able to stand on the path leading up to Sera monastery, idly watching some Tibetans rebuilding an accommodation block for the monks. More than twenty years had passed since the terror of the Cultural Revolution, when Sera, in common with virtually every other religious building in Tibet, had been dynamited, reduced to a miniature Dresden, and when those monks who had not already been shot or hustled off to labour camps had been driven away, defrocked, or casually murdered.

Before the Chinese invasion of 1950, Buddhist monasteries had been repositories of Tibetan civilisation and a principal pillar of Tibetan national identity. In the 1920s, Sir Charles Bell, British Political Officer in Sikkim, had estimated that they contained up to a quarter of the entire male population. And in Tibetan eyes this was quite logical. After all, if the religious life is superior to that of the layman, then a properly regulated society will enable as many of its members as possible to put aside the petty business of the world and to devote themselves to eternity.

This, however, was scarcely an attitude calculated to appeal to Maoist ideologues. By 1966 the pure flame of revolution was ablaze in China, purging the land – at least in theory – of the corrupt accretions of centuries. An attempt was underway to obliterate history: the same impetus to return to 'Year Zero' which a few years later would inspire Pol Pot to transform Cambodia into an overcrowded necropolis.

In China's colony, Tibet, the young zealots charged with carrying out the 'Destroy the Four Olds' campaign – ideology, culture, habits, and customs – ran amok and vented on the unfortunate Tibetans not just their political fervour, but that ancient hatred – born of fear and contempt – that the Han Chinese have, for immemorial centuries, felt for the 'barbarian' peoples of Asia. The same fear that induced them to build a defensive wall 1,500 miles long; the same contempt that obliged all ambassadors to the Middle Kingdom to kowtow before their emperor, who alone among rulers had been invested with divine authority to rule over the disparate peoples of the earth. By the time the fury of the Cultural Revolution had burnt itself out, around 5,000 monasteries and temples had been laid to waste: perhaps 95 per cent of the religious buildings in the entire country. In 1968, the year that modish apparatchiks took their Maoist banners to the streets of Paris, Tibet was a land of ashes, rubble, and mass graves – unreported, untelevised, and forgotten.

Things had certainly improved since then. Whether or not the Tibetans working on the reconstruction of Sera were doing so under Chinese orders (for Peking had belatedly recognised the power of the tourist dollar), or whether they had voluntarily donated their labour, seemed relatively unimportant. These people, happily toiling in the mild spring air, were clearly enjoying their work, doing what they felt to be needful and right. Ever since Hu Yaobang, then General Secretary of the Chinese Communist Party, had come to Lhasa in 1980 and pronounced himself shocked at what he had found, life for the Tibetans had, little by little, improved. To be sure the waves of Chinese colonists kept on coming and a system of apartheid continued in such minor matters as education and the provision of housing, but at least the frenzied iconoclasm was over and the midnight knock on the door had become somewhat less frequent. Possessing a photograph of the Dalai Lama was still theoretically a criminal offence – carrying a penalty of several years' imprisonment – but in fact they were freely available in the Barkor street market, at the centre of the ancient city.

The whole Barkor area was rapidly becoming a mini Kathmandu, with hundreds of young Americans and Europeans passing through on their way to Nepal. In the officially sanctioned bookshop there might still be large framed photographs of Mao and Stalin, but at the Hotel Banak Shöl there was a paperback library of insurrectionist Western literature, where every evening travellers would meet to trade useful information and virulently anti-Chinese opinions. Under the pretext of teaching English, one or two people even claimed to have been living in the hotel for a year or more.

Down the path towards me came a small party of monks, all dressed in coarsely woven, burgundy-coloured robes. They had evidently come to inspect the restoration work. There were six of them, but apart from one venerable figure, the crown of whose head was grizzled with silver stubble, they were all very young: certainly less than thirty years old. Only the older man would be able to remember a time before the arrival of the Chinese, when the young Dalai Lama was still on his throne and the Buddhist clergy were the real power in the land.

Plodding on up the hill I came to the main hall of the monastery. Its substantial masonry had emerged from the Cultural Revolution relatively intact, even though many images and books had been carted away to be smashed, burned or sold onto the international art market. Of the three great monasteries in or near Lhasa – Sera, Drepung, and Ganden – Sera is the best preserved, while of Ganden almost nothing remains. I stepped inside. There was no one else around. The dominant colour was a deep, rich red. Even the strong white light streaming in through windows high up near the roof became soaked with crimson before it had penetrated more than a few feet. From the massive supporting pillars hung long silk *thankas* – banners made of scarlet and gold appliqué, bearing religious images or motifs – while on the floor, rows of mats covered in reddish brown cloth led up to the gilded images of the Sera's fifteenth-century founder, several Dalai Lamas, and a colossal Buddha whose head disappeared through the ceiling into the building's upper storey.

Such prayer halls are undeniably impressive. On some occasions they strike me as mysterious and compelling – the product of an ancient and inscrutable civilisation – while at other times their magnificence speaks more of power and wealth than of sanctity and I find myself resenting the domination of an oppressive materialism. Religion was both Tibet's greatest achievement and its society's greatest bane. Tibetan Buddhism was both the inspiration of philosophy, music, art, and architecture, the cohesive influence which bound together Tibet's thinly scattered peoples, and the reactionary force which prevented the development of political institutions, the spread of education, the birth of a secular literature,and the acceptance of useful technology. Ultimately it was the church which insisted on Tibet's isolation from the rest of the world and it was her isolation more than her lack of military preparedness which in the end allowed the Chinese to occupy the country with impunity.

Outside again in the sunshine, I climbed a small hill and sat looking down over the site and the northern outskirts of Lhasa. Every summer, in the old days, the grassy fields around Sera, known as *lingkas*, were the stage for Lhasa's annual holiday. Groups of players, sponsored by the various aristocratic families, would perform the long Tibetan folk operas, or *lhamo*, in the open air. Tents were erected, picnics spread out, and for a week or more the inhabitants of the capital devoted themselves entirely to pleasure. Down by the Kyichu River, archery contests and horse racing provided rival attractions. The well-born and the affluent put on lavish clothes and went out on display, while the humbler citizens, in no way excluded, wandered idly among the competing distractions. The show was free. It was a time – or so I have been told – when class barriers came down and a spirit of licensed democracy prevailed. Such occasions perhaps presented Tibetan society in its most favourable light and saw the national character at its most cheerful, fun-loving and open-handed. Heedless of the outside world and desiring nothing more than to be left in peace, the Tibetans devoted themselves to gentle entertainments and harmless pastimes.

My efforts to imagine these lyrical scenes were rudely interrupted by a strident metallic voice, bolstered by martial music, coming from the grim concrete huddle of a nearby compound. Next to many surviving Tibetan monasteries, the Chinese, in their amiable way, have built either a factory or a barracks. Doubtless the monks were intended to reflect on the shame of absenting themselves from the task of socialist construction, or on their political impotence, or both.

One of the chief functions of public loudspeakers in Mao's China was to divide the day into work periods. The entire nation was supposed to leap from bed simultaneously and from then on until bedtime, to submit the pattern of their waking hours to the implacable regimen of a disembodied voice. No angelus bell or muezzin ever exercised an authority remotely as absolute. The one minor drawback to this system was that territory under Chinese control covered a very large area and when it was time to get up in Peking it was still the middle of the night in Lhasa: 1,500 miles to the west. No matter. The rules can't be changed just to accommodate a few Tibetans. And so to this day Tibet expresses temporal solidarity with the Chinese masses by keeping in step with Peking time.

Seldom can imperialism have been so blatant or have exposed itself quite so heedlessly to derision.

In the afternoon I cycled out to the Norbulingka, a walled park on the western edge of the city containing the Dalai Lama's summer residence. Leaving the old town with its low, white-washed buildings packed tight around the Jokhang, or central shrine, I pedalled beneath the gilded magnificence of the Potala, passed through the raw and ugly gap where the city gate once stood – before which illicit visitors to the 'Forbidden City' would pause in trepidation – and forked left beneath the rocky outcrop known as Chakpori Hill, scene of bloody fighting in the uprising of March 1959. Wretched shanty buildings, a parody of functional architecture with which the Chinese communist authorities have disfigured every town and city from Manchuria to Afghanistan, stretched away along the airport road. Tibet has not been included in the immense Chinese railway network – the terrain is too inhospitable and sparsely populated for such an enormous engineering effort to be worthwhile – so the elderly Boeing which arrives every day from China's nearest large city, Chengdu, is the primary link for Lhasa's Chinese inhabitants with (as they see it) civilisation.

There is a road of course, but lorries take between ten days and two weeks to cover the 1,500 hazardous miles of high passes and vertiginous drops.

At the entrance to the park, some soldiers in the baggy, olive-green uniforms of the People's Liberation Army were happily photographing one another in front of the ornate gateway to this famous tourist attraction. It was impossible not to feel pleased that they were enjoying themselves on such a beautiful afternoon. The sky was still as unblemished and luminous as it had been in the morning, the atmosphere just as fresh and clean and innocent. Sheltered by high walls, the park's trees were already blurred with green, and in their branches the local birds were serenading one another lustily. I scrunched along a gravel path.

The present, fourteenth, Dalai Lama's summer residence is a two-storey, flat-roofed building in a traditional Tibetan style with solid white-washed walls and elaborate woodwork painted in red, orange, and yellow. Only its ground floor rooms were open, the most impressive of which was the Reception Hall in which a large, intricately carved throne was almost submerged by *khatas*, the white scarves made from inexpensive cloth which Tibetans present to one another as a greeting, or mark of respect. The Norbulingka seemed a homely, peaceful place and it was not difficult to imagine why successive Dalai Lamas preferred its light and airy pavilions to their dark and oppressive winter quarters, high up in the forbidding Potala. More than two years after my visit, in autumn 1989, I talked to the present Dalai Lama at his home in India and he remarked that the one thing he really detested about the Potala was its ineradicable smell of rats.

On the same occasion he recalled the afternoon of 10 March 1959. He had been standing, he said, on the roof of his residence in the Norbulingka in the company of

Tibet's Lord Chamberlain. From early that morning a crowd had been forming outside the entrance to the park, until eventually it numbered about thirty thousand people. The citizens of Lhasa were afraid that the Chinese were intending to abduct him. Once in Peking he would be a hostage, ensuring the continued tractability of his people, and a puppet, his public statements carefully scripted. Circumstantial evidence suggests that this is indeed what the Chinese authorities had in mind. Whether they did or not, the crowd had no doubts. The gateway to the Norbulingka was blocked and the Dalai Lama effectively taken captive by the people for his own protection.

'I remember . . .' he said, in a cheery, unemotional, sort of way, '. . . it was a sunny spring day, with a very bright blue sky. In the distance I could hear the noise of the crowd. There was some shouting, but the Lord Chamberlain and I were talking very casually. Then I recall saying to him, suddenly, "Today might be a turning point in the history of Tibet. Maybe this is the beginning of a new era". Of course I had no idea what was shortly to happen, but at that moment I was, I think, conscious of history as it actually occurred.'

A week later, on the night of 17 March, the Dalai Lama fled from the Norbulingka disguised as a soldier and carrying a borrowed rifle. For seven days, the crowd had shown no sign of giving up. Messages had gone backwards and forwards between Tibetan officials and the Chinese military, but no resolution to the stalemate could be found. Vociferous demonstrations had been held in the streets of Lhasa itself, while the Chinese quietly strengthened their positions and brought their artillery to bear. The turning point finally came at four o'clock on the afternoon of 17 March, when two shells exploded within the park, one relatively close to the Dalai Lama's residence. It is not known exactly why the order was given at that particular moment, or why only two rounds were fired. Presumably it was thought that a limited display of force would serve to concentrate the minds of the Tibetan officials and to bring about their prompt capitulation. Instead, it was decided that the Dalai Lama should escape. It was not then being suggested that he should leave Tibet entirely, merely that he should move to an area south of Lhasa which was not yet under effective Chinese control. Once there he would be able to negotiate, free from coercion.

During the day of 19 March, while the Dalai Lama's party put as much distance between Lhasa and themselves as the difficult terrain would allow, the pattern of events established during the previous week continued outside the Norbulingka. The crowd had not diminished and protests continued; the guns were loaded but silent. It seems that the Chinese had no idea that the Dalai Lama had fled. It might be supposed, therefore, that at two o'clock on the morning of 20 March when the bombardment of the Norbulingka began, their commanders thought that in addition to putting down a civil insurrection, they were also assassinating a religious leader and head of state.

In the darkness there was mayhem. Next morning, when the sun rose in a bright sky over the rim of the Lhasa Valley, the killing fields were revealed. I have talked to a number of Tibetans who were there. Quite independently, two people gave me the same description. On that morning, they said, it was impossible to walk in a straight line near the Norbulingka because you had to find spaces for your feet between the bodies of the dead.

The slaughter of what had now become the Lhasa Uprising was anyway just beginning. The fighting went on for three days. Artillery began to shell Sera monastery, Chakpori Hill, and the Potala. In the streets of their capital the Tibetans tried desperately to engage the

Chinese in hand-to-hand fighting and were everywhere cut down with automatic weapons. Thousands of demonstrators who had survived the carnage at the Norbulingka took refuge in the Jokhang, the temple at the centre of the old city. There, finally, on the morning of 22 March they came under mortar and machine gun fire. At around noon, armoured cars smashed down the gates and troops began rounding up prisoners. The battle for Lhasa was over and the Tibetans were now a humiliated and subjugated people.

Hearing the news from his capital and realising that he himself was now a fugitive, the Dalai Lama decided that his only sensible course was to seek to influence events from the safety of another country. At four o'clock on the afternoon of 31 March he crossed the Indian border and began the life of an exile. Within days his people, or at least those who could escape from the tyranny, had begun to struggle across the Himalayas to join him.

I cycled back to the Barkor. It was a very pleasant ride in the insouciant sunshine. In front of the Jokhang, pilgrims from distant parts of Tibet, so coated in dust that they could have been the employees of a flour mill, were prostrating themselves before the entrance to the shrine. Small groups of off-duty soldiers, raw youths whose most fervent prayers were doubtless for a prompt posting back to China, looked on, nudging one another in a mixture of amusement and contempt. They clearly regarded the Tibetans as a species of life so alien as to be quite incomprehensible.

I sat on the ground with my back against a brick wall that the afternoon had soaked with the sun's warmth. Could any other two people be so utterly dissimilar as the Chinese and the Tibetans? If they stayed for a thousand years, would the Chinese ever see that the Tibetans had qualities which they themselves lacked? Probably not. In that case would the Chinese stay for a thousand years? Chinese dynasties – whether of the traditional or the communist variety – tend to take a long view of history. When asked what he thought of the consequences of the French Revolution, Mao is said to have replied – only half jokingly – that it was much too early to tell. But then during the early to mid '80s Peking had seemed to want some kind of *rapprochement.* Delegations of Tibetans from India had been allowed to visit their homeland and to report back to their government in exile. In 1985, to general amazement, several thousand Tibetans had even been allowed to visit Bodh Gaya in northern India to hear the Dalai Lama teach an important scripture, the Kalachakra, and although many of these people unaccountably failed to return, there had been no reprisals, no shrill denunciations of Tibetan perfidy and ingratitude, no indignant re-sealing of the border.

Alas, this new beginning was short-lived. In autumn 1987 political mid-winter returned to Tibet and oppression once more swallowed up its benighted people. There have been tanks again in front of the Jokhang; more Tibetans have been shot dead in the streets; the survivors live in fear of the midnight summons; prisoners sleep thirty to a cell; torture is not so much commonplace as routine. Demonstrators against injustice have their heads plunged in excrement, and their genitals electrified with cattle prods. Women have had their breasts amputated. One man has been given a sentence of twelve years' hard labour for singing a 'counter-revolutionary' song. There are no young Western travellers in Tibet any more and the Banak Shöl Hotel has been closed down.

I left Tibet in April 1987 – a few months before the nightmare returned – even then convinced that the world could provide no clearer instance of political injustice, nor a more blatant denial of a people's fundamental right to self-determination. In common with many other people who visited the country during that period, I told myself I would do my bit to help: report my experiences as widely and graphically as possible; write letters to the newspapers when occasion arose. After all, what else could be done when democratic governments chose to ignore iniquities about which they were fully informed?

It was on my way home through Nepal that I met Tenzin Choegyal for the first time. He was pleased I felt indignant about the sufferings of his country. For his own part, he said, he had got a bit out of touch. He had worked for the Dalai Lama's administration at one time, but not any more. Nowadays he lived in Kathmandu and had two young children and a living to make. Maybe I should visit some of the Tibetan settlements in India, to see how things were after thirty years of exile. To find out what had been salvaged from the general wreck.

'It might be fun,' he said, warming to the idea. 'We could go together.'

Chapter 1

DELHI – 1989

Coming down to breakfast, I found Tenzin at a table by the window, eating a boiled egg in a desultory way, and scanning the headlines of *The Hindustan Times*. His Tibetan features, to say nothing of his jeans and bright green polo shirt, made him immediately recognisable among the suited Indian businessmen, who formed a majority of the dining room's occupants.

When not engaged as my companion, guide, and translator, Tenzin is a businessman himself these days, but this is just the latest metamorphosis in a life of almost routine upheaval. If the Chinese had not invaded his homeland, he would, for the past thirty years, have been a monk in Lhasa's Sera monastery. Instead of which he is now a prosperous entrepreneur and family man. Things have worked out well for him. Alas, not all his exiled compatriots have been quite so fortunate.

'It says here it was forty-seven degrees yesterday.'

Morning pleasantries over, Tenzin handed me the paper and indicated a front-page story. During the past week in Delhi, five deaths had occurred which could definitely be attributed to heatstroke; the more affluent of the city's inhabitants were said to be leaving by the thousand for the Himalayan hill stations; and a promise had been extracted from Indian Airlines that they would somehow find an extra airbus to put on the route up to Srinagar. At the conclusion of the report, a senior Indian army officer was quoted as saying that his men were working flat out, but that unfortunately the road from Kashmir to Ladakh (a tiny portion of India on the Tibetan side of the Great Himalaya), would remain closed for at least another month. The Zoji-la, a 12,000 foot pass, had as usual been blocked to a depth of about a hundred feet and although they had been using dynamite to clear the drifts, there was still a risk of additional snowfall.

'Look at this egg,' Tenzin expostulated; 'it's always the same in India at this time of year. The yolk is so pale you can hardly tell where it ends and the white begins. It's because the chickens have nothing to eat.' He stared glumly out of the window, which was giving off a dull, steady heat like a central heating radiator. A layer of what appeared to be cayenne pepper covered the sill, the result of a short-lived wind that during the night had picked up a substantial amount of the Rajasthan desert, carried it fifty miles or so, and then fly-tipped it onto the city. In consequence, the air had a rather sinister ochre tinge, and the fronds of the palm trees at the far end of the drive appeared strangely insubstantial in the dust-filled haze. The hotel had plainly given up on its lawn which had been grilled to a toast-like colour and consistency. In the sky, pariah kites, sharp-eyed for carrion, spiralled smoothly on rapidly ascending thermals like scraps of burnt paper rising from a fire. Below, Delhi's unfortunate inhabitants roasted. It was eight o'clock on the morning of 12 May 1989, nearly halfway through the hottest month of the year.

A mere 300 miles to the north, in Tibet, the snowline

would be quickening its steady retreat to the glaciers. Teams of yaks, their horns decked out with red and gold tassels, would be ploughing the recently frozen soil, preparing the ground for the annual wheat and barley crops.

Tenzin had been born, forty-seven years before, in Kham, a region of eastern Tibet, near the town of Kanze. The eldest son of an established family of farmers and traders, he had passed his early years in the relative grandeur and comfort of a three-storey mud-brick house. It was a fiercely masculine society in which boys were taught to break wild horses and carried a rifle as soon as they reached their teens. The climate was harsh and in winter snow drifted up the side of the house, blocking out the ground floor windows. Sides of meat hung from the rafters would remain fresh indefinitely, preserved by the cold, dry air.

The communist Chinese army, the PLA, arrived in Kham in 1950, but it was not until 1956, when Tenzin was fourteen, that trouble really began. His parents had in any case planned to send him to Sera so, in the company of relatives, he was packed off to Lhasa in the back of a Chinese truck. His father and uncle meanwhile joined the resistance, lending their efforts to the struggle against Chinese domination.

Two years passed, during which Tenzin received the rudiments of a monastic education and Tibet descended steadily into chaos. By 1958, the resistance had been defeated in Kham and its leaders were trying to regroup their forces in the mountainous region of Lhoka, immediately to the south of Lhasa. The war had reached a decisive phase and as the Chinese clearly could not be defeated, his father decided that Tenzin should be sent to safety and freedom in India. Leaving Lhasa on the main road south to the town of Phari, he crossed the Himalayas by the Jelap-la ('la' is the Tibetan word for 'pass') and descended through the Sikkimese capital of Gangtok to the Indian hill town of Kalimpong. From there he soon made his way to nearby Darjeeling and resumed his education; this time learning not Tibetan Buddhist classics, but the Roman alphabet and conversational English under the instruction of American missionaries.

A few months later, the Dalai Lama crossed the Indian border and a general exodus from the mayhem of southern and central Tibet began to gather momentum.

In 1963, after a year of compulsory service in the Indian army, Tenzin began to earn a meagre living in Darjeeling as a translator for the Tibetan language newspaper, *Tibetan Freedom*, until one auspicious day in 1965 he was told that an American charity had awarded him a year's full scholarship to study civil and business administration at Cornell University. The young man who twenty-three years earlier had been born in one of the wildest and – for Westerners – most inaccessible places on earth, now found himself on board a Boeing 707 bound for Boston.

His studies completed, he returned to India to work for the Home Affairs Department of the Dalai Lama's exiled administration in Dharamsala. By 1968, however, he was back in Darjeeling: the new editor of *Tibetan Freedom*. Unfortunately, this journalistic career was brought to an abrupt end only two years later by a severe attack of pleurisy. To recuperate, he went to stay with a cousin in Kathmandu. There, health restored, he found work in the carpet business, eventually founding, with his brother Lobsang, a company manufacturing handwoven rugs for export to Britain and Germany.

*

'I guess we'd better go to find Athar,' Tenzin remarked without any obvious enthusiasm for braving the Delhi inferno. In the hotel driveway the taxi-drivers were asleep in the shade, spreadeagled on charpoys, their limbs flung out with almost matrimonial intimacy and abandon. No one seemed much inclined to wake up, let alone to take us anywhere. The light was so strong that even through sunglasses I was obliged to squint, and the air, still stirred by the remnants of a desert wind, gusted particles of dust into my eyes and mouth.

Eventually we found an elderly Sikh with the whiskers and profile of an Old Testament prophet, who was sufficiently unintimidated by the weather to risk driving us out to Majnu-ka-Tilla, the Tibetan refugee camp on Delhi's northern outskirts.

New Delhi is a strange city. Purpose-built as an imperial capital with triumphal avenues and monumental public buildings, it has been extended with planned housing enclaves, embassy districts and government offices, so that everywhere an incongruous sliderule order prevails. Not that the extempore can ever be wholly banished in India. To sustain the dignity of the nation's capital, even in the hot season water is pumped onto the public gardens so as to nurture the merest hint, the thinnest wash of green. Yet at every roundabout as we drove past, young men, each with a towel and bar of soap, queued patiently for their turn to stand under the sprinklers and to take a very public shower.

The Sikh, aggressive instincts apparently undimmed by advancing years, drove fast and carelessly through a mêlée of rickshaws and cyclists which mysteriously melted away in front of the bumper. Occasionally I glanced out of the rear window to see if any blood or wreckage had been left strewn upon the road behind, while Tenzin, who likes being driven in India even less than I do, clasped a handkerchief to his nose, wound his window tightly up, and relapsed into stoical silence.

New Delhi became Old Delhi, Lutyens's red sandstone was replaced by Mogul red sandstone, and abruptly we were plunged into the familiar melee of Chandni Chowk. Tongas, scooters, taxis, lorries, motorbikes, handcarts, trishaws, and countless thousands of people formed an apparently impenetrable mass into which Delhi's green and yellow buses, which daily strike terror into the hearts of the city's pedestrians, drove purposefully, spewing out smoke, horns blaring.

Beyond the Red Fort and the Railway Station, the throng of people gradually thinned, and after a few minutes the road began to run alongside a slow-moving body of muddy water, which frequently disappeared altogether behind a thick screen of encroaching reeds. Despite its unprepossessing appearance, this was the Yamuna, one of the holy rivers of India, flowing sluggishly down to its confluence with the Ganges at Allahabad.

The Hindu pilgrim bathes in the Yamuna and the Ganges because their waters have come from the Himalayas where, in Indian mythology, the gods are said to dwell. The most holy of these peaks, Kailas, the palace of the great god Shiva, a point of intersection between heaven and earth, is, however, fifty-five miles inside Tibet. Tibet for Hindus is a holy land.

Tibetans, on the other hand, being devout adherents to another Indian religion, Buddhism, have long made the pilgrimage in the opposite direction: down to the plains where the Buddha was enlightened and first set out the principles of his new religion.

The scummy waters of the Yamuna looked distinctly uninspiring. Outside the car window was just India at its worst: hot, filthy, pullulating, and wretched. The houses by the side of the road were lean-tos made of sheets of scavenged iron, abandoned metal tins beaten flat, card-board cartons, chicken wire, and straw. Here and there stood piles of disembowelled machinery, salvaged from derelict cars and trucks, and now standing each in its own black viscous puddle of oil: organs hacked from a redundant body.

I leant forward to talk to the driver. I knew we were heading north, but I wasn't sure precisely which road we were on.

'This is the road to Amritsar. Sikh holy city. Golden Temple. Very beautiful place.'

The Punjab crisis, regional separatism, hoodlums with AK 47s, murder, arson, corruption, extortion . . . this was what the newspapers were full of; this was what modern India really worried about. Who could be expected to concern themselves about a few Tibetans when the survival of India as a unified state was in question?

Suddenly, on the other side of the road, over what looked like a perfectly ordinary Indian shanty town, I could see tall bamboo masts from which flew strings of brightly coloured pennants. We had arrived. No Tibetan settlement is complete without its prayer flags: small rectangles of cheap cloth, illegibly printed with prayers, intended to distribute benediction indiscriminately on the breeze. Ignoring the oncoming traffic as an impertinent irrelevance, the taxi-driver swung the car across the road under the bumpers of a speeding lorry piled with sand, and pulled up underneath a stunted tree. This provided a patch of shade about the size of a small tablecloth. We all got out. The Sikh propped open the car bonnet, gingerly released the pressure from the boiling radiator, and announced that he would wait for us. Meanwhile, he said, he would go and get himself some tea at one of the stalls by the side of the road. So saying he locked the doors, removed the distributor cap as an added precaution against theft, and wandered off.

To reach the nearest of the Tibetan buildings it was first necessary to cross a small swamp, the confluence of several open sewers in which two black pigs were energetically and noisily truffling, the malodorous mire drying on their hairy flanks and backs in dull, crusty patches. As an experimental breeding centre for typhoid bacteria, the outskirts of the camp could clearly not be improved upon. After having been stopped short two or three times by deep pools of black slime, we found a narrow beaten path which eventually brought us into the street of two-storey buildings. These appeared to be of considerable permanence and grandeur when compared with the hovels on the perimeter, but were in fact just cubes of concrete held together by steel strengthening rods. Tenzin hailed the first person to come along and enquired where we might find the principal figure of authority: the camp's welfare officer.

Authority turned out to be represented by Jampa Choejor, a heavily built man in early middle-age, with glasses and a bold check shirt. In common with many Tibetan men he wore a substantial gold signet ring, in which was set a chunk of rough-cut turquoise, and a large watch strapped to his wrist by a metal bracelet of industrial strength. His ground-floor room was stuffy and almost dark as its windows were covered with wide strips of raffia matting in order to ward off the sun. An electric ceiling fan, which was apparently about to break free from its mounts and cause carnage in the room beneath, thrashed the air to remarkably little effect, while in one corner an elderly fridge was shaking itself rapidly to pieces. The walls were washed with pale blue emulsion and high up on one of them was a large, framed, hand-tinted photograph of the Dalai Lama as a young man.

It was only after a few minutes, when my eyes had

become sufficiently accustomed to the gloom, that I noticed the room's fourth occupant: a monk sitting cross-legged on a narrow bed, apparently meditating.

Interrupting Tenzin's explanation for our visit, Mr Choejor opened the cavernous fridge, produced three bottles of fizzy lemonade, and wiping the sweat from his eyebrows with a handkerchief, slumped down as if extremely glad of an opportunity for a few moments' rest. Tenzin began again. It was a speech that over the coming months I came to learn by heart.

We were, he said, researching a book about the Tibetan refugees who had fled to India and Nepal thirty years before. His job was both to translate and to enable me to talk freely with ordinary Tibetans in a way that would otherwise be extremely difficult. We wanted to find out why these people had left their homes, precisely how they had escaped, and what had happened to them in the ensuing years. We intended to investigate the human cost of exile: the effect of suddenly losing everything that was familiar and secure and being cast out into a world of terrifying uncertainty. We also wished to see what proportion of the refugees had retained their Tibetan identity and avoided assimilation into the great mass of the Indian poor. This would enable us to assess just what had survived of a unique culture which in its homeland had been so ruthlessly suppressed and persecuted as to be almost extinguished. In order to carry out our research we intended to visit all the main areas of Tibetan settlement on a journey lasting several months and to talk to as many prominent individuals as possible, including His Holiness the Dalai Lama.

Mr Choejor nodded affably as if nothing could be simpler or more reasonable.

'We're going up to Dharamsala tonight,' Tenzin continued, '. . . but I just thought we should make preliminary enquiries here in Delhi about Athar Norbu. Is he around?'

'I doubt it,' replied Mr Choejor cheerfully. 'He spends quite a lot of time in Kathmandu these days you know, especially during the hot weather, but we can go along to his room and look if you like.'

This was scarcely a very encouraging start, not least because we had only flown in from Kathmandu the night before. Athar Norbu was a person I particularly wanted to talk to as he was currently one of the leaders of the *Chushi Gandruk*, the guerrilla organisation which during the '50s and '60s had been responsible for most of the armed resistance to Chinese rule. Athar, Tenzin assured me, had not only been in the thick of the fighting, but had also been one of the first Tibetans taken to the United States to be trained by the CIA.

In order to allay my disappointment, I decided it would probably be sensible to extract some rather more mundane information from Mr Choejor. He responded with alacrity and a civil servant's enthusiasm for statistics:

'There are around two thousand people here now, 75 per cent of whom came to Delhi between 1963 and '64. . . .'

I began to have a faint foreboding that even with Tenzin's help it might be difficult to wean the Tibetans from facts and figures and to lure them onto more fertile but less predictable ground.

Recalling the fetid moat through which I had just been obliged to wade, I enquired about the camp's general state of health. Mr Choejor's affability and cheerfulness showed no sign of diminution.

'Oh, not too bad. Pretty good really. It's not like before. At the beginning the majority of the people were just living in tents. Many of them died. Now we have a dispensary, a school, a *gompa* (temple). . . . Things are completely different.'

India probably has a higher density of virulent bacteria than any other country on earth, whereas Tibet, at an average height of nearly 14,000 feet above sea level, is almost as sterile as an operating theatre. It is simply too harsh, too cold a place for the majority of microbes to survive. The Tibetans, therefore, despite being a tough, outdoor people in the main, had almost no immunity from infection. So when the first tattered groups struggled out of the mountains, exhausted and undernourished after their arduous journey, with little or no money and dressed in cold-weather clothing, many soon fell victim to disease. In particular, the plight of the first refugees who followed the Dalai Lama in April and May 1959 was made infinitely worse by the seasonal heat of the Indian plains. Death in many forms swept through them with the grapeshot ferocity of a medieval plague. Thousands succumbed to typhoid, cholera, but above all to tuberculosis. The first refugee camps, established by the Indian government, quickly turned into tenanted graveyards where almost the sole preoccupation of the living was anxiously searching the faces of family and friends for signs of incipient mortality. The monks from Lhasa's great monasteries who had immediately and instinctively followed their religious leader, found themselves confined to camps in the torrid climate of Assam. Missamari, the name of one such centre, still causes a shadow to pass across Tibetan faces whenever it is mentioned.

'Let's go and see if anyone knows where Athar is.' So saying Mr Choejor lifted up the matting which covered the doorway and let in a shaft of sunlight that struck the floor like a laser. We followed him along an uneven dirt path through a warren of small, murky dwellings, some built of durable materials, some evidently constructed out of whatever had come to hand. Looking at them, I couldn't really decide which would be worse: the winter cold, the suffocating spring heat, or the torrents of summer monsoon rain. Autumn would be tolerable – just.

All the faces that glanced at us as we passed seemed to have Tibetan features. India's population, if not its weather, had apparently been left outside on the road. How well did these people get on with their neighbours? Delhi, after all, is a city riven by communal strife, where the casual slaughter of Muslims and Sikhs, followed by bloody reprisals, has been far from an uncommon occurrence. Were they resented? After all, a shanty town of Tibetan refugees tends to attract the attention of UNICEF, while the average Indian slum dweller is generally left to fend for himself, or to rot. Mr Choejor seemed sanguine enough.

'There have been a few problems, but nothing serious.'

'Such as?'

'Well, for example, we are sometimes accused of brewing our Tibetan beer – *chang* – illegally and selling it to the local Hindus. That kind of thing.'

We stopped outside another anonymous two-storey building, this time made of brick. Clearly, being a prominent political figure had its privileges. Not that many however. Inside, several small dark rooms, each about ten feet square, led off a bleak central hallway. From one of them an ample woman of about thirty-five appeared hurriedly, rearranging her clothes and looking rather flustered. She had plainly been asleep. Yes, she said, this was Athar's room. No, he was not in Delhi. He was in Nepal. No, she didn't know a phone number, but when we got there we should just ask around. After all, everyone knew Athar. Tenzin groaned.

It had been dark for over an hour when we set out for Old Delhi station, though the air temperature seemed determined to ignore the sun's disappearance. Within a mile, sweat was trickling down my spine, my shirt having lost any capacity for further absorption. At roundabouts, small groups of Indian policemen, pensionable Lee Enfields slung across their shoulders on frayed webbing, were setting up road blocks with splintered planks and dented oil drums. These were intended to foil fanatical Sikh terrorists. On the whole they seemed more suited to the task of arresting elderly cyclists for riding without lights.

Indian railway porters are obliged to wear a distinctive uniform of ragged red cotton. As a result they look rather like inhabitants of hell who, having already done time in boiling pitch, are now being required to carry crushing loads up and down stairs on undernourished matchstick limbs. Whether this Sisyphean activity rates as promotion or demotion is hard to tell. We had no sooner set foot inside the station than our bags were seized by two of these unfortunates. 'Jammu Mail', said Tenzin firmly, adding one or two vaguely threatening riders to this instruction in fluent Hindi as our belongings swiftly disappeared. In addition to Tibetan (Kham and Lhasa dialects), Tenzin speaks better English than many of the inhabitants of England, Nepali, Hindi, and a smattering of sundry other Indian languages like Bengali and Urdu.

Despite the fact that not much seemed to be happening, a loudspeaker overhead, through demented electronic shrieks and cackles, gave out an unceasing stream of vital information, while away in the sidings an invisible herd of locomotives was rumbling about, shunting. Eventually the train clanked in and came to a halt with an excruciating shrieking and wailing of brakes. Tenzin and I struggled past a chai-wallah attempting to balance a tray of about thirty small cups of milky tea, while gesticulating violently with his other arm at a railway official who was refusing to let him on board to sell them.

Our section of the carriage was already occupied by a youth of about eighteen, who, rather self-consciously it seemed to me, was slipping on a pair of very natty pyjamas while being watched with extreme disfavour by a stout, perspiring, middle-aged man in an ill-fitting suit. The reason for the latter's annoyance soon became apparent, for sheltering behind his generous bulk was an exquisite young woman of refined and classical beauty. This, he lost no time in telling us, was his wife, whom he was taking on honeymoon to Kashmir. In a country of arranged marriages, the girl was looking less than convinced about the benefits to be expected from his solicitude. Down the corridor, two boys, children of the new India, were playing with a battery-powered Space Invaders machine which emitted a demented tweeting every time one of the hostile aliens was obliterated.

After eleven hours of clashing and jolting and being continuously assaulted by gale-force gusts of the hot night wind, we pulled into Pathankot on a still, humid, lethargic morning. A ten-minute rickshaw ride along a scrofulous street, populated chiefly by threadbare dogs with a pathological aversion to rickshaws, brought us to the bus station. Seeing Tenzin, and without asking where we wanted to go, the man selling tickets shouted at us to hurry up as the bus for Dharamsala was just leaving. The driver revved the engine mercilessly, enveloping bystanders in a noxious smog of fumes, leaned for some seconds on the horn, and then shot out into the main road, scattering browsing livestock and a dozen or so children, innocently playing cricket in the dung-filled gutter.

Although grateful to Nehru's government for giving him a home, the Dalai Lama must have greeted the news that it was to be Dharamsala with mixed emotions. Nehru had pronounced the place perfect; its tranquillity and remoteness were, he said, ideal for a spiritual leader like the Dalai Lama. Ideal for a spiritual leader perhaps; for a politician, less good.

Ever since Independence, the Indian government had prided itself on a foreign policy of peaceful coexistence. In the late 1940s the global order was manifestly changing. To the determined anti-communist, the new China might look threatening, but to those who considered themselves disinterested observers of the Asian political scene, Mao's moral fervour and desire for the betterment of his people appeared wholly admirable. China had been abused by the Western powers and invaded by the Japanese; India had been colonised. Both were now taking control of their own destinies after a century of political impotence. India's leaders doubtless felt some sense of common purpose with the new Chinese administration and hoped that together they might improve significantly the lives of nearly half the world's people. The high point of Sino–Indian conviviality came in 1954 with the conclusion of a trade agreement which included in its preamble the so-called Panch Shila, or 'Five Principles of Peaceful Co-existence'. The Chinese had of course invaded Tibet four years earlier in 1950, but so far there had been little resistance or repression. Anyway, the world had had other things on its mind, most notably the Korean War.

By 1956, however, a year in which the Chinese were prevailed upon to allow the Dalai Lama to visit India (in order to celebrate the 2,500th anniversary of the Buddha's birth), bitter fighting had broken out in Kham. As soon as he met Nehru, the Dalai Lama explained the situation that had now arisen and expressed his tentative opinion that it might be better for him not to go home. In the outside world he would be able to publicise the Tibetan cause, which was otherwise so easily dismissed or forgotten. But Nehru would have none of this. Despite his Indian government having inherited all the treaty obligations entered into by the British, he had no intention of endangering his country's entire foreign policy by provoking a crisis over Tibet. At his specific insistence the Dalai Lama returned to Lhasa, having been instructed to make the best of things and to try to arrive at a working relationship with his Chinese overlords.

It was, therefore, a considerable embarrassment to Nehru to have the Dalai Lama back on Indian territory a mere three years later. A fudged solution was concocted. The Dalai Lama would be given sanctuary, but he would not be recognised as the legitimate ruler of Tibet. He would be merely an exiled religious leader living in a remote and deserted hill station where it would be extremely difficult for him to make himself a nuisance. China had become a major piece on the chessboard of the world's affairs and pawns like Tibet had occasionally to be sacrificed.

So the Dalai Lama went to live quietly at Dharamsala and began to consider how best to provide for the thousands of Tibetans who had now joined him in exile. He had been there only two years when, to establish a border more to their own liking, the Chinese invaded northern India, humiliated the Indian army, and obliterated Nehru's vision of Asia united in peace and cooperation. It was a betrayal by which Nehru is said to have been embittered for the rest of his life.

After about three hours, I began to make out the dark bulk of the mountains looming up ahead through the thinning haze. During the summer, the Himalayan snowline retreats to about 17,000 feet, so only around the summits of these subordinate peaks were there dirty patches of greyish ice. The view in early spring – a jagged white wall rising abruptly out of the mustard fields of the Kangra Valley – is a sight to thin the blood with adrenalin. In mid-May it is nothing much to write home about.

The bus turned off the main road and began to climb with immense and noisy effort towards the main town of Lower Dharamsala. This is the Indian administrative centre for the district. Upper Dharamsala, (otherwise confusingly known as McCleod Ganj after the intrepid Scotsman who first decided to settle there), is the hill station, 2,500 feet above, which has become the unofficial Tibetan capital. We reached the bus station, just, and the engine died with a prolonged shudder and a rattle of glass. The passengers piled off and disappeared in the direction of the bazaar. Tenzin and I were apparently the only ones going any further. Fortunately, another bus for Upper Dharamsala was leaving shortly, so we sat on our bags to wait. The faces of the people passing by were still, without exception, Indian.

The 2,500 feet of extra altitude entail another six or seven laborious miles by road, which take at least half an hour to cover owing to the incline and the 370° bends. With each mile that passes the view down to the Kangra Valley becomes more majestic. Conifers thicken by the roadside, and the atmosphere and temperature become inescapably those of the mountains.

When the British abandoned Upper Dharamsala in 1947, they left little more than a village strung out along a narrow ridge, one section of which had been flattened to make a small public green. In the surrounding woods were scattered two or three dozen wooden bungalows, with corrugated iron roofs, stone chimneys, and wide verandahs to keep out the monsoon rain. Roses and marigolds grew as well in their gardens as they did in Sussex, and on chilly evenings, tucked into the corner of a chintz-covered sofa, warm within the influence of an established log fire, the simulacrum must have seemed reassuringly complete. Once it had been suggested that

Upper Dharamsala should become the summer capital of the Raj, but owing to an extremely destructive and confidence-sapping earthquake, this distinction had been awarded to Simla, which anyway had the additional virtue of being considerably closer to Delhi.

Shuddering and coughing, the bus reached the top of the hill and drew up in a small, crowded square. At least two thirds of the faces that were immediately visible had Tibetan features. The remainder were either Indian tourists, refugees from the heat, or young Westerners. A group of six monks was standing, chatting, presumably about to embark on the return journey to their monastery. One of them, a burly young man of about twenty, was cradling a Lhasa Apso puppy. Few sights could have more clearly signalled our abrupt transition to the Tibetan cultural world. Down on the plains, dogs are regarded as carriers of disease, useful only as scavengers. The Buddhist Tibetans on the other hand, who consider all forms of life to be interrelated and thus worthy of respect, frequently keep them as pets.

Along one side of the square was a low building of dark, weathered timber. 'That's Nowrojee's,' said Tenzin. 'When I was employed here by the government, we used to sit on the balcony and drink beer after work. It has the best view in McCleod Ganj.' I followed him into the gloomy interior of the shop. The Nowrojee family once prospered by supplying the British inhabitants of the bungalows with the material components of a comfortable existence. When the Raj departed, it was left in possession of virtually the whole town; a dramatic and wholly regrettable introduction to the property business, which very nearly proved ruinous. There was no one who wanted to rent the houses and now no one to sell things to either. Through the lean years the store stayed open, stocking everything from petrol to peppermints. Then, hearing that the Indian government was looking for somewhere for the Dalai Lama and his followers, N. N. Nowrogee, the fifth patriarch in this modest commercial dynasty, simply wrote to New Delhi and offered them a town.

Mrs Nowrojee, an elderly, white-haired, rather stern-looking woman in a brown sari was weighing out green chillis for one customer while keeping a suspicious eye on three Tibetan schoolchildren who had come in to buy chocolate. The idea of renting an old bungalow, even if dilapidated, struck me as an appealing one. Were there, I asked, any still unoccupied? Mrs Nowrojee looked at me as though I was a troublesome and perhaps slightly retarded child. 'No of course not. McCleod Ganj is completely full. There's nothing at all.'

And so indeed it proved. The hotels were all packed with Indian holidaymakers and foreign tourists and the semi-official guesthouse, Kashmir Cottage, the home until she died of the Dalai Lama's mother, had been booked out for weeks past. Various floors were offered by Tenzin's evidently extensive acquaintance, but this didn't seem a very appealing prospect after a night on Indian Railways.

Dispirited and tired we decided to go to have something to eat with Wangchen Dorje. Wangchen, Tenzin explained, had once been a radio operator with the Tibetan resistance in Mustang, but nowadays lived quietly on the proceeds of a small restaurant and hotel. As this was entirely managed by his young wife, his greatest exertion was the weekly screening he gave at the local cinema of a pirated BBC video about Tibet. He had been doing this for as long as Tenzin could remember and the quality of the tape had degenerated over the years to a point where a good deal of imagination was now required. But still, an audience could reliably be found and people seemed to go away satisfied.

Wangchen's hotel had been one of the first places we

had tried to find accommodation, but naturally it had been full. Its owner was said to be out on business. 'Playing mah-jong,' Tanzin had remarked disapprovingly. Mah-jong, like strong drink, was an indulgence best kept for later in the day. The game had clearly been suspended to allow time for lunch, as on this occasion we found Wangchen – a large, middle-aged man with a boxer's build running slightly to fat – sitting on the flat roof of the hotel eating *thukpa*, the Tibetan version of noodle soup, into which he was dropping strips of air-dried meat, *shakampo*, to the great interest of several kites and a white-tailed vulture, circling close overhead. In addition to a T-shirt and tracksuit trousers, he was wearing, improbably, a stetson. Catching sight of Tenzin, whom he hadn't seen for at least a decade, he looked briefly nonplussed, and then, chortling with laughter, grabbed him by the hair, in which one or two thin lines of grey had begun to appear. Tenzin did not look at all pleased to be subjected to this kind of treatment, but graciously refrained from protest.

'Have some *shakampo*.' Wangchen held out a long, gnarled piece of biltong. 'In Tibet we use yak meat; here it is lamb. I prefer beef but these Hindus' (he waved an arm in the general direction of the Indian plains), 'do not like to kill cows. You can only get beef if you agree to call it buffalo and sometimes not even then.'

It seemed an inappropriate moment to point out that as Buddhists the Tibetans should, strictly speaking, be vegetarians. In fact they are some of the world's most unrepentant carnivores. Owing to the climate, few vegetables were grown in Tibet, and a hard outdoor life anyway required the energy provided by a meat diet. Buddhist ethics were therefore dispensed with and a collective guilty conscience assuaged by the hypocritical practice of employing Muslims as butchers. The Tibetan exiles in India, where the climate is warm and vegetables are plentiful, have so far shown very little enthusiasm for culinary virtue.

'Is this meat dried in the sun?'

'Here in India, yes, but in Tibet the air itself is so dry that you can just hang up a side of meat in the shade and it will be cured. It tastes better like that. If you put it in the sun it dries too fast and becomes tough.'

As hunger wore off, the conversation shifted from food to another of life's necessities: a roof over one's head. Wangchen expressed great regret that he couldn't help us.

'Nowadays, so many of these young Westerners come here because they have heard of His Holiness, that there is never anywhere to stay in McCleod Ganj. Except in the middle of winter.' He paused to stare with evident distaste at one of his guests: a young man with long, lank hair and a generally epicene appearance, who had come up onto the roof to hang out his washing. 'I could throw someone out . . .' (the idea seemed to appeal to him briefly), '. . . but that kind of thing is bad for business in the long run.'

A complex and far-reaching search, loftily orchestrated by Wangchen, was soon underway to find us somewhere to sleep. After about three-quarters of an hour it emerged that a relative of a friend of one of Tenzin's distant relatives was presently in Delhi and that therefore his room was vacant.

'It's somewhere just beyond the offices of the Tibetan Youth Congress,' Wangchen explained. 'Tenzin will find it easily.'

'That's very convenient.'

'What is?'

'That it's next to the TYC. They're on my list of people to talk to.'

'Oh, they're good at that,' said Wangchen scornfully. 'That's all they ever do: talk. They're always talking big about all the terrible things they're going to do to the Chinese, and what happens? Nothing. They're always talking about going on hunger strike in front of the Chinese Embassy in Delhi. And they do. But then it comes to around lunchtime and they're not getting anywhere, no one seems to be taking much notice, so they give in. They'd have been a great deal of use up in Mustang. My generation had spirit. I tell you, this lot has been in India too long. They've all gone soft.'

Chapter 2

DHARAMSALA (I)

The following morning, Tenzin and I set out to walk to Gangchen Kyishong, the headquarters of the Tibetan government in exile, almost exactly halfway between McCleod Ganj and Lower Dharamsala. Due to the gradient, it takes about twenty-five minutes to amble down and about forty-five minutes to struggle back up.

Even at a less than ideal time of year, with hardly any snow on the Dhauladar and the Kangra Valley indistinct beneath the summer haze, the landscape around Dharamsala is actively beautiful. It does not have merely the passive prettiness of a postcard; it somehow makes you feel better just to look at it. Perhaps it is because the mountains rise so abruptly from the plains that one has the sensation of being on God's private balcony, overlooking India.

We strolled cheerfully down in the sunshine. Tenzin said that only the day before a man had been badly mauled by a bear. It was the talk of the bazaar. He had been collecting firewood quite near McCleod Ganj. Also there were supposed to be plenty of leopard around still. People sometimes saw them when they walked back up the hill at night. A thousand feet below a mountain torrent, still aggressive with glacier melt, chafed at lorry-sized boulders. Two grey langur monkeys wandered along the road in front of us, completely unperturbed.

Gangchen Kyishong, or the Tibetan Secretariat Compound as it is also less romantically known, houses a government which no state has so far recognised and which may not even fly its national flag for fear of upsetting its Indian hosts. These humiliating circumstances apart, its premises are quite extensive and impressive. There is a large hall in which the Assembly of Tibetan People's Deputies periodically convenes, various ministry buildings grouped around a central courtyard, the Library of Tibetan Works and Archives (which also contains a small museum), and accommodation for the civil servants and their families.

'Looks like they're putting up a new Information Office,' Tenzin observed. We stopped next to a large, anonymous concrete building still clad in scaffolding. A thin, greyish-haired man in his late fifties, wearing an extremely crumpled tweed jacket, was pottering about the roof, apparently taking a proprietorial interest in the construction. Tenzin called up to him.

'That's Sonam Topgyal. He's the General Secretary in charge of Information.'

Mr Topgyal came down a precarious wooden ramp and joined us by the side of the road. He immediately struck me as rather a quiet and diffident individual to be distributing propaganda. He also spoke no English. However, he seemed pleased to see Tenzin, whom he remembered well enough, even though they hadn't met for seventeen years. We were invited up to his office for tea.

The existing Information Office turned out to be three or four rooms stuck onto the roof of another department. In the first of these about a dozen people, most of whom looked as though they had not long since left college, were sitting behind ancient manual typewriters bashing out press releases and articles. There were a few ancient, Bakelite telephones scattered about, into one of which a young man was bellowing the same phrase repeatedly to no appreciable effect. Books, pamphlets, and magazines were piled up everywhere. Many of them written in English and had been produced by the Information Office itself. By the door was a board covered with sympathetic newspaper cuttings, while on the walls were posters carrying black-and-white photographs of young Tibetans. Even allowing for the poor quality of the printing, they looked ashen and harassed. These were contemporaries of the Information Office staff in Tibet who had made the mistake of expressing heterodox opinions and were now confined to Chinese gaols in consequence.

We were joined in Mr Topgyal's office by Tenpa Samkhar, the Assistant General Secretary. Whereas Mr Topgyal was slim, reserved, and monoglot, Mr Samkhar was plump, voluble, and polyglot. The older, senior man seemed to represent the Tibetan officialdom of a bygone age. Born, bred, and educated in Tibet, his vision of the world had acquired its particular tint in a very different era. If he lived out the rest of his life in India, it would remain an alien, rather uncomfortable place. Mr Samkhar on the other hand had either come to India as a very young child, or had been born there. He clearly felt no unease. He was comfortable with its languages and understood instinctively how things were done.

Would it be possible for Mr Samkhar to arrange for us to talk to one or two of the senior government officials? 'Of course.' He would have to ring up and ask, he said, but he did not foresee any problems. Could he give us a letter of introduction to the people in charge of the various resettlement camps elsewhere in India and Nepal? Certainly. Why not?

Tenzin was struck by a thought. 'Do you know what has happened to Mr Wangdu Dorje? Is he still in the government service?'

'I believe he is writing a book at the moment – an historical work – but you will probably find him at his office near the library.'

After a few more minutes of desultory conversation, Tenzin and I got up to leave, promising to return later in the day to find out if any appointments had been made for us.

'You could telephone me . . .' said Mr Samkhar, '. . . but for some reason, I don't know why, the system does not seem to be working very well at present.' Trying to run an administration with the infrastructure available in a remote Indian hill station was clearly not without its attendant problems.

'Wangdu Dorje used to be my boss,' Tenzin explained when we were outside again. 'He was in charge of the Home Affairs Department for years.'

The relevant office turned out to be on the ground floor of another austere, functional, concrete building. Tenzin put his head gingerly around the door and was immediately greeted with enthusiasm. The room's occupant was a man in his late sixties, with a domed forehead, a sallow complexion, receding black hair and a rather breathless voice. He did not seem to be at all reluctant to be disturbed; if anything, rather the reverse. His large, Formica-topped desk was covered with manuscript proofs which he was evidently in the process of correcting. Apart from a couple of wooden chairs, the room had no furniture. He beamed at Tenzin rather like a retired headmaster recalling the achievements of a favourite pupil.

Maybe, I said, when the pleasantries had subsided, he could tell us something about his long career in the

Tibetan administration? He nodded gravely, and paused for a moment, holding an enormous mug in front of his face, surveying, or so it seemed, the landscape of his past in its enamelled surface. Dressed in a woollen shirt and a crumpled, sleeveless cardigan, he looked every inch a man of the people. There was no hint of ministerial grandeur in either his appearance or surroundings. He seemed to be someone from whom life had stripped all non-essentials.

'You must understand that in Tibet I was nothing to do with the government. I was just an employee of an aristocratic family and I worked on their estate to the south of Lhasa. In fact I was their storekeeper. My family were what you would call middle-class. My father had paid for me to go to school, which was unusual in Tibet in the old days. Generally speaking, the only way ordinary people could receive any education was by joining a monastery.' He drew back in his chair with an expression akin to distaste. 'It was not a particularly good system.'

'Are there many exiled Tibetans in positions of authority who in the old days could never have hoped for advancement?'

'Oh yes, many. But before the Chinese came, Tibetan society was slowly changing. It would not have stayed the same. The Dalai Lama himself was anxious it should adapt to the modern world. Anyway I was fortunate. I had a job, a wife, four children; I was secure. So when the Dalai Lama fled to India it was hard to know what to do for the best. I knew that as I worked for the aristocracy, it would be dangerous for me to stay. The communists did not care for people like me. Also I had been helping the Tibetan resistance with supplies which perhaps the Chinese knew about. On the other hand it was difficult to take the actual decision to leave. Then one afternoon the Chinese soldiers arrived in our village. I remember watching them kicking down the doors of the houses, one by one, looking for people whom they suspected of being in contact with the guerrillas. That night we left for Bhutan.'

'What do you think would have happened to you if you had stayed?'

'I would probably have been shot.'

For a moment his face creased into a smile of almost mischievous amusement. Events which must have been terrifying at the time were now so far in the past as to seem part of an adventure story. Time had faded their emotional content and only a narrative outline remained.

'Was your journey very difficult?'

'It was not particularly hard, but it was quite dangerous. The Chinese, who at that time were consolidating their hold on southern Tibet, kept getting ahead of us and we could only move when it was dark. After fifteen days' walk we crossed safely into Bhutan – and were immediately arrested. The Bhutanese were not at all pleased to have hundreds of Tibetans coming across their northern frontier. I suppose they didn't feel very safe themselves and were worried that the Chinese might decide to occupy them as well. They kept us locked up for a week, which wasn't very pleasant as they only gave us one bowl of soup a day. Finally, they said that they would let us out of gaol just as long as we didn't try to stay in Bhutan. So we walked for another seven days down into Assam. There I tried to get work, but the only jobs available were those for labourers on road gangs up in the mountains. As I spoke Hindi reasonably well it occurred to me that I might be of some use to the Tibetan authorities who were trying to set up refugee camps with the help of the Indian government. I spoke to a Tibetan official and within a few weeks I had become a Relief Officer at Buxa.'

'Does Buxa deserve its grim reputation? Most people speak of it as if it were one of the outer circles of hell.'

Wangdu Dorje philosophically contemplated the

bottom of his mug. 'Actually, I think the thirteen months I spent there were the most unpleasant of my life. The conditions were very bad and many people died. It had originally been a prisoner of war camp, you see, and the whole place was surrounded by barbed wire. Eventually I was able to leave because I was elected as a representative for the people of U-Tsang, which is the administrative region of central and southern Tibet. From then on, my career was entirely in government. In 1963 I became Secretary to the Kashag, the Tibetan cabinet, and then a year later I was appointed Minister for Home Affairs. In 1968 I also became Minister for Security and I managed both portfolios until 1977 when I was sent down to Delhi to be the Dalai Lama's Representative, responsible for our relations with the Government of India.'

It struck me that representing an administration denied official recognition might be a complex task.

'In a sense the Government of India's relationship is with His Holiness personally. You see, this is actually an important question. There are many Tibetans nowadays who are great enthusiasts for democracy – democracy, democracy, all we hear about is democracy – and who say we must have a Prime Minister apppointed by elected officials. Even the Dalai Lama himself has supported this idea. People are also legitimately concerned with what might happen to the Tibetan cause if His Holiness were to die and we were left with no obvious leader. But there is no doubt that the attitude of the Government of India towards a Tibetan Prime Minister would be completely different.'

'Has the attitude of the Government of India altered over the years? Are they getting tired of you? After all they have enough problems of their own these days.'

'No, not really. They still partly finance new settlements. They also pay for the majority of our children to go to school. They have been very generous. Of course there have been some difficulties. A few years ago when the Chinese allowed the Tibetans to travel more freely, we started to get children coming from Tibet, mostly illegally, hoping to be educated in the schools here. There were up to a thousand annually, which did not please the Indian government very much.'

'Do you think the system of government that the Tibetans have evolved in exile is a satisfactory one? After all, you must know as much about it as anyone.'

'Well, it works. The Kashag, which up until now has been directly appointed by the Dalai Lama, does the day-to-day administration, but the elected Peoples' Deputies control the budget and in the last resort can veto proposals. So we have established a kind of democracy. And under this system there's no doubt that the Tibetans in India, even though they are refugees, are doing much better than those left behind in Tibet itself.'

Leaving him to grapple with his proofs unmolested, we struggled back up the hill to McCleod Ganj for a lunch appointment with one of the new breed of Tibetan politicians. A friend of Tenzin's – they were at university together in the '60s – Lodi Gyari had risen over the years to become the exiled administration's Minister for International Relations. Thanks to increasing sympathy for the Tibetan cause, this is a position which guarantees public prominence, and his is a name now frequently to be found in the quality dailies of Europe and America. A disturbance in Lhasa, a detonation of outrage in Peking, and the world's newsrooms are hungry for a quotation. On those occasions when they manage to get through on the phone, Lodi Gyari is invariably the man to supply it.

We had agreed to meet at the Hotel Tibet, a modern two-storey building at the far end of McCleod Ganj, owned by the Tibetan government and having a slightly inappropriate reputation for the best Chinese food in town.

Lodi Gyari, a large, black-haired man in early middle age, greeted me courteously, slapped Tenzin affectionately on the back, and said that he had already ordered the house speciality – twice-cooked pork with white cabbage – as well as a variety of side dishes. Did I like sweet and sour? Despite being one of the members of the Tibetan Kashag he was casually dressed in a white open-necked shirt and grey flannel trousers. His instructions nonetheless had an electrifying effect on the staff, who scurried about energetically, even when there didn't seem to be much that needed doing, and whose natural Tibetan affability was quite submerged beneath an attitude of exaggerated deference. The object of their respect and concern settled back in his chair, exuding the quiet confidence of someone accustomed to getting his own way. Having lunch with inquisitive foreigners was plainly an everyday occurrence.

I quickly concluded that he was a natural politician, a man who irrespective of time and place would have found himself drawn to public life as inevitably as a salmon smolt to the sea. It was his natural habitat.

As an opening conversational gambit I remarked what a pretty place Upper Dharamsala was. So tranquil, so unspoiled, such a wonderful view down to the plains. If one had to be an exile, then there were doubtless many worse places that one could have ended up. Lodi Gyari agreed that indeed it was an attractive town, even if nowadays rather crowded. Something would have to be done about its infrastructure: its open drains were a health hazard and general disgrace. As to its being tranquil, that was a matter of opinion. To an outsider it might well appear so, but if you were involved in Tibetan politics then it seldom seemed particularly peaceful.

What, I wondered, were the political issues presently

exercising the corridors of power? He thought for a moment, took a sip of tea, and then with what seemed to be a note of weary resignation in his voice replied that the Strasburg Proposal, or at least its implications, remained close to the top of the agenda and unfortunately showed few signs of descending it.

A little less than a year before – on 15 June 1988 – the Dalai Lama had addressed the European Parliament in Strasburg and set out what he described as a 'realistic solution' to the Tibetan problem. (It was a speech that, a few months after our lunch with Lodi Gyari, was to help win him the Nobel Peace Prize.) In it, he had offered the Chinese government several major concessions. Rather than insisting on full Tibetan independence, his administration had declared itself willing for Tibet to become 'a self-governing democratic political entity . . . in association with the People's Republic of China.' Furthermore, China could remain responsible for Tibet's foreign policy, stationing a limited number of troops on Tibetan soil for defensive purposes.

The Tibetans had been starting to get desperate. Nothing much had happened to further their cause since the brief flurry of activity at the beginning of the decade, when effective contact had been re-established between Peking and Dharamsala. China's programme of economic liberalisation had continued, but politically her gerontocrats had remained as obdurate and self-righteous as ever. Worst of all, rather than seeking compromise through negotiation, it seemed that they had decided to rid themselves of their Tibetan embarrassment once and for all by encouraging large scale immigration. The tourist industry, a provider of desirable white-collar jobs, had been developed specifically to encourage Han Chinese to settle in Lhasa and the other major Tibetan towns. There were six million Tibetans in Tibet and 1,200 million Chinese in China. If only half a per cent of the

Han population could be induced to move westwards onto the Tibetan plateau then the immigrants would find themselves in the ethnic majority. This, many Tibetans believed, was precisely what had already happened. Certainly in the eastern parts of their country, in areas which had once been parts of Kham and Amdo, the Tibetans were by now heavily outnumbered.

Tourism had, however, proved to be a double-edged sword. With foreigners providing moral support and acting as witnesses, the Tibetans had become unexpectedly rebellious. There had been riots in Lhasa in October 1987 and again the following March. To the Dalai Lama – Buddhist monk and admirer of Mahatma Gandhi – such developments were anathema. He deplored violence, yet his nation was faced with oblivion and some kind of action plainly had to be taken. The result was the infamous proposal with its unforced concessions on Tibetan sovereignty. These, so critics insisted, undermined thirty years of work and virtually the entire justification for the existence of a government in exile.

'It went down particularly badly in Tibet itself,' Lodi Gyari observed glumly, while doling out rice from a large metal bowl.

'It was unpopular enough here, but in Tibet it was a disaster. They were particularly upset by the Dalai Lama's remark that he did not want to take an active part in a future Tibetan government; that all he wanted was the establishment of a democratic system. Democracy's all very well, but you can't simply impose it on people. You have to take them along with you. Here in India the Tibetans understand the idea, though frankly the majority would much rather the Dalai Lama just told them what to do. Much rather.'

He paused for a moment as if briefly to consider this lamentable state of affairs.

'In Tibet they couldn't see what we were trying to

achieve at all. They said "Independence and the return of the Dalai Lama to rule over us are everything we've been fighting for. Why are we giving in now?" They felt betrayed. And of course we can't just disregard their opinions. They're the ones who have to live with the Chinese.'

'Does the Dharamsala administration have much influence over what goes on in Tibet?'

'No, not really. It's the Dalai Lama who has the power. Whether we like it or not we're stuck with the consequences of this extraordinary loyalty that Tibetans have to His Holiness. It is the dominant political factor both here and in Tibet. And of course this particular Dalai Lama has more influence than any other in history. More even than his predecessor, the Thirteenth.'

He hesitated for a moment, as if conscious of an impending indiscretion, and then plunged on regardless.

'Let's face it, Tibet was *not* a united nation in 1949. The Lhasa government did not exercise its authority uniformly over the whole country. Large areas of Kham were under the control of local chiefs. Even today it is only the Dalai Lama who keeps the Khampas in tow.' For confirmation of this scandalous opinion he glanced across at Tenzin, who seemed taken aback to hear such a frank admission of the inadmissible. United by language and culture, the Tibetans are nonetheless plagued by factionalism – both religious and political – the greatest source of schism being the animosity felt by some Khampas for their compatriots in Lhasa and Central Tibet. But in conversation with outsiders, such problems are usually circumvented. Rather like a family disgrace, they are considered unsuitable for general discussion and are diligently avoided.

Who, I wondered, had been its most vehement detractors in Dharmsala?

'Well, a lot of people are worried about such developments, but I suppose a focus for discontent is the Tibetan Youth Congress.'

Back in 1970, a group of young Tibetans, dissatisfied with the cosy way in which the exiled government was then being run, had inaugurated a youth movement to raise the pressure of political debate. Whether or not they realised it at the time, they were creating an equivalent to a parliamentary opposition. The Tibetan establishment, which had then had less than a decade to get used to the theory of democracy, was not best pleased to find itself being subjected so soon to a practical demonstration of its methods.

In March 1977, when the President of the TYC was an ambitious young activist called Lodi Gyari, a hunger strike was organised in Delhi next to offices of the United Nations, its aim being to oblige the UN to reopen its dust-coated files on Tibet. Quite coincidentally, an Indian general election was then underway, bringing to an end the State of Emergency unwisely declared by Indira Gandhi eighteen months earlier. The Janata Party, which had long been supportive of the Tibetan cause from the safety of the opposition benches, was victorious at the polls and abruptly the Tibetans found themselves in the novel position of being the guests of a broadly sympathetic regime. In order to take maximum advantage of the situation, Lodi Gyari went to call on members of the new administration and extracted from them promises of support.

Returning to Dharamsala, presumably not a little pleased at his own cleverness, he soon discovered that far from his initiative being applauded, it was regarded as insufferably presumptuous and liable to endanger the entire relationship between the Tibetan government in exile and their Indian hosts. Triumph turned into fiasco and he and three of his colleagues were forced to resign from their positions within the TYC.

Even without his ignominy their glory would have been short-lived, for within a few weeks the Janata government had thought better of its impetuosity and reverted to the cautious foreign policy of the previous administration.

I was just about to observe that the indiscretions of his youth had clearly not damaged his career in the long term, when lunch was brought abruptly to an end. A small clump of deferential officials materialised at the side of the table. Hurried consultation was followed by profuse apologies. Pressing matters of state required his attention. One of the Dalai Lama's brothers had arrived from America – where he is an academic – and was seeking his opinion on a difficult subject. He was sure that we would understand. Another time. No. Absolutely not. He wouldn't hear of it. The bill was already settled.

'The Chinese regard us as their Number One Enemy.'

Tashi Namgyal, the Secretary General of the Tibetan Youth Congress, seemed rather taken with the glamour of this remark. He paused for the sake of emphasis, and stared at Tenzin with a good deal of pride and just a hint, or so it seemed to me, of complacency. He was a sturdy, black-haired man in his early thirties, dressed in olive-green fatigues.

'Why is that?'

'Because we are outspoken. We talk complete independence and are sworn to struggle for it even at the cost of our lives.' He seemed to survey his own violent death with complete equanimity, as well he might, it being an extremely distant prospect.

We were sitting in a small, tidy office on the second floor of a building just up the road from the Hotel Tibet. It was a fresh, clear morning and the sun was shining confidently in through the open window. The sultry heat that presages the arrival of the monsoon had, for the moment, lifted. Taking advantage of the fine weather a colony of crows in a nearby tree was having a pitched battle over nesting rights and their outraged cawing at times made conversation almost impossible.

Was he, I enquired, a full-time politician? If so, how were his activities financed? The exiled government itself was, by all accounts, chronically short of funds.

'Oh, we manage. The TYC has over ten thousand members. Until a few years ago we had only a president and a secretary general who were full-time officers. Nowadays there are five of us.'

'So how did you reach your present position?'

'I was a child at the time of the '59 Uprising and I was brought to safety in India by one of our neighbours. While the TYC was being set up, I was at school in Madhya Pradesh, right in the middle of India. A very long way from Tibet.'

He hesitated, as if uncertain whether or not to digress.

'Actually, I heard a short while ago that my parents are still alive. They live in Kham, in Chinghai Province. It's part of China now.'

I suggested that it must be difficult to feel strong emotions for people who are just names – rather than a flesh-and-blood reality – even if they are one's parents. He shrugged. Living in a community of exiles, where fragmented families are the rule rather than the exception, perhaps it didn't do to make a fuss about such things.

'I finished school and went to work in Bhutan. The Bhutanese government offered me a job. They said they would train me as a forestry officer. But I felt that I had only been given this opportunity because of the education provided by the Tibetan government. I decided that I should give something back to the system that had helped me, so I talked to the Dalai Lama's Representative and obtained his permission to come to Dharamsala.'

It struck me that this principled stand might have had something to do with a disinclination to be a forestry officer in the wilds of Bhutan, but he wouldn't hear of it.

'I wrote to the director of Swiss Aid to Tibetans to ask for his help and he replied that his organisation would give me a scholarship. So I did a degree: Bachelor of Commerce. After that I wanted to do law, but I was told that this would be pointless because in India if you obtain a law degree by correspondence course you are not allowed to practise. So I joined the Tibetan government service. That was the beginning of my political career.'

Turning to a more general topic, I said that I'd heard the TYC were opposed to compromise with the Chinese. Tashi Namgyal suddenly became very indignant and passionate.

'We disagree strongly with the administration and we try to present this matter to the public. We are a democratic society and the people must decide. Public opinion is in favour of *full* independence.'

'But isn't your government just being practical: trying to find a workable compromise with the Chinese: allowing them to save face, and at the same time giving the Tibetans control over their own affairs.'

'We can't follow a middle way. You cannot compromise with the Chinese. They will make an agreement on paper – like the "One Country, Two Systems" deal for Hong Kong – but one slight excuse and they will do precisely as they like.'

'So how will you win independence if you are not prepared to negotiate and to compromise?'

'The first and most important thing is to make the Chinese settlers go back to China, otherwise Tibet is finished. This will involve force. We must make them feel uneasy by taking direct action: burning their shops and so on. If it is inevitable, we may have to attack them personally. Also you should remember that these settlers are very obedient. If the Chinese government tells them to go, they will pack up and leave within twenty-four hours.'

I glanced across at Tenzin to see how he was coping with this heresy. Not well apparently. He seemed to have been rendered not only speechless, but also temporarily immobile. Led by a Buddhist monk, an unwavering advocate of non-violent resistance, the Tibetans, whatever their private opinions about the likelihood of its success, generally profess complete loyalty to the official policy. A Tibetan terrorist is a complete impossibility as he or she would be instantly disowned by the Dalai Lama, the government in exile, and 90 per cent of the Tibetan population. Which is not to say that the majority of Tibetans are under any illusions about the readiness of the Chinese to bow down before superior moral example. Mao's famous dictum that power comes from the barrel of a gun is frequently admitted to bear an unpleasant resemblance to the truth. And the fact that representatives of less scrupulous organisations often receive a sympathetic hearing from governments which cavil at issuing the Dalai Lama with an entry visa arouses some bitterness but increasingly little surprise.

There is, however, an additional factor which invariably complicates the discussion of such matters. When the Tibetan refugees fled to India in 1959 they found themselves the guests of a country which only twelve years earlier had won its independence from a colonial power. Unsurprisingly, they studied how this had been achieved and were pleased to note the obvious compatibility between Gandhi's non-violent protests and their own Buddhist pacifism. Not only was non-violence morally right; it actually appeared to work. In consequence the Tibetans have tended to believe ever since that their highly ethical stance will in the end yield results, pragmatism and principle enjoying a joyful consummation at some future date so far unspecified.

Alas, events may not prove to be quite so tractable. Although Gandhi undoubtedly made himself a considerable nuisance to the British colonial authorities, it is debatable to what extent he was responsible for their ultimate departure. There is reason to suppose that the British left India chiefly because they had lost the will to power. Events at home were more pressing and an empire had suddenly become an expensive encumbrance. Anyway, by 1928 the franchise had been extended to the entire adult British population and a fully democratic legislature was having twinges of conscience about suppressing the political rights of subject peoples. All of which is rather different from the present situation in China and Tibet. Were a Tibetan Gandhi to have the temerity to lead a contemporary Salt March, there seems every reason to suppose that he would be arrested, imprisoned, tortured, and shot.

'Don't your views about violent action in Tibet bring you into conflict with the Dalai Lama?' Tenzin had evidently recovered the power of speech.

'Oh no. Definitely not. We don't oppose non-violence. The TYC believes very strongly that non-violence is very effective – particularly given the size of China and the strength of its army – but we also feel that violence has a role to play.'

'But surely the two methods cannot be complementary? They are mutually incompatible.'

'We do not disagree with the Dalai Lama, we just think that violence is one method by which our goal may be achieved. Take the recent risings in Lhasa for example. We feel they have been very constructive and very timely. Before, many people thought there were just a few Tibetans in India who wanted independence.'

'So did the TYC help organise the riots?'

'We keep contact with people in Tibet, but we cannot go into the details of these things. But there should definitely be more demonstrations. We must involve ourselves so that an outside power could help us. Look what happened in Afghanistan. We could fight a guerrilla war again. After all, we had a guerrilla army in Nepal until 1972. And it was not broken by the Chinese. The CIA stopped supplying us so that Nixon could visit Peking. That is all. If the guerrillas were still active, I tell you I would go there. I would fight.'

Somewhat bemused by this mixture of energy, hope, naivity, and self-delusion, Tenzin and I made our way down to Thekchen Choling, the Dalai Lama's Residence, where we had an appointment with his Private Secretary. We hoped to be able to arrange an audience for when we returned to Dharamsala in the autumn. As we were a quarter of an hour early we sat on a bench beside the main entrance under the watchful eye of an Indian security guard.

In general, Tenzin had little time for Tashi Namgyal's incendiary plan of action. It contained, he said, exactly the kind of ideas Tibetans tended to come up with when they lived comfortably and didn't have enough to do. Dharamsala specialised in producing such amateur heroics. Demonstrations in Lhasa were one thing – they generated publicity – but talk of regrouping guerrilla armies and murdering Chinese civilians was so much nonsense. As far as he was concerned, if anything was to be saved from the wreckage of Tibet, then the Dalai Lama's policy of occupying the high moral ground and attempting to negotiate with the Chinese was the only option available. Though, he conceded, there were many of his compatriots who thought differently, including one or two whose opinion he respected.

At eleven o'clock sharp we approached the guard at the gate, stated our business, and were escorted to a small reception room just inside the Residence compound. This was neat, recently dusted, and immediately conveyed an impression of competence and order. On a polished table, next to a scale model of the Potala in a glass case, there was a selection of magazines and sober academic journals with articles on all aspects of Tibetan life: from studies of polyandry among nomadic yak herders, to learned comparisons of the Chinese and Tibetan translations of the Sanskrit Buddhist scriptures. I was still trying to decide whether I was more interested in Ladakhi shamans than Himalayan homoeopathy when a young man from the secretariat arrived to take us to our meeting.

We crossed the smooth metalled driveway that led up to the front entrance of the Dalai Lama's Residence, skirted round some gaudy flower beds, climbed a steep flight of stone steps and came to a modest complex of single-storey office buildings. Through the first open doorway, two robed and shaven-headed monks could be seen struggling to separate the screen of a desk-top computer from its polystyrene protective container. One of them looked up as my shadow fell across him. 'Apple,' he said, and grinned.

Tenzin Tethong, the Dalai Lama's Private Secretary, had himself been a monk for many years and although his duties are nowadays chiefly secular, in both his voice and demeanour there remained unmistakable traces of clerical gravitas. Of medium build, bespectacled, dressed in formal black robes, he greeted us in perfect English, with studied politeness. Tenzin, whom he had known since they were both in their teens, was the recipient of an ironical smile.

'I'm glad to see you're returning to the fold. Despite all

these years making money in Kathmandu, I knew you'd come back to the government service sooner or later. I'm sure we can find you a post in the Department of Economic Affairs. Your experience will be invaluable.'

Tenzin, aghast at the thought of returning to a civil servant's life – to say nothing of a civil servant's salary – sat down and declined to be amused.

The question of an audience with the Dalai Lama was briefly discussed and our request acceded to, on the understanding that we wouldn't just turn up in five months' time and expect to be slotted into the schedule on the afternoon of our arrival.

'So many Westerners want to see the Dalai Lama nowadays . . .' Tenzin Tethong observed with asperity, '. . . that I get quite a few complaints from Tibetans. They ask me if they need a foreign passport to have an audience with His Holiness.'

In addition to being the Dalai Lama's Private Secretary, Tenzin Tethong is also a politician: in his youth a founder of the TYC and for years subsequently a fixture in the Kashag, or cabinet. The Kashag is the Executive of the Tibetan government in exile, a group of approximately seven people, which takes the day-to-day policy decisions, directs the work of the civil serice, and whose actions are then subject to the scrutiny and approval of the elected assembly of Tibetan Peoples' Deputies. Its members, known as *Kalons*, have traditionally been appointed by the Dalai Lama, but nowadays – after the unexpected vogue for democracy in both China and Eastern Europe – they too have become subject to election by a conference of peoples' representatives.

What, I wondered, did the establishment think about TYC's dislike of its policies? And what of their enthusiasm for violent protest in Tibet? Tenzin Tethong stiffened visibly and his habitual gravity grew a shade darker.

'What exactly did they say?' he enquired suspiciously, as if fearing the worst.

'They were in favour of driving out the Chinese settlers by the use of force.'

'Who said that?' His voice took on a headmasterly tone, only to be quickly suppressed. 'Oh, never mind. There are differences of opinion among Tibetans. There always have been. It's healthy that people should say what they really feel. Unfortunately, the TYC are right in many ways. It is difficult to do a deal with the Chinese. The British are finding this out with Hong Kong. At least the people in Hong Kong *are* Chinese and, unlike Tibet, Hong Kong *was* part of China. And then there's no doubt that the riots in Lhasa have done more to create awareness of the Tibetan situation than anything we have been able to do during the last thirty years. The media are only interested in violence. Governments – your government, the British government – say terrorism must be eradicated, but do they support peaceful movements and men of peace like His Holiness the Dalai Lama? No, they do not. And the British government, because of British India's relations with Tibet earlier this century, is one of the few that fully understands the truth about the Tibetan situation.'

'Do you yourself believe wholeheartedly in negotiations?'

'It's not really a question of being wholehearted. I want full independence; we all do. But this is very difficult to achieve immediately. In exile it is not difficult to hold strong opinions. We would like to go home, but for the present we have enough to eat, our children go to school. Meanwhile inside Tibet itself the people suffer and the transfer of population continues. Soon Tibet will be gone, so we must take some action now.'

Tea was called for and we sat drinking it, calmly discussing the destiny of nations. In the background there was the steady clatter of typewriters and the murmur of conversation. Every now and then a phone rang. For the staff of the Dalai Lama's secretariat, it was just another day at the office.

Juchen Thupten, the senior Kalon (and hence the nearest thing the exiled government has to a Prime Minister), was a burly man in his fifties, greying hair brushed back from his forehead to reveal a furrowed and criss-crossed brow. Sleeves rolled up, he looked rather like a trade union leader, the hard-bargaining representative of men engaged in some routinely arduous and sporadically dangerous employment. Sitting stolid and impassive, he might have been hewn from a block of particularly unyielding granite, an angular sculpture from some workshop of socialist realism. On the whole, I decided, he didn't look very Tibetan at all. But then there is no particular Tibetan physical stereotype. Insofar as it is possible to generalise, the Khampas tend to be taller and broader than the Central Tibetans, while the Lhasa people are often quite lightly built, with a more delicate (they might say refined) bone structure. Some Tibetans have an unequivocally Mongoloid appearance, while others, like Juchen Thupten, seem to have inherited vaguely Caucasian characteristics.

There is no universal agreement about where the Tibetans originally came from, although it is generally held that they migrated from eastern Central Asia (a term imprecise enough to allow for a generous margin of error), south towards the Himalayas round about the beginning of the Christian era. More specific information is hard to come by.

We had returned to Gangchen Kyishong, the offices of the government in exile, and were sitting in the reception chamber of the Kashag building. Juchen Thupten had agreed to give us half an hour of his time before lunch. It was a large and colourful room with a peony-red carpet, sofas scattered with embroidered bolsters, and a dozen or so low tables on which intricate carvings of flowers and auspicious symbols had been picked out in an entire shade-card of brilliant gloss. The most striking decoration was a large heraldic device, supported by snow lions – Tibet's contribution to the international bestiary of mythological animals – while next to the window, above a relatively modest throne, hung a full-length lifesize colour photograph of the Dalai Lama, beaming beatifically.

Juchen Thupten was harassed. This soon became obvious. His manner might be stoical, but behind the severe and unadorned façade, a bedlam of thoughts was in tumultuous contention. There was only a week to go before the biennial Gyalong Tsogchen, or General Assembly, which would be attended by not only the entire Tibetan government, but also the welfare officers of the various settlements in India and Nepal, the Dalai Lama's Representatives abroad, religious leaders, and the heads of important educational institutions. In short, just about everyone of consequence in exiled Tibetan society.

Being both an extremely busy and an incorrigibly modest man, he was finding it difficult to understand why I was so interested in the minutiae of his life-history. He had been born in Kham, he said, of a modest background. His father had worked for the local chieftain. As a young man he had joined the guerrillas fighting the Chinese. Yes, he had seen some fighting. He had then escaped to India. What more could I possibly wish to know? After coming to India? Well, he had been one of the first settlers at Bylakuppe down in the south, near Mysore. Then in 1972 he had been elected to the Assembly of Tibetan Peoples' Deputies where he had served for four years, being elevated to the Kashag by the Dalai Lama in 1976.

Was it usual for members of the Kashag to have served as elected deputies beforehand? It was not *un*usual, he said, but such experience was by no means compulsory. So did ordinary Tibetans regularly attain high office, or were the most important posts still distributed among the members of a self-perpetuating oligarchy as had formerly been the case in Tibet?

A flicker of interest passed across Juchen Thupten's face. Here, it seemed, was a subject sufficiently important to displace, albeit briefly, his anxieties about the General Assembly. Leaning forward for emphasis, he placed a broad hand on his right thigh to steady himself.

'Since we came into exile, our social and governmental structures have undergone dramatic changes. People like me would not have dreamt of achieving high office before. In Tibet it would have been impossible for an ordinary man to become a Kalon. Inconceivable.'

He slumped back against the cushions and stared at me to see if his words had taken sufficient effect. I decided to be slightly provocative:

'So there is no truth in the Chinese accusation that the people in Dharamsala are just remnants of the old feudal system; a system which they would ideally like to see re-established?'

Juchen Thupten didn't actually smile, but he seemed to come as close to doing so as present adverse circumstances would permit.

'You would scarcely expect me to agree with the Chinese. But in answer to your question, no, we are not fighting for the restoration of the feudal system. We are concerned for the welfare of six million Tibetans.'

Despite such laudable sentiments, one does not have to spend more than a few days in Dharamsala to become aware of the fragility of the political system which the Tibetans have established there. The whole edifice – democratic ambitions notwithstanding – is all too plainly held together by the will of one man. It was the Dalai Lama, under the tutelage of Nehru, who originally insisted that the exiled Tibetans should draw up a constitution in order to present a clear ideological alternative to Maoism. Nowadays it is the Dalai Lama who insists that they should further democratise their administration, and place less reliance on his own opinions and advice. Obedience to authority, or more specifically to religious authority, is engrained in the national character and the self-assertion required of a citizen in a democracy does not come easily to most Tibetans, particularly those of the older generation. They now find themselves in the curious position of being ordered to be less acquiescent.

I put this point to Juchen Thupten who became suddenly rather morose.

'Right now we are trying to make our government a democracy in the true sense of the term, but this is dependent on His Holiness the Dalai Lama remaining at the head of the administration.' He paused for a moment to contemplate this uncomfortable paradox. 'Nowadays His Holiness has to visit foreign countries, to receive foreign visitors, so generally he has less time for the Kashag. But there is still constant contact and he is consulted on every major issue. His Holiness attaches extreme importance to the institutions of democracy.'

'So if the Dalai Lama were to die would you be able to carry on? Could the government in exile continue without him? Is your democracy sufficiently well established?'

Juchen Thupten frowned and looked disinclined to answer. Eventually, with the look of a man who had decided, somewhat against his better judgement, to reply to one last troublesome question, he said: 'I don't know what would happen, but certainly it would be more difficult for us. Very, very difficult indeed.'

*

Tenzin and I went to have lunch in the staff canteen. At long, bare trestle tables the foot soldiers of the administration were crammed shoulder to shoulder, eating large steamed dumplings, each about the size of an orange, and a lank green vegetable, apparently a kind of spinach. This bland and frugal menu only became palatable when dunked in an irascible red chilli sauce, puddles of which were dotted about on old earthenware saucers. On their own the greyish dumplings tasted of nothing in particular. Still, after four or five of them it seemed unlikely that one would need to eat again for a week. Hunger suffocated rather than satisfied, I gazed around. Most of the faces were young and animated and the atmosphere reminded me agreeably of a college dining hall.

Things had not changed very much in twenty years, Tenzin remarked indistinctly between mouthfuls, showing few obvious signs of nostalgia for his former life. It was all just the same as when he had worked for the Department for Home Affairs in the 1960s.

'The only difference is that all of us had been born in Tibet. None of this lot has ever been near the place.'

I was impressed that so many bright, young, educated Tibetans obviously chose to take ill-paid government jobs in order to be part of the cause, to work for the independence of their country. I detected, I said, an atmosphere of selfless dedication to public service. Tenzin looked doubtful. There was, he agreed, still a resilient strain of idealism among young Tibetans in Dharamsala, but then it was also extremely difficult to get well-paid employment in India; with or without a university degree. Naturally, Indians tended to get preference in the job market – after all it was their country – and even for them getting started in life was seldom easy without the right connections.

Having followed the general example and rinsed our dirty plates under a cold-water tap by the door, we wandered across to the library where we had agreed to meet Choedak Gyatso, a member of the Assembly of Tibetan Peoples' Deputies. The library itself was a handsome and substantial two-storey building, constructed from modern materials in a traditional Tibetan style: the white-washed walls tapering inward slightly towards the flat roof, a pleasing modification of the basic rectangle echoed by the scarlet window frames. Shielding the main entrance was a carved and filigreed porch. Unlike many of the government offices which were anonymous, flimsy, and had clearly been put up at the minimum possible expense, the library seemed solid and permanent; a tacit admission that the Tibetans were unlikely to be returning home – at least in the immediate future.

Although having no preconception of what Choedak Gyatso might look like, I was definitely not expecting him to be a monk. In fact it took quite a few moments for me to be convinced that I was actually talking to the right person. Fortunately, he did not appear to be in the least offended by my temporary confusion. Indeed, he seemed to find it extremely amusing. I soon realised that he was a man naturally disposed to be amused by life in general. Not for him the wan and wasting melancholia of an exile pining for home. Or for that matter the solemn, withdrawn, and otherworldly demeanour one might expect from a religious contemplative. In robust good humour, he exuded prodigious amounts of energy, and was plainly delighted to enthuse about his work as an elected representative of the people.

We agreed to sit in the shade of the library porch. I explained that we had just been to see a senior member of the Kashag. What, I wondered, was the state of relations between the Executive and those democratically appointed to keep an eye on it?

Choedak Gyatso was immediately convulsed with mirth. At length, having recovered sufficiently to be able to speak, he replied: 'Oh we have our disagreements you know,' before once again succumbing to immoderate laughter.

'So who gets the final say?'

'We do.' He became abruptly serious. 'Generally things are settled by consensus, but only the Peoples' Deputies have voting rights. For example, we are just about to have our General Assembly. It happens every two years. The decisions taken will have to be implemented by the government agencies. Tibetans from all walks of life attend the conference, but the final decisions rest with us.'

He beamed at me, apparently with Panglossian confidence that everything was for the best in the best of all possible worlds. I was rather taken aback, being unprepared for quite this degree of assurance and optimism.

'So how are the deputies appointed and how many are there of them?'

'We are elected by universal franchise over the age of eighteen. Voting takes place in the Tibetan settlements throughout India. We have an electoral register maintained by regional commissions. Just now there are twelve deputies. Formerly it was seventeen. Now the number is to be increased again.'

'Only twelve?' This struck me as rather a half-hearted commitment to democratic accountability.

'Well, democracy costs money. The deputies have to be paid and our administration is very short of finance. Besides, there are only around a hundred thousand of us in India and Nepal.'

A brief calculation on the back page of my notebook confirmed that this was indeed a comparatively generous ratio. If 55 million Britons are represented by 650

Members of Parliament, then each MP may crudely be said to have a constituency of 84,600 people. Whereas each Tibetan deputy would be accountable to only 8,330 of his compatriots.

'At the moment . . .' Choedak Gyatso continued serenely, clearly impervious to any hint of criticism, '. . . six of the deputies represent the three regions of Tibet; two each for U-Tsang, Kham and Amdo. Then five more are elected by the members of our religious groups. I myself was elected by the Nyingma-pa Buddhist sect.'

'So the clergy still have a big say in Tibetan political life?'

'Certainly, though not as much as they did in Tibet. There, as you probably know, we had two parallel administrations, each responsible to the Dalai Lama, one run by the nobility and one by the monks.'

I said that I was dimly aware that such had been the arrangement, but that I had never been at all clear how it had actually worked.

'No. . .' Choedak Gyatso chuckled, '. . .I daresay not.'

'So do the monasteries feel that they nowadays have sufficient say in politics or do they resent their loss of power?'

'Oh no. They are quite content. Besides, the monks still have a privileged position. You see they can vote for monastic representatives and also in their regional elections.'

'So they can vote twice?' I enquired, vainly trying to stifle my incredulity.

'Yes, yes of course,' Ghoedak Gyatso assented equably, as if nothing could be more tediously normal.

There was a slight pause while I digested this surprising information, until I was suddenly struck by an arithmetical anomaly:

'What happened to the twelfth deputy?'

'I beg your pardon?'

'The twelfth deputy. We have only accounted for eleven of them. Six for the Tibetan regions and five for the religious orders.'

'Oh, one is nominated by His Holiness the Dalai Lama. He is generally an expert of some kind. At the moment he is an authority on Tibetan literature.'

Again the ubiquitous presence of the Dalai Lama. Surely the Tibetans realised how vulnerable they were leaving themselves by not building a system independent of any one individual? It seemed to me that given the existing system all the Chinese had to do was to wait until the Dalai Lama died, at which point, in all probability, the Dharamsala government would collapse and effective organised resistance promptly cease.

Choedak Gyatso listened with no evident sign of alarm to my dire predictions for the future. 'You're exactly right. . .' he said in a soothing voice, '. . .and this is just what His Holiness feels and why he is so insistent that there should be democratic change.'

Determined not to give in without a struggle, I persevered with no great expectation of success: 'Have you ever considered having a multi-party system with the leader of the victorious group becoming Prime Minister?'

'Yes, this has been proposed – the Dalai Lama has supported the idea for several years – but we cannot develop so fast. We cannot merely impose our ideas from the top. There must be a general will among the mass of the population. After all . . .' Choedak Gyatso smiled broadly as if conscious of irrevocably clinching the argument, '. . .what is the point of democracy if it does not express the will of the people?'

The following morning we took a taxi to the neighbouring hamlet of Forsyth Ganj. Surmounting a small hill, we drove onto a large, open playground where a couple of hundred blue-uniformed schoolchildren were noisily at play. We had arrived at the Dharamsala Tibetan Childrens' Village, a residential orphanage and school, at which one of Tenzin's nephews was currently a pupil.

Despite frequent attemps at elucidation, my understanding of Choegyal genealogy was still a coin-sized circle of light surrounded by a continent of darkness.

'When my brothers and fathers fled from Tibet,' Tenzin began again wearily as we climbed a steep flight of steps up the school office, '. . . they were forced to leave behind my mother and three sisters. My second eldest sister, Yatuk, subsequently married and had eight children, six of whom still live in Kham. However, two have managed to come to India. One is a monk in Sera monastery down near Mysore; the other, the youngest, is here at TCV. He's twelve now. We smuggled him out in 1985. My sister wanted at least one of her children to have a proper education. Despite all these improvements the Chinese claim to have made in Tibet, teaching Tibetan children to read still doesn't seem to be much of a priority.'

Inside the office two young women teachers were getting down to some paperwork. They looked up quizzically as we entered. Tenzin explained the purpose of our visit and one of them pulled down a large, grey box-file marked 'Children from Tibet – 85'. A young boy peering round the door was then instructed to put his curiosity to good use by taking us to the relevant accommodation block.

The school's buildings, dotted up and down the hillside, appeared basic but adequate. Through the glassless windows of the classrooms drifted the sound of multiplication tables being enthusiastically chanted and I was conscious of a cheerful, energetic atmosphere. The melancholy fact that most of the children had lost one or both parents seemed to have been miraculously dissipated. They looked healthy and happy, and in some respects the place struck me as distinctly preferable to the schools I myself had attended in England.

Despite the prevailing mood, Tenzin's nephew turned out to be a shy, silent, wild-looking boy, with crumpled clothes and a mop of tousled hair. Assiduously avoiding eye contact, he stared down at his hands as if hoping to find there a script for this distressing interview. Deciding that the presence of a stranger might well be intimidating, I wandered off to a grassy bank with a view down over the basketball court to the Forsyth Ganj army camp and the distant Kangra Valley.

After about ten minutes I was rejoined by Tenzin who remarked in a tone of suppressed exasperation that the boy was a difficult case. Although he seemed sullen and obstinate, he doubtless had a good heart. It was just that his early years seemed to have left him cowed. No matter how fortunate his present circumstances might be, his early childhood in Tibet seemed to have permanently stifled his capacity for happiness.

'He's coming to Kathmandu for the holidays. While he's there he can play with my brothers' children. They're his age. Maybe that will make a difference.'

I replied that it might be imagination, but I thought that I could already distinguish between children who had come from Tibet and those born in adverse circumstances in India. Even if the latter were orphans and had lived in the most spirit-crushing poverty, their natural exuberance seemed somehow to be capable of resucitation. It might be lying dormant, but it had not become extinct. Whereas the Tibetan children had apparently been irreversibly repressed by uncertainty and fear.

Tenzin declined to endorse this generalisation, but politely conceded that I might have a point.

As an incontrovertible statement of fact, I reminded him that we had better be moving if we were going to be on time for our appointment with Mrs Pema Gyalpo, the

Dalai Lama's sister, and since 1964 the Director of the Children's Village. Tenzin looked suddenly gloomy. Why, I wondered, was he showing so few signs of enthusiasm for this encounter? Was there something that he hadn't told me? Had his relationship with this eminent lady suffered, at some point in the distant past, some calamitous and irreparable fracture? On the contrary, Tenzin replied, he held her in the highest esteem and had had the honour of knowing her for the best part of thirty years. It was just that she was, well . . . Although never normally at a loss for English vocabulary, words seemed temporarily to fail him.

'A bit of a dragon?' I suggested.

'No, no, not all, certainly not,' Tenzin replied brusquely and set off rapidly back down the hillside. Feeling vaguely contrite, I lamely followed.

The Dalai Lama actually had two sisters. The elder, Mrs Tsering Dolma, was the first director of the Dharamsala orphanage, but after her untimely death in 1964 she was succeeded by her younger sibling, Pema Gyalpo. Although the story of the Dalai Lama's discovery is relatively well-known – the identification of the two-year-old son of peasant farmers, living in a remote village in north-eastern Tibet, not far from the (then) Chinese border – the other members of his large family, whose lives were of course utterly transformed by this momentous recognition, have been written about surprisingly little. The Dalai Lama's mother, who died in Dharamsala in 1981, actually gave birth to no fewer than sixteen children, of whom nine died in infancy. Among the seven who survived, there were five boys (the Dalai Lama, originally called Lhamo Dhondrub, was the fourth), and two girls.

Half a century as a scholar monk and political leader has endowed the Dalai Lama with a cultivated and commanding manner, yet in his rugged, almost earthy appearance there are still intimations of a peasant background. In consequence I was taken aback, on being ushered into her office, to find that his sister was a handsome woman of decidedly aristocratic demeanour. Sitting very upright at a large neat desk behind a portable typewriter, she was dressed in an immaculately laundered pale yellow blouse and charcoal grey gown. Her thick black hair was pinned back severely into a chignon, not a strand, not a whisp, apparently having given a moment's thought to disobedience. I was instantly reminded of a fierce, but kindly headmistress who had inspired in me at the age of five a complex mixture of affection and terror.

As Tenzin seemed to be unusually slow in coming forward, I began to explain as succinctly as possible what we were doing in Dharamsala, expecting every moment to be reproved for repeating myself, or mumbling, or contravening some elementary requirement of English grammar. To my relief, and somewhat to my surprise, she graciously replied that she was delighted to hear I was interested in the Tibetan cause, looked forward to discussing the present situation with me at length, but as she was unexpectedly pressed for time, perhaps we would care to come round to her bungalow for lunch.

'Then I can find out what Tenzin's been up to all this while,' she remarked as she accompanied us to the door. Tenzin flinched slightly, smiled thinly, and said nothing.

The bungalow in question turned out to be of a classic colonial type built at the turn of the century with a painted tin roof, a substantial brick chimney, and a long wooden verandah angled to allow leisurely and tranquil contemplation of the Indian plains. The forest, which had been thinned slightly but not felled, gathered protectively around this fragile capsule of past time, while a mile above, clearly etched against the greyish surviving snow, a vulture circled the grim crags of the Dhauladar. Tenzin and I paused at the garden gate while a motley collection of dogs – which had been enjoying the run of the lawn and in general took a dim view of visitors – was hustled away by the gardener.

Pema Gyalpo emerged from the living room and suggested that as it was a sunny day and not too hot we might care to sit outside.

'Unfortunately, this year some hornets have built a nest under the eaves, but they cause no trouble if they are left alone.'

I said how impressed I had been with my brief visit to the Children's Village. How orderly it had all looked. And what a congenial, constructive atmosphere the place had seemed to have. Pema Gyalpo allowed herself a sliver of a smile.

'I am glad you formed a good impression. Nonetheless we still have many problems. There are still financial constraints – despite the generosity of foreign sponsors – and the school is badly overcrowded. We have about fifteen hundred pupils who are supposed to be accommodated in "families" of about twenty students. At the moment, each home is obliged to care for at least thirty-five children. I'm afraid they cannot be looked after properly under such conditions.'

'But surely there are many fewer orphans than there once were? The material condition of the Tibetan exiles must have improved out of all recognition since the early days in the 1960s.'

'Not everywhere the Tibetans find themselves is quite as comfortable as Dharamsala. You will see that for yourself if you are going to travel with Tenzin to our settlements elsewhere in India. Of course things *have* changed. Originally the children who came here were orphans whose parents had been killed by the Chinese, or who died on the journey from Tibet, or who had succumbed to disease because of the sudden change in the climate. As you probably know, many Tibetan men and women were employed by the Indian authorities building roads in the mountains. There was nothing else for them to do. But many of those people died from the harsh and unfamiliar conditions. Their offspring were sent here. However, since 1979 we have had an influx of over a thousand children from Tibet. The year before last over four hundred came here; last year there were three hundred more. Only this year, because of the disturbances in Lhasa, they have stopped coming. This means that, at present, half of all the children in this school were born in Tibet not in India.'

For nearly twenty years, Tibetan exile was absolute. Those who had successfully escaped to India and Nepal were completely cut off from the family and friends they had left behind. They were aware that thousands had died, especially during the atrocious years of the Cultural Revolution, but just who had perished and who had survived, there was no way of knowing. Then in 1978, two years after the arrest of the Gang of Four, the thaw came.

The Chinese announced that, for the first time since 1959, Tibetans separated by the Himalayas would be allowed to resume contact. They would even be permitted to visit one another; provided they agreed to travel on Chinese passports. Even more surprisingly, the Chinese invited a delegation from Dharamsala to see conditions in Tibet for themselves. In August 1979, such a group, which included Lobsang Samten, one of the Dalai Lama's elder brothers, flew into Canton. In May the following year the General Secretary of the Communist Party, Hu Yaobang, publicly criticised the effect of Chinese policies on the Tibetan plateau. (He was forced to resign in January 1987 after student democracy demonstrations and has since died, still in official disgrace.) At the same time a second delegation from Dharamsala was making its way through the Tibetan region of Amdo. In June 1980 this was joined by a third group, led by Pema Gyalpo, which had been sent specifically to investigate educational standards among the mass of the Tibetan population.

It was too much to hope that such propitious developments would continue indefinitely. Large, enthusiastic crowds greeted the second delegation when it arrived in Lhasa. The Dalai Lama's name was vociferously chanted and one or two individuals, for whom discretion was clearly not the better part of valour, shouted out, 'Tibet is an independent country!' Immediately accused of being responsible for these 'splittist' demonstrations, the delegation was hustled out of the city and flown back to China on the first plane. Pema Gyalpo was allowed to complete her tour, but no more such dangerous invitations were issued, and Peking and Dharamsala returned to less adventurous forms of diplomacy.

Why, I wondered, had the Chinese ever embarked on this curious policy? Surely they could have anticipated such (from their point of view) disturbing results? Or were they so blinded by ideological self-righteousness that they assumed their guests would just stand and applaud the many achievements of their beneficent rule?

Pema Gyalpo, looking extremely stern, considered her answer at length.

'I think a decision of this importance – whether or not to invite a Tibetan delegation – would only be taken in Peking and very often the politicians in Peking do not know what the situation in Tibet is really like. They have probably never been there and the information they receive is mostly what their subordinates think they would like to hear, rather than what is actually the case.'

'So what do you feel nowadays about your mission to Tibet? Did it serve any useful purpose?'

'Certainly it was important that we knew what conditions in Tibet were really like. Things were so much worse than I had expected. For three months, most of the time I was in tears. I have never seen anything so awful. Nowadays it helps me to understand the background of the children who have come here to Dharamsala. Many of them have seen terrible things. For example, one little boy who arrived last year had been forced to watch his elder brother being executed. If children have gone through such experiences when they are very young there is a lot of healing we have to do to ensure that they grow up to be whole and balanced people. Of course the book-learning part of education is important, but here it is not everything.'

'So do you find the children from Tibet to be very different from those born in India? Or after a short while here do they become indistinguishable?'

'Oh no, they are very different. The children from Tibet are much more Tibetan. When I look at the children who have always lived in this country, I can see that they are part Indian. Such things are inevitable. How could they be otherwise? The other major difference is that although education in Tibet has not improved at all during the past thirty years and most of the children who come here cannot even write, they are so keen to learn. They progress very fast and think of nothing but learning. They are quite different from the children born and brought up here in Dharamsala. *They* think of nothing but playing.'

Sitting on the sun-dappled verandah, drowsy with the midday warmth, I could readily understand why. Tibet and its suffering began to seem extremely remote. Bees bumbled about among the marigolds and a languid breeze fumbled the stray tresses of creeper hanging down from the roof. It could not always be easy, I suggested, to sustain one's indignation, living in such tranquil and congenial surroundings. Dharamsala was so pretty, so peaceful.

Pema Gyalpo eyed me severely, her expression leaving me in little doubt that she herself experienced very few problems in this respect. Anxious to recover her good opinion, I assumed what I hoped was an expression of great earnestness. How, I wondered, had Tibetan social organisation been affected by the tribulations of life in India? Was the family unit managing to survive the stresses and strains of exile?

This was evidently a suitable subject, as Pema Gyalpo looked somewhat mollified.

'Well, in Tibet there were extended families. People were very close-knit. Generally there was no shortage of land, so if two young people got married, or if there were children, often it was possible just to build extra accommodation. But here, in India, a family may have only one room, two rooms. Suppose there are five children, which is probably about average, then they can hardly all stay together when they grow up. The children have to find a job – which may be a long way away – and a place to live, and therefore contact with their parents and grandparents is lost. Of course I realise it is like this in the West, but for us it is different. We want to keep the Tibetans together so that our cultural identity can be preserved. Unfortunately this is sometimes very difficult.'

'Five children sounds a lot. Do Tibetans regard contraception as irreligious?'

'No. At any rate not the young ones. I imagine all Buddhists would consider abortion to be sinful, but contraception is a different matter because it is the prevention of life not the destruction of it. Nowadays the more educated girls tend to put off having a family. But many people think that since so many thousands of Tibetans have been killed by the Chinese we must have as many children as possible. They have a point don't they?'

I agreed that they did.

'Personally, I am very aware of the financial constraints and try to persuade people that quality is more important than quantity. But I understand why others think differently.'

'So what is the average age at which Tibetan girls marry nowadays?'

'On average, around twenty-one, twenty-two. But many wait much longer, especially as I said the better-educated ones.'

'There is no difference then between the educational opportunities available to boys and to girls?'

'No, although a slightly higher proportion of boys do go on to take specialised courses at college or university. But this is to do with social attitudes; no educational authority dictates that this should be so.'

One of the things which strikes nearly all Westerners when they first encounter Tibetans is their great amiability, even in adverse circumstances. To me, this national character has always seemed to stem partly from the nature of the relations between the sexes. Tibetan men and women do not appear to struggle within the confines of repressive social conventions or taboos, and there is a naturalness in their behaviour which is perhaps a little surprising in the context of an otherwise conservative society.

I referred this general observation to Pema Gyalpo. Clearly the Dalai Lama's sister would be treated with exaggerated respect and deference, but did she not agree that the position of Tibetan women was, on the whole, quite favourable? For a moment she said nothing, being, or so it seemed, reluctant to apply the vocabulary of Western feminism to Tibetan social attitudes.

'Well, yes. I suppose so. I think Tibetan women are

quite . . .', she paused, '. . . liberated.' The word clearly struck her as being fraught with danger. It doubtless had treacherous layers of meaning, of which she was unaware, and to which she was therefore disagreeably vulnerable. 'We certainly never think of ourselves as being inferior – although to be honest some people do pray to be reborn as a man – and women's equality is not really an issue with us. Perhaps this is because we are preoccupied with national survival and other issues seem, at best, secondary. On the other hand, two seats in the Assembly of Tibetan People's Deputies used to be set aside for women, but this arrangement was abandoned because we felt it was unnecessary. We preferred to compete on equal terms.'

'So have women subsequently been elected in open competition with men?'

'Oh yes. There have been female deputies, and at the moment three out of the thirteen General Secretaries in our civil service are women. It is quite possible for women to reach senior positions in Tibetan society.'

'Which is very different from the way it was before the Chinese invasion?'

'True. But women were not treated badly in Tibet. The government and the bureaucracy may have been staffed entirely by men, but women had authority in the home and were in a much better situation than was traditionally the case in Asia.'

I was about to embark on a pet theory of mine – namely, that it was the struggle to survive in the harsh Tibetan climate which had required women to be active members of society, and which had refused to permit the corrupt indulgence of the zenana – but the conversation was interrupted by the arrival of a pair of irate orange hornets, neither of which seemed to have overheard the previous testament to their good character. When order was finally restored it became apparent that Pema Gyalpo had decided to change the subject.

'Now Tenzin . . . ,' she said firmly, 'What have you been doing with yourself since I was last in Kathmandu?'

'Eh? . . . Me?' Tenzin started violently, rather like a dreaming schoolboy suddenly required to name the six wives of Henry VIII. 'Oh nothing. Nothing much, you know.'

At nine the following morning, we had an appointment with the General Secretary of the Office of Economic Affairs, Tenzin having pertinently remarked that if we were going to see half the Tibetan settlements in India, it might be as well to know in advance how exactly they were all paid for. It was a Sunday morning and Mr Dawa Tsering had agreed to open his office down at Gangchen Kyishong solely to make himself available for interview.

We found him in a large empty room – which six days a week would have been filled, in excess of capacity, by the ranks of his junior officials – wandering forlornly from desk to desk, trying vainly to find a phone that worked. He had, he said, a message for the Dalai Lama's Private Secretary, which in the absence of any other more convenient form of communication looked as though it was going to have to be carried up the hill to McCleod Ganj and delivered by hand. In order to cheer him up, for he really did look extremely miserable, I thanked him effusively for finding time to see us on his day off and said that I considered the devotion to public service of the members of the Dharamsala administration to be quite remarkable; indeed exemplary. He stared back at me with a puzzled expression.

How much, I enquired did the average civil servant get paid for his labours on behalf of the Tibetan cause?

'Oh, between 650 and 1,200 rupees a month.' (£25–£45)

'How about the Welfare Officers in charge of the various settlements?'

'Maybe 800 rupees.'

'And the senior ministers, Kalons for instance?'

Dawa Tsering looked at me glumly, his face clearly registering the opinion that journalists were extremely dangerous, likely to trick you into telling them all sorts of things that you weren't supposed to, and in general a very poor substitute for a quiet Sunday morning at home.

'About 1,500 rupees is the maximum for Kalons, though there are added benefits such as free education for their children at the TCV.'

Was money a perpetual problem, I wondered, or after thirty years of exile had the Tibetans managed to provide a reliable, if meagre, living for themselves?

'It's certainly a problem still, but we survive. Of course we are constantly trying to think of new ways in which to increase our income: new enterprises and so on. At the beginning, when we were setting up our settlements, we had a great deal of help from international charities and aid agencies, but as time goes by such organisations expect you to look after yourself: they have a new set of problems to deal with. And then again you must distinguish between the budget of the government in exile, which we must finance ourselves, and that for, say, education, which to a large extent is still funded by the Government of India.'

'So what is the total annual budget of the Dharamsala administration?'

All Dawa Tsering's fears about how the conversation might turn out were now clearly coming true. He shot Tenzin an imploring glance. Surely a fellow countryman could be relied upon to help him out of this disagreeable predicament? Unfortunately, Tenzin showed every sign of being even more interested in the minutiae of government expenditure than I was.

'I am not sure I can tell you.' His natural Tibetan instinct to be obliging fought a pitched battle with his discretion. And lost. 'No, this I am not authorised to disclose. You see we have sources which we keep to ourselves.'

An awkward silence settled on the room.

'But I am sure I could tell you about *some* major sources of our revenue and then you will have a better idea.' I smiled encouragingly. Seizing hold of this compromise with obvious gratitude. Dawa Tsering began, almost volubly.

'First of all, every Tibetan in exile pays one rupee a month. Some people say we should call this a tax, but we prefer to describe it as a "voluntary contribution". The Indian authorities do not recognise Dharamsala to be a fully fledged government in exile, so probably they would not like us collecting taxes. Anyway the most important point about this contribution is that it indicates the allegiance of the people.'

'One rupee doesn't sound like very much allegiance.'

'Well, in some places it is two rupees. Because of inflation the government's costs have risen. Altogether this brings in about 165,000 rupees a month. [£6,350.] Then, of course, we have business profits from our carpet factories, our hotels, and so on. In India we have about twenty enterprises and together these earn us about twenty lakhs of rupees.' (£75,000 a year.)

'So which is your most profitable business?'

'Oh, the carpet business, by a long way.'

'I'm not surprised!' Tenzin remarked unexpectedly, with considerable warmth. 'Here in India the government gives a 20 per cent cash incentive to exporters who bring in foreign currency. In Nepal, I don't get anything – not a rupee, not a paisa – and I still have to compete with you people. I have to be 20 per cent more efficient than you are before I earn a cent.'

Dawa Tsering looked taken aback by this outburst and uncertain whether to apologise or not. I tried to lead him back onto safer ground.

'So are your businesses all state-run, or do you get involved in joint ventures with private capital?'

Unfortunately, this well-intentioned enquiry seemed only to deepen his anxiety.

'Just recently we have been getting so many Americans coming to Dharamsala, telling us that we are very inefficient, very out of date, that everything must be decentralised and run by private entrepreneurs. We are trying to adapt to this new ideology, but I tell you it is not always easy.'

In India, I suggested, since Independence the government had favoured state economic planning, so perhaps it was unsurprising that the Tibetans had inherited this preference.

Dawa Tsering nodded glumly. 'Fortunately, our ventures are very successful, otherwise. . . .' His voice trailed away.

'So what new projects do you have in hand?'

'Oh, we are trying to build a food-processing plant. We are taking advice from a man in Delhi; an expert. Then we would like to collaborate with the Japanese on a software factory. They are doing a feasibility study. You see we have a serious problem. His Holiness the Dalai Lama is very concerned about our education system. He thinks that education is crucial to our cultural survival. But unfortunately we are producing too many educated young people. There is nothing for them to do: they cannot get jobs. Unemployment among the exiled Tibetans must be tackled. So we are trying to start a watch assembly unit – we are being helped in this by a Tibetan who has set up a similar project for the Sikkimese authorities – but this is not specialised work. It is not suitable for young people who have spent three, four, five years at university.'

One of the more colourful stories told about the exiled Tibetans concerns a hidden treasure of gold and silver, said to have been brought across the Himalayas in 1950 by a train of a thousand pack animals and then stored in stables belonging to the ruler, or 'Choegyal', of Sikkim. Intended as a contingency fund, to be used in the event of the Dalai Lama having to leave Tibet in a hurry, it came in very handy only ten years later. In 1960, the bullion was taken down to Calcutta where it realised close to a million dollars. This was subsequently invested, or so I had been told, in 'The Dalai Lama's Charitable Trust'. What, I wondered, had happened to it since? Was it still a mainstay of the Tibetan economy in exile?

'No, that's all gone'.

'*All* of it?'

'Well, nearly all. From the money we got for the gold and silver, the trust received seventy-nine lakhs of rupees [£304,000]. Unfortunately, a certain portion of this was invested in an iron and steel company which went bankrupt and we lost about twenty lakhs. Then another portion was entrusted to some Marwaris in Calcutta. They were supposed to know all about the stock market, but they cheated us and we lost everything. The Marwaris, you know, have a reputation for this kind of thing in India. Perhaps my predecessors were not sufficiently aware of it.'

At this point, Tenzin, who had been sitting on the edge of his seat, aghast at this tale of gullibility and financial incompetence, could restrain himself no longer.

'You mean to say the seventy-nine lakhs just disappeared? How? It's impossible! Unbelievable.' Dawa Tsering, who of course bore no personal responsibility for this débâcle, which had occurred long before his arrival at the

Tibetan Treasury, promptly closed departmental ranks and became abruptly defensive.

'Well, we had invested some additional funds with a paper mill in Bhopal, and we were able to recover this money with a dividend also. The trust was then merged with the Paljor (Treasury) Office to keep it under direct supervision. There were about eleven lakhs left [£42,000], and with these we started the Tibetan Woollen Yarn Centre in Amritsar – which supplied all our carpet factories – and the Export Office in Delhi. From the moment it came under the control of the government, everything was managed very successfully.'

Tenzin's indignation, however, could not be so easily stilled.

'So how much did they lose altogether?'

'About sixty lakhs [£230,000],' Dawa Tsering conceded ruefully. 'It's true: the only money we held onto came from the paper mill shares. Other than that everything was gone. Lost.'

Chapter 3

MANALI

By the time we had climbed back up to the McCleod Ganj bazaar it was raining. Or rather a kind of waterlogged atmosphere, mid-way between cloud and drizzle, had descended on the town, making it look sodden, dingy, rubbish-strewn, and cheerless. Even at the height of the hot season, the mountain climate was maintaining its prerogative to be unpredictable. Nearly everyone was indoors and both the plains and the Dhauladar were invisible. It was time to be off.

The evening before we had agreed to give a lift to the Dalai Lama's Representative in Manali, Dawa Thargay, who we now found sheltering in a doorway next to the bus stand, a slight, spare man, apparently in his late fifties. The uncertainty surrounding his age was greatly increased by the results of a disastrous experiment with hair dye. This had left some patches of his head a statesmanlike silvery-grey, while the remainder was as black and glistening as a newly tarred road. The overall effect was that of a diminutive but sprightly panda, dressed in an old tweed jacket and carrying a canvas shoulder-bag.

'You can sit in the front to absorb the impact . . .' Tenzin remarked affably to our new travelling companion, '. . . I know these Indian drivers.' The driver in question, who had huddled up under a blanket, looked exceedingly morose to me, and more disinclined to move at all than about to indulge a craving for reckless speed.

'He's worried . . . ,' Dawa Thargay explained, '. . . that we may not get any petrol. The day before yesterday some Sikh terrorists let off a bomb in the bus station at Pathankot and killed nine people. The authorities in Punjab have closed all the state borders, so the tankers can't get through to Himachal.'

Eventually, with the greatest reluctance, the driver consented to make a start, and under extremely specific instructions from Tenzin about braking at corners, free-wheeled gingerly down the hill into Lower Dharamsala in order to economise on fuel. Fortunately, news of the local energy crisis had not reached the first garage we came to, so we duly filled up the tank and then set off in earnest.

It is a truth generally acknowledged that India polarises her admirers and detractors to a greater extent than any other country. There are people who, despite acid experience of its failings, wilfully persist in looking at the place with romantic affection. And then there are those who think the former group are either blind or mad and who can see nothing but violence, filth, superstition, and venality. I count myself as a member of the first demented category; Tenzin, on the other hand, very definitely belongs to the latter group. If anything is capable of reconciling these two, otherwise incompatible points of view, it is a leisurely drive, on a sunny day, along quiet country roads, through the Kangra Valley.

A few miles out of Dharamsala, the sky cleared, and the long, majestic rock wall of the Dhauladar re-emerged, the summits of its jagged peaks freshly white-washed and gleaming.

We drove eastwards, parallel to the mountains, between flower-speckled meadows, past neatly clipped tea gardens, and through long dappled corridors of overhanging trees. At Kangra itself, the old Rajput fortress, earthquake-shattered and teetering on its sandy crag, introduced a brief note of melodrama to this Arcadia, but after only a few miles the countryside levelled out and resumed a benign, fecund, and generally cornucopian appearance. Even the taxi-driver thawed out and produced a photograph of the Dalai Lama from his wallet, which he stuck on the dashboard dangerously close to the dagger-wielding arms of Kali, an alarming Hindu goddess of antisocial habits and disagreeable appearance.

'The Tibetans and the local Hindus get along fairly well these days . . .', Dawa Thargay observed placidly, drawing on his cigarette and stretching out of the window to snatch at a passing leaf, '. . . certainly much better than they did when we first arrived. And then of course the mountain people have always revered His Holiness.' Tenzin immediately concurred with this optimistic assessment, adding quite unprompted that our driver seemed a pleasant enough individual and, furthermore, surprisingly competent.

We paused for lunch in Mandi, a town built precariously on the sides of a steep valley gouged out by the tumultuous River Beas, and then turned directly north, upriver, until the road came to a narrow opening, blasted through the foothills with dynamite. Here the driver stopped the car, walked over to a small ochre-coloured temple, clanged the entrance bell, and disappeared inside. He returned about five minutes later, looking extremely cheerful, with some grimy nuggets of consecrated sugar wrapped up in a screw of old newspaper. These he offered to each of us in turn.

'We'd better eat it . . .', sighed Tenzin, '. . . otherwise he probably won't go anywhere. He claims that the next few miles are very dangerous, but that since they put up the temple hardly anyone's been killed. If you believe that. . . .'

'A lot of Tibetans died when the road was built,' Dawa Thargay interrupted, suddenly very serious. 'You'll see. It's cut out of a cliff-face. People lost their footing. Lorries went over the edge. There were landslides when the snow melted in the spring. Sometimes they weren't very careful with explosives.'

Content that his passengers were now spiritually prepared, the driver started the engine, revved it up furiously, and then pulled away in third gear causing consumptive spasms to shake and rattle the ancient bodywork. Although the road was wide enough for two lorries to pass abreast, the drop of several hundred feet down into the racing waters of the Beas looked distinctly uninviting.

I said that I'd heard about the Kulu Valley's notorious roadgangs, but that as my knowledge was very limited, perhaps Dawa Thargay could tell me more. He nodded, keeping one eye on the driver, who, rather unnervingly, had started to sing.

'Well, when the Tibetans came out in '59 there was nothing for them to do. Most had no money, so they had to earn a few rupees just in order to survive. As they had the reputation of being tough people, and of course they were used to high altitude, they were put to work building mountain roads for the Indian government. What you must understand is that hardly anyone came into the Kulu Valley from the south until the 1950s. These hills were impassable for any kind of vehicle during the British colonial time. But after the Chinese invaded Tibet, the Indians started pushing strategic roads up to the border, right along their Himalayan frontier. After the Sino–Indian War in '62, of course, the programme of construction was accelerated. The Tibetans were very useful. They broke rocks, did all the heavy labouring. The problem was that they had no immunity to the local diseases. People thought they would be better off in the mountains rather than down on the plains. It was cooler and seemed to be cleaner. But still they died. Tuberculosis was the biggest killer. Many of the children who ended up at the TCV in Dharamsala were orphaned here.'

'So how long did this go on?'

'It still does. By which I mean there are still over fifteen hundred Tibetans in the Kulu Valley and many of them still work on the roads. Fortunately their health is not as bad as it was, though we still have many problems. Around 1962, camps were set up in South India. Everyone was supposed to leave here, but the resettlement areas soon filled up. Some people had the opportunity to go, but preferred to stay close to the Tibetan border. They thought they'd been going home, you see. Time went by, but for a long while they were not discouraged. They thought the Chinese would stay, maybe three, four, five years. Eventually they realised it wasn't going to be like that, but by then it was too late to move somewhere better.'

It was late afternoon when the valley finally opened out and the road descended through apple orchards to the banks of the Beas and the crowded little town of Kulu. The people in the streets were nearly all fair-skinned, noticeably paler than the Indians of the plains, and for a moment it seemed as though we had taken the wrong turning and ended up in the Kashmir Valley by mistake. For the next hour, we followed the meandering course of the greenish, tumbling river.

Just before it got dark we came to a sharp bend where several strings of Tibetan prayer flags were flapping vigorously in a gusting breeze. Beneath them some tatty huts built of tin and tarpaulin (the less affluent had to make do with carboard and sacking), clung to the river-bank twenty feet or so from the swirling snowmelt. For the first time since the suffocating heat of Majnu-ka-Tilla, I felt myself moved by pity, rather than mere sympathy. Here were poor people, far from home, driven out of their own country, and through no fault of their own living a wretched existence on the brink of oblivion.

Tenzin, despite a normally imperturbable manner, was obviously shocked. 'I had no idea it was still as bad as this up here,' he whispered across to me.

'This . . .', said Dawa Thargay with what sounded suspiciously like proprietorial pride, '. . . is Fifteen Mile Camp. You should come here tomorrow.'

'Why is it called Fifteen Mile Camp?'

'Because it's fifteen miles from Manali. Why else?'

The name's chilly functionalism seemed only to emphasise the bleakness of the place. Dawa Thargay caught sight of Tenzin's grim expression and his manner became immediately defensive.

'We'd like to relocate these people, but we have many difficulties. For one thing, Manali is a holiday resort. This makes land very expensive and rents very high. Without land it is also impossible to start some kind of small industry which would provide alternative employment to the roads. Anyway, come down tomorrow in the daylight and see for yourself. Talk to Tsewang Rinzin; he's in charge.' He paused for a moment, as if wondering whether it would be wise to continue or not.

'You'd better be careful though: the local authorities don't like foreigners visiting the Tibetans. Last month, they arrested two American ladies who have been sponsoring the education of some children here and put them on a bus back to Delhi.'

'Why on earth did they do that?'

'Oh, I don't know really. The central government in

Delhi doesn't like too much attention being paid to the Tibetans because they want to maintain good relations with China. And of course the Indian security services have always worried that the Tibetan camps, especially in militarily sensitive border areas, might be used by foreign spies. But in this case it was probably just local politics. As I said, the Indians and the Tibetans generally get on well together, but some politicians like to stir up trouble in order to get themselves elected. They tell the people that if they're unemployed it's because the Tibetans have taken all the jobs. Then they say the local Indians are so poor because the government is spending all its money looking after us. According to them, we get so much money from foreigners that we don't need any help at all.'

The following morning was crisp and clear, the peaks of the Great Himalaya, an encampment of dazzling white tents set against a background of flawless Wedgwood blue. Although Manali is at a height of only about 6,500 feet – little more than Dharamsala – the sides of the mountains are steep, and cold air seems to be trapped down on the valley floor, like the chill of winter at the bottom of a warming pond. Manali itself is an unlovely town. Rapid expansion as an alpine resort has thrown up the kind of building that probably doesn't look too bad with snow up to the eaves, but which, when exposed to full public view, induces a mood of acute depression. Still, it is one of the principal gateways to the high Himalaya and the mountain people, the inhabitants of the Kulu Valley, and Indians from the plains all mingle in its grubby alleys, jostle in its sooty teashops, and cram onto the ancient, stinking buses of the much reviled Himachal Pradesh Transport Department.

Fifteen miles out of town to the north is the 14,000 foot

Rohtang Pass, snow-bound each year from October to June, one of the subcontinent's great cultural watersheds. To the south of the Rohtang are the green rice paddies of Hindu India; to the north are the high, arid lands of Lahaul, Spiti, Zanskar and Ladakh, where barren, tawny hills roll on into the Tibetan province of Ngari, and where the Buddhist population has, immemorially, looked north to Shigatse and Lhasa for guidance and inspiration. To the south is the country of the cow; to the north is the land of the yak. Tibet is very close in Manali and I can readily understand why her dispossessed offspring chose to stay there, when materially they would have been better off in resettlement areas 1,000 miles from home.

Tenzin and I took a bus back down to Fifteen Mile Camp, where we found Tsewang Rinzin sitting on the river bank, looking down philosophically at the ruins of a *chorten* (a small reliquary monument), which had collapsed during some recent floods and was now steadily breaking up in the churning rapids below. Two Lhasa Apsos, insensitive to the prevailing mood of gloom, gambolled around him, only suspending their tussles to chase after a large brown lizard which had unwisely decided to sunbathe on the beaten footpath nearby. A slight figure, about sixty-five years old, Tsewang Rinzin was wearing a pink woolly bobble hat pulled well down over his ears in order (or so it seemed) to shut out the uncouth clamour of reality and to leave him to his thoughts in peace. He looked to be a simple, honest man, frankly rather baffled by the perfidy of the world, but still determined to salvage some shreds of order from the general wreck.

Seven huts, together with their inhabitants' belongings, had also been washed away, he informed us, but of these there was no sign whatever.

We sat on an old wooden bench in the sunshine (which

by now was quite hot), watching the flashing river race head over heels down to the distant plains. The Beas is well known in India for its trout fishing, but Tsewang Rinzin disavowed any knowledge of this reputation and said that personally he had caught nothing. Shielding his eyes from the glare, he pointed up to the smooth contours of the snow-bowl on the slopes of the mountain opposite.

'They say they're going to build a ski resort up there,' he remarked, with an air of considerable scepticism. 'The Tourism Minister went to Europe on holiday. Came back full of ideas. Told the newspapers he's going to turn Himachal into the Switzerland of Asia.' He paused for a moment, to savour the full absurdity of this suggestion. 'Some hope.' In order to distract him from the spectacle of ministerial *folie de grandeur*, I asked him how he came to be living in the precarious and disagreeable circumstances of Fifteen Mile Camp.

'I come from the Kailash area. It's not very far from here really. Just across these mountains.' He waved his arm vaguely north-east, in a gesture as eloquent as it was imprecise. 'I used to work some land that belonged to Sera monastery and so I knew that sooner or later the Chinese would come for me. Everyone who had been connected with the monasteries was a "class enemy". People were always being arrested. I used to watch them go, one by one, and wonder when my time would come. So I ran away. It wasn't very difficult. I went to Ladakh and stayed there for three years. But there was no work. Nothing at all. So I reckoned maybe Manali would be better. At least, I thought, it'd be warmer in winter. The cold in Leh is terrible. Minus forty degrees – for weeks.'

'But surely Tibet must be just as cold?'

'It never seemed to be. There's something about the cold in Ladakh that gets into you, and however many clothes you wear, whatever you do, you can't get it out till spring. Anyway I came to Manali. There were about twenty camps in the Kulu Valley then and I was put in Camp C. I started work on the roads at one rupee, fifty paisa a day [six pence]. It doesn't sound much – and it wasn't – but money was worth more then and you could get by. Sometimes we were given milk powder and sometimes crushed wheat. We don't get anything like that any more. I've worked here ever since. Twenty-six years now.'

His acceptance of this miserable fate was, as far as I could tell, complete. There was no trace of resentment in his voice. Hope, it seemed, had perished and with it much of the exile's pain and desolation. A numb fatalism made daily life tolerable.

Tenzin, however, was not so easily satisfied.

'But surely you must have been given opportunities to leave, to go down south. You were quite young then, able-bodied, unattached. Why did you stay here, living in a hut, breaking rocks, and freezing half to death?'

'I had the chance to leave, it's true. And I would have gone to South India. But during those three years in Ladakh, I had to borrow money to survive. So I couldn't leave without repaying my debts. Even today I am still paying it off.' He grimaced and shook his head.

'What about the other people still in this camp? Were they in similar circumstances?'

'Many of the older people here now were given the chance to leave. Some were sick and didn't want to travel; some were afraid of the heat in the south; many just wanted to stay close to Tibet. They thought that if they stuck it out for a couple more years then they'd be able to go back.'

'So who's here now? Many of the original inhabitants must have died over the past thirty years.'

'Come and see for yourself. Of course the younger ones aren't here. They leave the children with the grandparents while they go off to work on the roads.'

We strolled down a path between huts, the roofs of which were mostly made out of old tins beaten flat. I spotted several varieties of biscuit as well as two brands of mustard oil. It had turned out to be a glorious day and the exceptional beauty of the surroundings – acid-green rice paddies, willow trees bending over the milky river, pine forests on the upper slopes extending to the pristine snow – mocked the desperation of the camp's inhabitants. If their homeland had not been invaded and pillaged, I kept reminding myself, these people would probably now be farmers, living in dignity behind their own solid walls, with a few animals, their own small patch of land, the safety net of their extended family spread around them, secure within the unquestioned values of their society and their religion.

We stopped at a doorway and Tsewang Rinzin lifted a piece of sacking for us to step inside. At first I could see only a patch of wall where a shaft of light from the single polythene window struck a shelf of pots and pans and mugs. Within a few seconds, however, my eyes began to adjust to the darkness. There wasn't much to see. My first impression was that the place was surprisingly neat: the earthen floor had been swept that morning – you could still make out the marks of the brush in the dust – and the few possessions had been put away tidily in corners. A photograph of the Dalai Lama, the sole object of decoration, was tacked up on the far wall. In the centre of the room were four large stones and a pile of white ash. There was no chimney and consequently the roof, which was only about nine inches above my head, was carpeted with soot. Spiders' webs hung down like black feather boas.

On a narrow bed lay a middle-aged woman. At first I thought she might be dead. A sturdy child of about two was jumping vigorously up and down on her stomach – using her as a kind of trampette – and yet she made no attempt to stop it, gave no sign of pain, uttered no word of protest. Suddenly she heaved herself fully upright and was convulsed with coughing. Wave after wave the spasms hit her like the sea smashing itself against an old rotten pier. The child retreated to the end of the bed to wait for a propitious moment to continue its exercise. The woman coughed and coughed so hard I thought she might dislocate her neck. Then the attack was over and she fell back like a sack of logs. Thwack. Her head hit the pillow, where it lay inert and silent. The child crept forward, paused, listened, and resumed its bouncing, tentatively at first, building up a rhythm, gaining height.

'She's got TB,' Tsewang Rinzin observed, superfluously. 'It's still a big problem here. The wife of the man next door died from it last week. I said I'd drop in to see him this morning.' He lifted the sacking and we stepped out into the callous sunshine.

The man next door had heard us coming and was standing outside, waiting.

'This chap's very lucky in one respect. He has a six-year-old boy who we managed to get into the TCV in Dharamsala. Someone from the school came over to pick him up yesterday.'

The recipient of this piece of good fortune didn't really seem to be in a mood to appreciate it. Having lost a young wife (permanently) and a child (temporarily) and consequently finding himself entirely alone in the world, he looked more miserable than anyone else I have ever seen. He was clearly on the brink of tears throughout our brief interview. I asked a few questions, trying to be as sympathetic as is possible for someone who is well fed, well clothed, and in possession of an air ticket back to London. The man didn't reply. He heard me all right, but my voice just couldn't punch a hole in the wall of pain. He just kept staring wildly round, stricken with horror that life could do such things, could inflict such devastation. Indeed, he seemed so agonised, so destitute, so utterly bereft, that it appeared to be only a matter of time before he was further deprived; this time of his sanity. I wondered whether this might not be merciful; whether in a twilit world he might not suffer less.

Tenzin and I walked back to the bus stop in silence. A group of children playing by the river shouted cheerfully after us. 'Inje, inje, inje.' As the English were the first Europeans the Tibetans encountered in any numbers, the word for Englishman and foreigner is the same. 'Inje, inje, inje.'

The woman on the bus back to Manali was less enthusiastic. 'Injes,' she grumbled. 'Always injes. More and more injes. Never any room to sit down on the bus because of injes.'

The declining afternoon sun enveloped Manali's Tibetan *gompa* in a comforting roseate glow. We were sitting fifteen feet up on the flat roof of an out-building, protected from the wind by the gnarled arms of an elderly apple tree. Monks crossing the courtyard beneath looked up at us quizzically. One or two smiled and waved. It had been Mr Lobsang Thondup's idea to clamber up a ladder to get out of the mud, and eventually, with the aid of a couple of friends and a good deal of swearing, he had succeeded in providing us with folding chairs and a table. There was also, he said, a clear view from the roof of the land which the Tibetan business community had rented from the town council. A robust, burly man of about fifty, he was obviously good at organising things. He was a survivor, a fixer, a practitioner of self-reliance. In the teeth of misfortune he had succeeded in making his life in Manali at least tolerably comfortable. For some years his small shop had been turning in a reasonable income, and he and family were now housed, fed, and clothed. All things considered, this was no mean achievement.

How, I wondered, did his standard of living now compare with that of the majority of the local population?

'Most of them are still much better off than we are. They own land and property. Often they also have a few fruit trees which yield a small income. Still, compared with the time when we worked as labourers we cannot complain. We manage.'

'Do you feel accepted here after all this time? Or are you still an outsider?'

'I have never felt particularly welcome here. There is a lot of resentment of Tibetans, especially when we are allowed to rent land. People go to the town planning committee to complain. "They used to work on the roads," they say. "Why don't they go back there? Then they were useful." I suppose I do wonder sometimes if I shouldn't have stayed behind. It hasn't been very pleasant here for the past thirty years. But there is no knowing what would have happened. I might be dead by now. I don't have any regrets, but I can tell you, no matter how successful I might become here, I would go home at the first opportunity. I would rather be poor in an independent Tibet than a rich man in India.'

In Dharamsala the uncharitable thought had crossed my mind more than once that a minority of Tibetans had made themselves so comfortable and prosperous in exile that there might not be exactly a stampede back to the climatic and topographical rigours of their homeland should the Chinese ever think better of their inglorious occupation. Lobsang Thondup's intention to return, however, didn't seem to be much in doubt. His face showed no obvious emotion, but just for a moment he lifted his gaze to the mountains and let it rest there.

'How do you get on with the authorities?'

'Not too bad. We have trouble with the tax people, but then so does everyone else. After all this is India.'

'What kind of trouble?'

'Well, for example, we have to pay sales tax. But there are no official rates for anything. The inspector comes round to my shop and says, "Good heavens! Look at all this stuff. I've never seen anything like it. I thought you Tibetans were supposed to be poor. You must pay 5,000 rupees at once." This is probably more than the entire stock is worth, so we have to negotiate, give him some presents, try to work out how big a bribe he is expecting.'

Tenzin, who over the years has become more than a little disillusioned with the probity of Indian and Nepalese officialdom, sighed sympathetically and shook his head.

'So how did you get started in business?'

'Well, when I first came to Manali I worked on the road with everyone else. There was no choice. Many of my friends didn't stay long in the Kulu Valley: just a couple of years. They went to the camps in South India. I put my name down for resettlement, but unfortunately I was not selected. They did not have enough land down there for everyone. Sometimes only two or three members of a family were chosen and in those circumstances people often decided to stick together. Anyway, for one reason or another, quite a few of us were left behind in Manali. First we had to learn the language; then gradually we began to understand the local system, the local law. After about fifteen years — '

'Fifteen years!'

'Sure. It took time to get established. It wasn't easy. After about fifteen years we had managed to do some petty business here and there, save a little money, so we went down to Ludiana in Punjab. Ludiana is famous throughout India for making clothing; especially sweaters; the cheap polyester kind that Indians buy each winter as soon as it gets a bit chilly on the plains. There are many factories there. We bought as much merchandise as we could afford, put it on our backs, and set off to sell it in the northern cities. We always travelled in groups of three or four – we still do – because there are many thieves. They carry knives and often work in gangs. I myself have been robbed several times. It's a very risky business; especially on the trains.'

'You say you still do this?'

'Of course. Business in Manali is only seasonal. The Indian tourists come in spring and summer and buy our things, but in winter nothing happens here. So we go down to Ludiana, just the same, only these days I take about 10,000 rupees with me. With that amount of cash, I can get another 4,000 rupees worth of merchandise on credit. But even if I do badly – say it is a mild winter and there is little demand – I must still pay the supplier the full amount so that next year I will get the same favourable terms.'

'So what is a good year?'

'Oh, if I sell everything I make between 30 and 40 per cent on my total investment; maybe 5,000 rupees [£190].'

'That doesn't sound so much for a winter's work.'

'Maybe not, but I make as much again, maybe a little more, from the shop in the summer. So we survive. You see over there . . .' He pointed in the direction of scrubby patch of land on the southern outskirts of town, where rows of lean-tos formed an impromptu shopping mall. 'The land the council allocated to us is now completely full up. When we first decided to go into business, there were very few people who had sufficient capital to get going. Those of us who had managed to save and borrow enough money were able to set up shop in the centre of Manali, by the bus station. But gradually the numbers increased and the Indian traders began to complain about the competition. So they shifted all the Tibetans down to the edge of town. They thought no customers would come down here and we'd all go bankrupt. As you can see, it didn't happen. Tibetans are very good business people – hardworking, very shrewd, careful with their money – and so if we are given half a chance we will always get on.'

Chapter 4

SIMLA

Simla, the state capital of Himachal Pradesh and one-time summer quarters of the British Raj, lies south-east of the Kulu Valley, 7,000 feet up on a range of hummocky green foothills, recently much vandalised by deforestation. Being further from the high mountains than Manali, its streets do not display quite the same varied mixture of peoples and although after the monsoon there is a view of distant snow peaks, during April and May the town is immured by a dust haze rising from the infernal plains. In *Kim*, Kipling makes Simla seem a dangerous and intriguing place, home of the mysterious Lurgan Sahib, a command centre of the Great Game being played out in Central Asia and Tibet. But today it is a holiday resort for India's new middle class and headquarters of the state bureaucracy.

After five hours on the road, during which time we had miraculously avoided two head-on collisions – a pleasantly uneventful trip by Indian standards – we joined a malodorous queue of cars and buses tailing back three or four miles from the centre of town. It was the height of the season and Simla had apparently succumbed to gridlock.

Clutching handkerchiefs to our faces – exhaust fumes in India are even more noxious than elsewhere, the fuel being adulterated with kerosene – Tenzin and I sat in stoical silence, envious of the passengers on the old narrow-gauge railway who swept past, waving derisively.

At the beginning of the nineteenth century the British colonial authorities had found it necessary to go to war with the expansionist Nepalese Gurkha dynasty, which, much to the annoyance of the Manchu Chinese, had invaded southern Tibet in 1788. Having been thwarted on that occasion, the Gurkhas plainly now wished to extend their dominion over the petty pricipalities of the central Indian Himalaya, an ambition of which the British strongly disapproved.

In 1819, the war over, the Raj found itself unexpectedly in control of a new chunk of empire. Owing to its moderate climate and attractive position, a small village began to attract the attention of British army officers on leave. Simla grew rapidly along a series of interconnected ridges and soon acquired a long promenade – The Mall – a baronial castle, an imposing gothic church, and, in 1888, a viceregal lodge.

Having eventually forced an entry into the town and abandoned our bags at an hotel, Tenzin and I went out for an evening stroll. The hillside down which the main part of Simla has been built is extremely steep and the houses are stacked precariously on top of one another. In the monsoon, landslides are frequent, and everyone lives in fear of the neighbour dropping in unexpectedly through the ceiling. The whole place looks as though it would only need a very modest earth tremor to send it crashing a couple of thousand feet down into the valley below. As indeed it would.

Perhaps more than anywhere else in India, Simla is purely a British colonial creation, yet the remnants of empire, such as they are, are nowadays forlorn islands of suburban gentility surrounded, and all but overwhelmed, by a surging ocean of Indian life. Even Christ Church – where not so very long ago the great and the good weekly renewed their contract with a pukka British divinity – is now painted saffron yellow, its European identity effectively suppressed, the ascendancy of an indigenous Hindu pantheon quietly but unmistakably advertised. Various services were announced on a tatty noticeboard, but it was a Sunday evening and all the doors were firmly locked.

There are still one or two half-timbered, mock-Tudor buildings along The Mall, indistinguishable from their cousins in Hazelmere, and in the doorway of one of them, the Gaiety Theatre, we found some Tibetans, both men and women, perhaps fifteen people in all, selling woollen scarves and Kulu shawls to ward off the evening chill. The temperature seemed to me to be in the low eighties Fahrenheit, but they were still doing brisk business with thin-blooded holidaymakers from the plains. Although none of the Tibetans had ever set eyes on Tenzin before, he was greeted like a dear relative, long absent, presumed dead. His prosperity and independence – the fact that he had made good in the outside world and in so doing reasserted Tibetan dignity – seemed to cause them particular satisfaction. They were doing all right, they said, in response to enquiries about their material well-being. At least they were doing all right at this time of year, because of the tourists. Autum and winter were more of a problem, but then, like the people from Manali, they went down into the northern cities to sell their merchandise there.

Unfortunately, just as our new acquaintance was reaching that degree of intimacy at which interesting information begins to be divulged, we found ourselves being hustled along the pavement by police with long truncheons, or *lathis*, with which they were enthusiastically thwacking the poorer and more obviously inoffensive members of the crowd. The President of India had come to Simla for the day and as he, like everyone else, wanted an evening stroll, a boulevard had to be cleared for his convenience by the heavy-handed minions of the law. Presumably unaware of the actual bodily harm that was being dealt out on his behalf, the President sailed past, smiling and bowing in that transparently insincere manner of politicians everywhere.

Early the following morning, Tenzin and I set off for Kasumpti, an outlying district of Simla, where an official Tibetan camp had been established in 1975. The Tibetans had originally been settled in an area with the congenial name of Summer Hill, but in 1972 they had been informed that as the state had other plans for the land – they were going to build a zoo – their presence was no longer required.

Fortunately, the indignities of exile did not seem to have entirely cowed the spirit of the local Welfare Officer, Mr Pasang Tsering, a small, breathless, timid-looking man of about forty-five. When we arrived he was in earnest conclave with his assistant, composing a letter of protest to India's then Prime Minister, Rajiv Gandhi. It seemed faintly ludicrous that from his tiny, sparsely furnished office he should be indignantly petitioning the distant corridors of power. The room itself was almost a perfect cube, painted white, inside a souless concrete block which served the settlement as factory, warehouse, and administrative centre. On his desk there was an ancient manual typewriter of the kind which takes a grown man to lift, a black Bakelite telephone that looked as though it had been pilfered from a museum, and a brass bell. He himself was wearing what I later came to recognise as the uniform of harassed Tibetan officialdom: white open-necked shirt, sleeveless grey pullover, baggy cotton trousers (man of the people with no use for fripperies); enormous battered wrist watch (lots to be done, no time to waste); and a large gold ring set with a hunk of Tibetan turquoise (statement of national identity and sole concession to vanity).

'I am so busy,' he said, eyes flicking down to the draft letter on his Formica-topped desk, which even from ten feet away I could see to be mostly crossings-out. 'I have to inform Mr Gandhi of our disgust at the Indian government's craven reaction to the recent slaughter of Tibetans in Lhasa. Also I have to finish my speech for this afternoon: we are having a demonstration. And then I must talk to our accountant. . . .' He paused for a moment as if suddenly aware that he wasn't being particularly hospitable. 'Would you care for some tea?'

'Thank you, that would be very nice,' I thoughtlessly replied from reflex politeness.

A shadow of disappointment passed swiftly over Mr Tsering's face, but finding himself irretrievably committed to this unwelcome social event, he bravely thumped the bell beside his typewriter and resigned himself to the interruption. In response a very old, very thin, very tall Tibetan shuffled in carrying a Thermos flask the size of a small milk churn and some battered cups. Another man, whose spectacles gave him a studious appearance, and who looked as though in better times he would have been a kindly village schoolmaster, quietly followed him into the room and was introduced as the settlement's accountant.

'We will all be demonstrating,' Mr Tsering continued importantly. 'I trust you will be joining us.' Tenzin mumbled something to the effect that he supposed we would.

'You too?' I asked the accountant, who didn't seem to be

anticipating an afternoon's political activism with any great enthusiasm.

'I have to,' came the mournful reply. Clearly he thought making a fuss in public likely to prove hideously embarrassing.

To take his mind off his impending humiliation, I tried to change the subject. I said that I understood that the principal reason for the settlements – other than the original one of preventing people from starving to death – was to keep all the Tibetans in the same place and thereby to minimise the erosion of their cultural identity. India with its uncounted millions and unimaginable poverty was an unfortunate place in which to be a refugee, especially if one were charged with preserving the soul of an entire civilisation.

Mr Tsering looked at me in an unfocused kind of way, his mind apparently still far off, perhaps imagining the impact of some memorable and cutting phrase when his letter was read aloud to the Prime Minister.

'Ah, settlements, settlements, settlements,' he sighed wearily, as the sound of the word, tolling from somewhere towards the rear of his brain, brought him inexorably back from a glittering horizon to the sticky mud of reality. 'My wife is a nurse you know . . .', he remarked apropos of nothing at all, '. . . she works in Dharamsala. I haven't seen her for over three months.'

Silence fell upon the room as we solemnly considered this sad estrangement. Tenzin was the first to speak, brightly explaining that twenty years before he himself had worked for the Tibetan administration in Simla, managing a carpet factory.

'How are you doing these days? Are you making good money? Does it finance the settlement adequately?'

Mr Tsering seemed much impressed by Tenzin's work experience and altogether less inclined to regard us as an inconvenience.

'Come,' he said grandly. 'I will show you,' all his other duties, both literary and administrative, swept aside by a sudden wave of generosity.

We trooped out into a bleak hallway, descended a flight of concrete steps and entered an enormous workroom – one entire floor of the building – seven-eighths empty.

'We built this with German aid,' said Mr Tsering, with an expansive gesture, his voice ricocheting eerily off the bare walls and floor. In one corner a dozen Tibetan ladies, most in early middle age, sat on carpet-covered benches before their wooden looms, working away steadily, their hands moving mechanically, needing no conscious instruction. Three small children, each about two years old, looked at the strangers shyly, standing first on one leg, then the other. Providing you could put up with the monotony of the task, it occurred to me that it wouldn't be such a bad place to work. At least it was light and airy, the very opposite of the stifling, tenebrous sweatshops of which India is unfortunately full.

How long, I wondered, did it take someone to learn how to make carpets? The physical process of weaving seemed easy enough, but following a traditional multi-coloured pattern of dragons and snow lions looked far from simple.

'About three months. Then they are fully trained. It is not difficult,' said Mr Tsering, with the confidence of a man who, having not attempted something personally, is wholly unacquainted with failure. 'Women have always woven carpets in Tibet: for the home; for the lamas in the monasteries; for saddle bags. . . . Here of course they work full-time; maybe eight or nine hours a day.'

'How much do they get paid?'

'Of course it depends how much they weave, but on average they earn about two hundred and eighty rupees a month [£10.50].'

Tenzin raised an eyebrow quizzically. 'You can get them to work for that?'

'Well, there are other benefits. They have free accommodation and water and get help with their children's schooling. Anyone who wants a job can have one. There are about forty-five people weaving at the moment. We have another workshop down the hill.'

'Actually . . .', confided the accountant, '. . . we'd like to pay them more, but the finances of the settlement don't permit it. Many of the Tibetans around Simla prefer to live in terrible conditions in the town – near the bus station in particular – because they earn much more money selling scarves and souvenirs to tourists than they could out here weaving carpets. This is a major problem. Others, especially the young girls, work for building contractors, which I believe is very well paid.'

'The young *girls*? Surely you mean young men.'

'No, the girls are considered easier to manage. They are also said to take more trouble when mixing concrete. If you don't mix the concrete properly, I'm told the buildings fall down, you know.'

I said that I could well believe it, but what I couldn't understand was why people didn't live in the settlement and still go to work in Simla each day.

'Well, they would have to walk sixteen kilometres there and back which is quite tiring, and while there is a bus part of the way, fares are then an additional expense. We'd like to keep everyone together – you're right, that is the whole point of the settlement – but we simply can't generate enough money to make it work. In a way it's fortunate that not everyone wants to live here, because we couldn't afford it. Simla is a holiday resort, so land is expensive and to build a house for a family of five costs around 21,000 rupees [£850]. We could get some help from the Government of India – they may not support us politically, but they are quite generous about such things as housing and education – and Dharamsala and certain international agencies would also contribute, but it would not be enough. There are perhaps three hundred and fifty Tibetans in Simla who live in really appalling conditions, but to rehouse them all, even in simple accommodation, would require about one and a half million rupees [£60,000]. This is quite impossible. Unthinkable. As it is we have six or seven people living to a room. In these circumstances if one person gets tuberculosis, they all get it.'

Tenzin, who had been listening to this sorry tale with some agitation, at last had the opportunity to speak.

'The problem is that you don't have enough money. Right? If you did have enough you could afford to provide more houses and to pay people properly in the factory. Then all the Tibetans could be together. Yes?'

The accountant nodded glumly.

'So the important thing is to get the business side working properly. The carpet business can be very profitable. *Very*. In Nepal there are lots of us doing it and we all make a good living. And here in India it should be easier, because the government provides export incentives which we don't get.'

'Yes, yes . . .', the accountant interrupted with unexpected animation, '. . . but we buy our wool from the office in Delhi run by Dharamsala and we sell them back the finished carpets at a fixed rate. So we are not in the same position as you are in Nepal. We are not entrepreneurs. We are not exporters. The profit from our carpets goes to fund our government and bureaucracy. Then what is left over it is up to them to distribute as they see fit.'

Presented with this working model of the merits of centralisation and government intervention versus those of decentralisation and a free market, there seemed little doubt with which side Tenzin was inclined to sympathise. He looked thoroughly exasperated.

'Besides . . .', the accountant continued defensively, '. . . there are advantages to this system. A central authority which buys in bulk can get a much better price for wool than a number of individuals acting independently.'

Tenzin appeared unconvinced. 'Maybe so, maybe not. The system can't be that good if it leaves three hundred and fifty people in dire poverty without adequate housing and proper jobs and doesn't enable you to run the settlement in the way the Dalai Lama intended.'

I looked round to see how Mr Tsering was coping with the developing argument, but he had a vacant expression, his mind having returned to higher things. Given the intractable problems by which his settlement was beset, I began to understand why.

The demonstration was due to begin at three-thirty on the steep slope leading up to Clarke's Hotel. A few days before the Indian newspapers had carried reports of Tibetans having been executed for their part in riots following demonstrations to mark the thirtieth anniversary of the Lhasa Uprising. The papers had also carried reports of Gorbachev's visit to Peking and the embarrassing student occupation of Tiananmen Square. The massacre was then little more than a week away.

When Tenzin and I arrived, about fifteen minutes before the scheduled departure time, about two hundred and fifty Tibetans had already assembled in the afternoon sunshine. They seemed a cheerful crowd – the young women especially – among whom there was a great deal of horseplay and boisterous laughter. One hapless girl was being teased about some peccadillo by her companions, their verbal assault being augmented by playful pokes in the ribs and the occasional sly tug at her long black pigtail. The victim wriggled a good deal, trying vainly to escape, a crimson blush glowing on her suntanned cheeks. More sedate middle-aged ladies sat patiently by the side of the road, moving only to evade the cars of important people in a hurry hurtling out of the grounds of the nearby High Court building. The leaders of the demonstration, Mr Pasang Tsering among them, were struggling to untangle the cable of a public address system, blowing hopefully into the microphone and shaking their heads at the resulting silence.

'Oh dear,' said Tenzin sadly. 'We had these demonstrations when I was in Simla twenty years ago. Nothing's changed. The Tibetans are still here, still poor, still protesting, still nobody taking any notice.' He was cheered up, however, by the arrival of three friends from the 1960s, who wrung him by the hand for at least five minutes. Streaks of grey hair were laughingly acknowledged and resumés of the past two decades exchanged with much incredulity and back-slapping.

Eventually, after letting out a number of piercing shrieks, the loudspeaker condescended to work, the microphone was repeatedly blown into – now with tremendous effect – and impressively amplified shouts of 'One, two, three' scattered the crows in the trees overhead and sent them flapping off towards the centre of town in search of a quieter life. A man then came down the line of demonstrators handing out Xeroxed copies of Mr Tsering's speech. This, Tenzin informed me, was written in an elevated, rhetorical style and condemned Chinese repression in the most outspoken terms.

Suddenly we were off, Mr Tsering leading the way next to a burly man carrying a large, gold-framed photograph of the Dalai Lama, the young women taking up a practised chant with startling collective lung power. Two uniformed policemen, whom I hadn't noticed before, attached themselves unobtrusively to the back of the procession.

If I had considered what effect the demonstration would be likely to have on the local Indian population, I would probably have anticipated a reaction of blank indifference. To my surprise polite applause greeted our entry into the warren of narrow streets below the bazaar. People leaned out of first-floor windows, waved, clapped, and shouted encouragement. By the time we had been walking for a quarter of an hour or so, the procession contained at least as many Indians as it did Tibetans. Whether they had joined up out of sympathy for the Tibetans' plight, shared antipathy towards the Chinese (the Indians had, after all, lost the war of 1962, a fact generally invisible to politicians, but not one overlooked by Everyman), or simply for want of anything better or more pleasant to do on a warm, sunny afternoon, it was impossible to tell.

Reaching the top of a steep hill, and being therefore in a good position to survey his by now considerable audience jammed into the street below, Mr Pasang Tsering stopped, set up his microphone on a stand, and began to deliver his speech with admirable fluency and passion. By now several more policemen had appeared, carrying *lathis*, and looking around them with that calculated insolence which is the gift of a uniform the world over. Fleetingly it occurred to me that they might use Mr Tsering's peroration as an excuse to lay into one or two of the more inoffensive by-standers, but even they, it seemed, were sufficiently mastered by goodwill to pass up this splendid opportunity for a little recreative self-assertion.

The speech concluded and applauded, the crowd melted peacefully away into the bazaar. The Tibetans had made their point, demonstrated their unity and common purpose, and the indigenous inhabitants of Simla (not to mention quite a few affluent holidaymakers from Delhi and Chandigarh) had shown a modest degree of solidarity. Meanwhile the Chinese leadership was considering whether the benefits of using machine guns on their own citizens would be outweighed by the international repercussions and concluding, ultimately, that they wouldn't.

Tenzin and I had decided to go down to the bus station in order to investigate the bottom end of Simla's housing market. The Mall, even at ten o'clock in the morning, was choked with Indian tourists, many with the disconsolate air of people haunted by an obligation to enjoy themselves. The most British thing about Simla nowadays, I decided, is not the half-timbered architecture, or the names of hotels, (Clarke's, The Cecil), but the general atmosphere, which, despite the town being 7,000 feet up, is unmistakably that of an English seaside resort. The place feels tacky, brash, over made-up; the noticeboards for 'Kwality Ice-Cream' and 'Roller Skating' and 'Dodgems' are more insistent and shout louder than could ever be required simply for reasons of commercial advantage. Crass materialism, and more specifically the odious self-satisfaction of the newly emergent Indian middle class, are everywhere on display. To take a spring holiday in Simla is a clear sign that you have made it in the brave new India, and while it is doubtless cheap to sneer at those who have just hauled themselves out of the slums, it can only be said that collectively they are not a pretty sight.

'A seedy pleasure garden, obsessed with status and display. What a place to be homeless and poverty stricken.' I observed sententiously to Tenzin as we strolled past the statue of Mahatma Gandhi. 'I wonder what Gandhi would have thought of the values independent India has adopted. Not much I reckon.'

'Maybe he wouldn't . . .', Tenzin replied equably, '. . . but this country has come a long way in the past forty years. They've made tremendous progress since you Brits pushed off home.'

Coming from someone whose opinions of India do not usually err on the side of flattery, I took this to be a mild rebuke and an invitation to change the subject.

Thirty or forty single-deck buses were drawn up on a large, flat, open space. As nature does not provide large, flat, open spaces in Simla, the bus station defied the terrain and gravity with massive concrete retaining walls and at its outer edge there was consequently a vertical drop of some fifty or sixty feet. Stopping a bus company official, we said we'd been told that some Tibetan refugees lived nearby and did he happen to know precisely where.

'Over there,' the official replied, indicating with a jerk of his head empty space beyond the parapet.

'I beg your pardon?'

'Over there.' So saying he hurried off to watch the beginning of a punch-up between two bus drivers, one of whom had just reversed his already battered vehicle into the side of another, equally dilapidated.

Tenzin and I went up to the wall and peered over. Down below, roofs speckled by a miscellany of refuse, was a small collection of wretched huts, made mostly of sacking and cardboard. Now that we knew where we were going, it wasn't hard to find the beaten pathway which led down directly beneath the bus station walls.

The first person we came across was sitting on a rock next to an open drain, looking at nothing in particular, and ignoring the ragged and exhausted coolies who filed interminably past, grunting. Kalsang, who certainly occupied a social level some way above these unfortunates, looked up at the sound of Tenzin's Tibetan greeting and smiled amiably. He seemed to be a man in his sixties, unkempt, but apparently in reasonable health.

(Having steep slopes and thousands of visitors with heavy cases, Simla maintains an entire class (probably caste) of people, earning a meagre and precarious livelihood humping heavy bags up and down hill. They are called coolies by one and all, the word coming either from *quli*, Urdu for hired labourer, or *Kuli*, the name of an aboriginal tribe from the state of Gujerat.)

Why, Tenzin asked, a note of incredulity creeping into his voice, was he living here in such obviously disagreeable surroundings? Why wasn't he down at the settlement in Kasumpti?

Kalsang explained patiently that he lived with his two children, who sold scarves and souvenirs to tourists and that while admittedly living conditions were not ideal, in terms of hard cash, they weren't that badly off. Kasumpti was undoubtedly a good place to live, but it was miles out of town, very inconvenient, and weaving carpets was not only a tedious form of drudgery, but also an ill-paid one. Besides . . . His voice tailed away.

Would he, we wondered, be willing to show us round his present home, assuming that he had nothing more urgent to attend to?

Kalsang looked positively pleased at this suggestion and rising stiffly to his feet waved proprietorially at a scene of unmitigated squalor.

'This place used to be a graveyard,' he began. 'When we first came here, we were always digging up bones. Some local Hindu people got very annoyed with us and asked the council to chuck us out. But they've stopped trying now. The big problem nowadays is people in the bus station throwing things over the wall. Tins and so on.'

Right on cue a cigarette packet bounced off a nearby roof and landed a few feet away.

'There you are. I told you so,' remarked Kalsang with evident pleasure at the punctuality of his corroborative evidence.

We walked down the path – which was partly beaten dry and partly swampy thanks to the drain – into the middle of the encampment. Anyone who has not encountered a really nasty Indian slum is first of all very fortunate and secondly quite incapable, unless they have an uncommonly powerful imagination, of appreciating the full horror of it.

We picked our way between puddles of bacteria soup, each of which, evaporating in the strong sun, was ringed by a slimy, yellow, high-water mark. Next to them lay assorted dogs and kittens, panting, too weak and emaciated to move, patched and tattered with mange, an adventure playground for the flies. The flies themselves weren't like European houseflies. They were smaller, more persistent, and came in swarms so thick that I found myself spitting them off my lips and dashing them out of my eyes with a sleeve. Human excrement was everywhere, drying out in innocent little coils. And then there was the smell: a sweet, sinister smell, far more insidious and threatening than any honest-to-God stench.

'Enough,' I called to Tenzin. 'I get the point.'

Kalsang looked rather put out at his tour being called off almost before it had begun, so Tenzin diplomatically suggested that we all should go to one of the bus station's teashops and continue our conversation in comfort. Somewhat appeased, Kalsang led the way back up the path, picked his way expertly through the quarrelling, gesticulating mayhem of arriving and departing passengers, and disappeared into the darkened doorway of a small and anonymous restaurant. It was not at all easy to follow him because the narrow passage leading to the dining room was nearly blocked by unsteady piles of inexpertly dismembered meat – goat by the look of it – and the floor was slippery with blood. Eventually, however, we slithered through to a table at the back and sat down next to a small window with a broken pane. Beyond the rusty iron roofs and rubbish strewn alleys, receding corrugations of evanescent foothills, layer upon layer of powder-blue haze, blended imperceptibly with the sky. Outside, buses and lorries thundered past.

It turned out that Kalsang hadn't had any breakfast, so Tenzin urged him to accept a bowl of meat curry with a pile of chapattis. We then sat sipping tea while he feasted. Beside my right elbow was an open range made of clay, not unlike a converted termite mound, on which half a dozen blackened cauldrons simmered, steamed, and spat. Every now and then the cook would stop hacking up bits of goat (without any obvious reference to anatomy) and drop another log through a wragged hole onto the fire beneath. The room would then fill with smoke, making the brightly coloured posters of Hindu deities on the wall opposite invisible for two or three minutes at a time.

'So you live with your family?' Tenzin prompted as soon as Kalsang seemed to have had enough.

'Three of my sons live in Manali and work on the roads, but my youngest son and his sister are here in Simla. I live with them.'

'So whereabouts in Tibet do you come from?'

'I come from Tinggri. It's in southern Tibet, about fifty miles from the border with Nepal.'

I said that I knew Tinggri well, that I had stayed there a couple of years before, and that I had longed to follow the old mountaineers' trail to Rongbuk under the north face of Everest. I would do it one day, I went on, spurring my hobby-horse to a gallop, I was sure of that. On a clear day the view of the great mountains from Tinggri – the highest group of peaks on earth – was unforgettable. It created an attraction, a longing, that could not forever remain unrequited. Kalsang grew thoughtful during this effusion. He didn't, I afterwards decided, look annoyed, or even sad, merely bemused that this curious foreigner should have such a vivid recollection of the town he had left half a lifetime before.

'What did you do there in Tinggri?' Tenzin asked.

'I was a farmer. I had a share in a farm with my four brothers. We used to grow barley and wheat. We employed a few people to work for us. At harvest time we couldn't manage without. That was the trouble. When the Chinese came, they said I was in the "serf owner" category and had to be punished for my former crimes. They said I would have to earn the forgiveness of The People. By 1964, things were getting really bad, so I ran away. I had to leave in a hurry without my wife and children. I thought, I'll go to find the Dalai Lama. What are we going to do in Tibet without His Holiness anyway?

'First of all, though, I went to Walung in Nepal and tried to get word to my family. I soon heard that they'd already gone to Sikkim. I went off to look for them, but almost immediately I was arrested by the Indian military police. They said I was a Chinese spy. I was in gaol for a fortnight and every day they beat me up to make me confess. At last they decided I couldn't be a spy after all and let me go.

'Eventually I got to Sikkim and found my wife and children. We then went to Dharamsala and saw His Holiness. It didn't feel so bad after that. Wherever the Dalai Lama lives is home for Tibetans.' Kalsang paused, took a swig of tea, and smiled.

'Things really seemed to be going quite well. The authorities in Dharamsala arranged for us to be resettled in a new camp in Madhya Pradesh, right in the middle of India, and we went down there to begin work on the land. But then my wife became ill. It seemed that while she had been in Sikkim she had caught tuberculosis, and the hot climate in India was very bad for her. The Indian doctor said there was no hope; that she was going to die.

'We decided that the only thing to do was to go back up to Dharamsala, to ask the advice of the people at the

Tibetan hospital. They were more helpful and gave her some pills, but they said she'd be better off living in a hill station; that if she went back to the plains it would be the end of her. So I enquired if it would be possible for us to get a place in a hill settlement; preferably Dharamsala. Unfortunately, the authorities said that the Indians didn't want Tibetans moving from settlement to settlement all over India and therefore they'd made this rule that you could only be resettled once. After that you were on your own. There was nothing else for me to do except to take a job on the roads in the Kulu Valley. It was hard work and we were very poor, but at least my wife lived for another twenty-two years. So you see I couldn't go to live in Kasumpti even if I wanted to. I've been resettled once already.'

The most remarkable thing about Kalsang, I suggested to Tenzin on the way back to our hotel, was his complete lack of self-pity. Living in atrocious conditions, he seemed to have reached a plateau of acceptance that bordered on contentment. Having known persecution, pain, penury, and bereavement, he had acquired a stoical and fatalistic cast of mind which daily protected him from rigours that would have reduced most people to an agony of despair. Yet he had not been dehumanised. He was still alert, perceptive, and had held onto a sense of humour. He had been happy to talk to us, but had had no use for sympathy. Indeed, I had formed the distinct impression that he couldn't understand what we were making such a fuss about.

At lunchtime we went back to see Mr Pasang Tsering, to congratulate him on his speech and the general success of the rally. We found him in high good humour: public oratory seemed to agree with him and yesterday's adrenalin had not so far been dissipated.

I was just about to begin a sobering account of our morning in the bus station, when the elderly telephone on his desk had a brief spasm, quivered, rattled, and then gave an inoffensive, almost apologetic tinkle. Beaming, Mr Tsering picked up the receiver with a flourish and bellowed 'HELLO!' into it several times. Suddenly, his manner changed entirely and he became silent and respectful. After listening intently for two or three minutes, he placed one hand over the mouthpiece in the best Hollywood manner and whispered loudly:

'Simla CID want to know who is this Andrew Powell and why he is being accompanied by Mr Tenzin Choegyal, a Tibetan national. What shall I tell them?'

Chapter 5

MUSSOORIE

Tenzin being convinced that as far as the Indian police were concerned, discretion was much the better part of valour, we decided to carry on to Mussoorie with the least possible delay. Providence was clearly of the same opinion, as the man on reception at our hotel turned out to have a brother with a minibus who was going down to Ambala near Chandigarh that afternoon and who was delighted (for a fee adjusted to take account of our fugitive status), to give us a lift. An hour later we were coasting down the hill on our way to the plains.

As we descended, the temperature began to rise inexorably. It had been a warm day in Simla, in the upper eighties Fahrenheit, but the wind that now began to blow in through the window had a life-denying, predatory quality I had never experienced before; not even on particularly torrid days in Delhi. I could feel the water in my skin, deep down close to the bone, being sucked out by an atmosphere ravenous for rain. We reached Kalka, where the terminus for Simla's narrow-gauge railway ends, returning to the flat land, home to the mass of India's toiling, suffering millions. The ground, the buildings, the sky, even the people (who were covered in dust), could be distinguished only by their varying shades of brown. It was like being on a planet with an orbit too close to the sun. Instead of our pleasantly mottled blue and green world, we were in one of those pitiless landscapes to be found in children's encyclopedias, over which a monstrous fiery star looms, melting the rocks and making rivers flow with molten lead.

A routine number of bodies had, the driver nervously informed us, turned up in Chandigarh the night before: victims of the Sikh terror squads.

We stopped eventually at a small shop belonging to the driver's relations and sought sanctuary in its dark and windowless storeroom. Most of the family were in there, out of the sun, crouching down among packing cases as if sheltering from an air raid. Following a short negotiation, the driver's younger brother's friend, who owned an Ambassador car, agreed to drive us up to Mussoorie.

After three more hours bumping and jolting around the outer circles of hell, we began to climb imperceptibly at first, then at an angle sufficient to make the engine labour and to put the driver to the trouble – which he greatly resented – of occasionally changing gear. By early evening we had reached Dehra Dun at the bottom of Mussoorie hill. There at least inhaling no longer seemed likely to cause severe internal burns. The road now began to rise dramatically, gaining 4,500 feet in a series of tight loops before coming out on the top of a ridge in a busy square.

Tenzin, who had also never been to Mussoorie before, disappeared into the milling crowd in search of directions.

'The Tibetans are in a part of town called Happy Valley,' he said, clambering back into the car with a puzzled expression. 'It seems a strange name to me, especially as we're on top of a hill, but that old Khampa over there swears that's what it's called.'

I explained that although my fellow countrymen had not been entirely without merits as colonial administrators, they were as a rule astonishingly unimaginative when it came to names. In consequence both Africa and Asia are still dotted with Happy Valleys, some distinctly more felicitous than others, some on hillsides, some on flat ground, and some, presumably, in valleys.

Tenzin fixed me with a stare which eloquently expressed growing wonder at the extent of Anglo-Saxon folly.

After about five minutes winding round a forested hilltop we came to a dead end, where the driver, who with night approaching was impatient to be getting back to Ambala, insisted on leaving us, absolutely refusing to drive anywhere other than back down the hill to the plains. Fortunately, Tenzin and I were prevented from any rash act of coercive violence by the appearance of a tall, heavily built Tibetan, evidently on his way home from a trip to the local shops.

'Anan Dawa?' enquired Tenzin hesitantly of the approaching shade. In response the figure stopped, peered though the gloom, uttered some Tibetan expression corresponding to 'Well I never!' and wrapped him in a rib-bending bear-hug.

Anan Dawa, Tenzin explained, when five minutes later we were sitting in his living room, our host having gone to the kitchen to fetch some glasses, had for many years been one of the Dalai Lama's bodyguards. He had helped him to escape from the Norbulingka and then been part of the armed escort that had chaperoned his flight to India. Later his duties had continued in Dharamsala. Nowadays he enjoyed a less stressful existence as a housefather at the Tibetan Homes Foundation, residential orphanage and school.

'I have fifty-two children. . .', remarked Anan Dawa beaming, as he came into the room with a litre bottle of Black Label Scotch, the greater part of which he proceeded to pour into three tumblers, '. . . but fortunately my wife doesn't mind. She'll be along in a minute. She's just supervising evening prayers.'

Through the wall came the muffled sound of Buddhist devotions being chanted with all the verve and depth of religious feeling that adolescents generally summon up on such occasions.

'They're all behaving themselves tonight. They've got exams tomorrow.'

'Fifty-two? Where do they all sleep?'

'Good question,' Anan Dawa replied, gulping down a couple of inches of neat Scotch. 'We're so overcrowded that we have to put triple-decker bunks in the dormitories. Each house is supposed to be looking after twenty-five children, but we've got more than twice our allocation. They keep on coming and we can't turn them away. We had a big influx from Tibet two or three years ago. I shouldn't really say so, but it's just as well that it's stopped, otherwise I don't know where we'd be putting them by now.' He paused reflectively. 'The main thing is that, overcrowded or not, here they get brought up to be good Tibetans.'

I said that Tenzin had just told me about his role in the Dalai Lama's escape into exile.

'Oh, that.'

'And that you were with His Holiness when he was smuggled out of the Norbulingka.'

'Uh.'

'And when he crossed the border into India.'

'Mm.'

'I think . . .' said Tenzin in a soothing voice, '. . . that for Anan Dawa it's a very old story. To foreigners I suppose it still sounds exciting, all that stuff, but for us Tibetans, well, we've heard it so many times, it's a bit boring by now.'

Anan Dawa grinned at this explanation. 'I suppose you'll need somewhere to sleep,' he said, being helpful in the practical manner that clearly came easiest to him. 'We have an official guesthouse here. I'll just nip down and ask the woman who runs it if she's got any spare rooms. I won't be long. Help yourself to a drink while I'm gone.'

Morning revealed the Homes Foundation to be a neat collection of solid, well-maintained buildings scattered about a wooded hillside. Built largely with money provided by Western charities, it was immediately obvious that foreign aid had on this occasion been well spent. There were no large roads anywhere nearby, and the setting seemed very calm, far from the workaday world; a good place to forget about politics, to be at school, or even to write a book. The guesthouse itself was an uncomplicated two-storey building with a large canteen on the ground floor and five or six simply furnished bedrooms upstairs. Outside a dozen or so Tibetan boys in blue uniforms were playing football. A pack of local mongrels had joined in the game and judging by the amount of possession they were getting, the dogs were winning easily.

The administrative offices of the Homes Foundation were only about two hundred yards away, so after breakfast, Tenzin and I wandered over to speak to the Director, Mr Tsering Dorje. Although the name had not struck me as familiar, I immediately recognised the intelligent, good-natured face which responded to my hesitant knock. Mr Dorje had for many years been the Dalai Lama's Representative in Switzerland – the European country with the largest number of Tibetan refugees – and I had met him in London two or three years before. Although a loyal and obedient public servant, his Swiss posting had left a great impression and it was not, I gathered, with unconfined joy that he had received the news of his recall to India. The enthusiasm of his wife and family had, he explained, been still more muted. Still, here they all were; making the best of things. If Dharamsala said his duty lay in Mussoorie, then who was he to demur. Rather like a man who has been promoted from First Secretary in Paris to Ambassador in Kampala, Mr Dorje spoke of Zurich with a catch in his voice, eyes shiny with nostalgia. I felt quite sorry for him, in a dispassionate sort of way. He was by no means the first educated Tibetan I had met who, after a brief spell in Europe or America, had been left with a painfully distinct vision of the Promised Land and whose dreams had been turned to ashes by an enforced return to obscurity and (relative) poverty in Asia. The Dharamsala ministeries contained, in my experience, quite a few such unhappy souls, tormented by the stream of impressionable Westerners who visited India, said how marvellous it was, how spiritual, how blessed by fate such Tibetans were to be living up a mountainside, and who then promptly flew home to the material nirvana of Los Angeles. Or Toronto. Or Sydney. Or Zurich, for that matter.

After we had chatted for a while and drunk the usual excess of sweet, milky tea, Mr Dorje said that as he hadn't been in Mussoorie for all that long, the best person to talk to us and to show us round was one of his subordinates, a man coincidentally called Dorje – Dorje means 'thunderbolt' in Tibetan – Mr Dorje Namgyal. If we would care to return to the guesthouse, he suggested, where we could sit on the verandah, relax, and have some tea, Mr Namgyal would be found and sent over to take charge of us.

Mr Namgyal, when he arrived, was a short, middle-aged man with heavy black-rimmed glasses and an expression which, if it wasn't exactly timid, was certainly self-effacing. He had a quiet voice, and although he spoke English with colloquial fluency, it was often quite hard to catch what he was saying. In England, I decided, he would have worked for a high street bank, or perhaps for one of the more prosaic bits of the Civil Service. A model employee – thorough, reliable, punctual, undemanding – he would have travelled home each night by train to a modest house in Metroland.

Still immersed in this fantasy, I asked Mr Namgyal where he lived, half expecting him to name some unremarkable commuter town in Kent or Surrey. He paused for a moment, looking puzzled. 'Why, here of course: in Mussoorie.'

'Oh, sorry. Where did you live in Tibet?'

'That is a bit difficult to say precisely: I come from a nomad family. Actually we lived on the southern edge of the Changtang. You know what that is? The great wilderness that covers the whole of northern Tibet.'

This was wholly unexpected: quite a revelation in fact. The nomads were the toughest of all the Tibetans, living an uncompromising outdoor life at high altitude in an extreme climate. Furthermore, their independent ways had not endeared them to the Chinese and it is often said that they have been treated with particular contempt and brutality. So much for Metroland.

'It's funny . . . ,' Dorje Namgyal continued, '. . . I meet all these foreigners nowadays who have been to Lhasa and Shigatse and Gyantse, whereas I myself know nothing of southern Tibet. I have never been there. I have never seen the Potala, except in photographs taken by Westerners.'

'So how much do you remember nowadays of your nomadic childhood?'

'Quite a lot, although I was still only a boy when my

family came to India. The memories are quite vivid really, considering how long ago it was. I particularly remember the great open plains, covered with grass and flowers in the spring. That time of year was the best. During winter we lived in houses made from mud and stones, but in spring we would set off with our animals, living in yak-hair tents – which had partitions inside and were actually quite comfortable – dressed in our sheep-skin clothes.'

'Did you come from a very poor family?'

'Well, we lived a hard, simple life, and we were not *ed–u–ca–ted* people (he stressed the word heavily, and spoke it slowly, reverentially, giving each of the four syllables his individual care and attention), but my family had quite large herds: about a thousand sheep, five hundred yaks, and maybe twenty horses. So we were quite prosperous really. We certainly had plenty to eat: meat, cheese, curd and tsampa barley flour. Also my elder father – it was customary among the nomads for a woman to have two husbands – used to go to trade in Lhasa, sometimes twice a year. As the return journey took six months, we didn't see very much of him. Occasionally he would make additional trips into the Changtang to fetch salt. This trading meant that our family had a little money as well as animals. As a result my parents were very frightened when they knew that the Chinese were coming. They had heard of terrible atrocities and were sure that because we were well-off we would be made to suffer.'

That semi-literate nomads living in yak-hair tents might fear persecution as the unacceptable face of bourgeois privilege cast an interesting new light onto Chinese ideological fanaticism.

'Did you actually see the Chinese yourself?'

'Oh yes. It was the autumn of 1958, when I was about eight years old. For several days groups of Tibetan guerrillas had been straggling through, fleeing from the fighting in Kham. We gave them food and they told us of the battles that had been fought and of the destruction and the killing. Then one afternoon my mother ran to me and said – she was crying – that the Chinese soldiers were coming and that I had to hide. She had heard stories of Tibetan children being forcibly carried off by the Chinese. To be educated they said. She told me to get in among our sheep and, if the soldiers came nearby, to crawl underneath one and to hang onto the wool on its stomach. So I went up onto the hillside and sat on the ground among the animals, looking down towards our camp. It wasn't long before the Chinese arrived: a column of soldiers. I recall being puzzled by their green uniforms: all exactly the same. They seemed to have no individual identity; not like the men I was used to. I lay on the grass and watched them, framed by the legs of the sheep. I remember that like a picture, a photograph, just as if it were yesterday.'

Unlike the majority of Tibetans who are generally reluctant to talk about themselves and who find it difficult to understand why their lives should be of such consuming interest to foreigners, Dorje Namgyal seemed to suffer from few such inhibitions. He was a fluent and willing storyteller, evidently not at all displeased to find himself with a captive audience and a morning off work.

'So what happened then:'

'Oh, the soldiers went away after an hour or so. They were more interested in tracking down the guerrillas than bothering with us. My parents would have liked to leave immediately, before any more of them turned up, but they knew we could not get our animals to the Himalayan passes before the snow arrived. Besides, the Chinese weren't likely to give us any trouble in winter. They would be shut up in their barracks, trying to keep warm.

'Spring came and we packed our belongings onto the yaks just as we always had. But that year the men saddled up the horses and went on ahead with their rifles and long knives. I suppose it must have been about the time of the Lhasa Uprising, but of course on the edge of the Changtang, we knew little of such things. We travelled to the north-west, hoping to make a big loop away from the inhabited areas, eventually turning directly south towards Mount Kailas and the Indian frontier. After about three months, our sheep had lambs, so we stopped and rested, waiting for them to grow strong. It was summertime; my last summer in Tibet.

'By autumn we had reached the border, close to the Khampa guerrilla base at Mustang in Nepal. There was just one high pass between us and safety. By this time, of course, the Dalai Lama was in Mussoorie, at Birla House, about five hundred yards from where we are sitting now. We rounded up our animals and began to climb steadily up to the pass. During the seven-month journey, we had not had the slightest problem with the Chinese; we hadn't even met any. I suppose they were too busy in Kham and Lhasa. But then disaster hit us. A terrible blizzard that went on for days completely buried us in snow. Although all my family survived, we could not save the animals and nearly all of them died. We arrived in Mustang with just a few yaks.

'At that time, everything was uncertain. Nobody knew what was likely to happen. I suppose people thought then that a political solution might be found; that the Dalai Lama would return and that we could all go home. After what they had heard of the fighting in Kham and Lhasa, maybe in their hearts they thought this was unlikely, but they didn't say so. Anyway, my family stayed in Mustang for over a year and a half. First of all they lived off their savings; then later the women had to sell their jewellery and the men their rifles.

'It was very uncomfortable. There were five or six thousand refugees there, and the price of barley was very high. Eventually my father decided that we had to move, otherwise we were going to run out of money and probably starve to death. So in April 1961 we set off down the gorge of the Kali Gandaki to Pokhara, about ten days' walk away, in the southern foothills of the Annapurna range. I was eleven years old.

'Pokhara was also full of Tibetans and conditions there were very bad. It was just like Mustang, except that because of the heat there was much more disease, so we kept on going until we came to Lumbini, the birthplace of Lord Buddha, down on the plains, close to the Indian border. There we tried to get Indian visas, but this was quite impossible. By now we had nothing left to sell and we had no food. All the time the heat grew worse. Thirteen of the elder members of our party died that May.

'My senior father decided that as things were desperate we would have to evade the police and enter India illegally. So one evening we left Lumbini and walked all night through the paddy fields. In the morning, soon after sunrise, we stopped and made tea. Suddenly we saw a group of policemen with long sticks, *lathis*, walking towards us, shouting. Then they charged us and beat us until we ran away, back into Nepal.

'Obviously, my father said, we were going to have to make a longer detour, and this time, if we didn't want to starve, we might have to fight our way into India. So again we left at night, walking for nine or ten hours. During the following day we hid in a wood until darkness fell again; then we set out once more. None of us had eaten for at least a week. At dawn we came to a village where we bumped into two Tibetan traders. They said that the border was just a few miles away and that there was no check-post. So on the third night we finally crossed the frontier.

'Unfortunately, our journey was not yet over, because we were now in a very remote area and it took us five more days to reach a small railway junction. We just ate whatever we could find in the fields along the way.

'At the station a crowd gathered to look at us. They were very inquisitive. I suppose they had never seen any Tibetans before. I remember they poked and prodded us and shouted to try to make us understand their language. We were very dirty and our clothes were just rags. Even the local buffaloes would come up to sniff us and then run away at the unfamiliar smell.

'We got on a train going to Banaras, where we knew there would be many Tibetans because of the Buddhist shrine at Sarnath nearby. Having no money, we could not buy tickets. We just jumped on board. Fortunately, the inspectors did not throw us off. They knew we were refugees and had nothing. On the way we begged for food.

'In Banaras the Tibetan officials told us that the only way for us to earn a living was for us to work on the roads and they sent us up to the Kulu Valley. My younger brother and sister were admitted to a Tibetan nursery school, but as I was eleven, they said I was old enough to work.

'After six or seven months the whole family was ill. It was not the hard life: we were used to that. It was the food – just chapattis, rice, and dal [lentils] – and the hot climate. Within a year, both my fathers were dead. My mother was in despair. But then she heard that my brother and sister had been sent to school in Mussoorie. So we came here. Of course nothing that you see now – the Homes Foundation, the Childrens' Village, the school – had been built then. There was just a lady and her husband: Mr and Mrs Taring.'

Dorje Namgyal smiled. The name seemed to rouse within him some deep affection.

I was still finding it extremely difficult to connect his

slight, dapper figure and neat clean clothes with the unfolding tale of endurance and suffering. In an attempt to forget about this dilemma, I said that I'd heard of Mrs Taring already and had read her book, *Daughter of Tibet*. Mr Namgyal looked pleased.

'I'm sure you'll want to meet them. They live halfway down the hill, in Rajpur. I'll telephone when we go over to my office and make an appointment for you. She is a remarkable women and they have both been very kind to me. When my mother and I first arrived in Mussoorie, they were already hard at work, getting this place started. We went to see Mrs Taring and she was very sympathetic and said she would find some financial assistance for us. In fact she found my mother a job in a nursery. Then she arranged for me to go to school in Dharamsala.

'The only trouble was, when I got there the authorities still insisted that I was too old – I was twelve – and that they had as much work as they could manage just looking after the very youngest children. Eventually they agreed that I could go to the Transit School in Kangra. There the conditions were appalling – overcrowding, disease, insufficient food – but at least I began to learn English. About a year later Mrs Taring wrote to say that she now had room at the Homes Foundation in Mussoorie and would I like to take up a place there. Of course I went as soon as I possibly could.

'I will never forget the day I arrived. I thought I had gone to heaven. I had been allocated a place in Home 20, which had just been built with money provided by the British charity, Save the Children Fund. Everything was new and clean. There was running water and enough to eat. There was furniture in the living room; even sheets on my bed. I had never slept in sheets before. It was the most wonderful day, perhaps of my entire life.

'The next morning I went to the Tibetan Central School

where Mr Taring was the headmaster. After a while it was decided that as well as receiving a general education I should be sent for intensive training in English. You see, at that time the Tibetans needed to be able to talk both to the Indians, who had given them a home, and to the international agencies which were providing them with aid. English was potentially the common language, but few Tibetans could speak it. So I went to study under a Mr Dexter. He was a kind and understanding man, as, in my experience, were all the foreign teachers who had volunteered to help us.

'Not having had any education as a child, it was decided that I should follow a vocational rather than an academic path, so I was sent to a college in Simla for a year. There I studied office management, book-keeping, and typing. At the end of the course I returned to Mussoorie to work for Mrs Taring, writing letters in English to foreign people who had agreed to sponsor the education of Tibetan children. Then, in 1972, I was appointed assistant to the head of Swiss Aid to Tibetans, and for the next eleven years I travelled with him all over India. This organisation alone has trained several hundred Tibetan teachers, fifty or sixty nurses and many Tibetan doctors. Nowadays I'm working with Save the Children Fund who sponsor around seven hundred and fifty children in Mussoorie.'

Dorje Namgyal smiled shyly. 'So now you know about my life.'

'What happened to your brother and sister? Did things work out well for them in the end?'

'Oh yes. After her schooling here in Mussoorie, my sister went to university. She now works for a firm of architects in Delhi. My brother studied for his Bachelor of Commerce exam at St Joseph's College, Darjeeling and he now works for Mr Tenzin.'

'Mr Tenzin who?'

'Mr Tenzin Choegyal. This Mr Tenzin.'

'You mean your brother works for Tenzin in Kathmandu?'

'Yes, yes,' said Tenzin chipping in hurriedly, to minimise any further confusion. 'He works for us as an accountant. Mr Namgyal told me about him when he arrived, since when I haven't had a chance to explain.'

'So all three of you, despite the suffering that went before, have benefited from the educational opportunities that have been available in exile.'

'Yes, that's true.'

'What do you suppose would have happened to you if your family had remained in Tibet?'

'Well, if my fathers had stayed. I am sure they would have been imprisoned or killed by the Chinese. But if you mean what would have happened if the Chinese had never invaded, if life had continued as before, if the old Tibet that is now gone forever still existed, then of course I would have been a simple nomad all my life and my children would have been simple nomads too. In our area education was unknown. There were some lamas, who taught us to recite basic scriptures, but there were no schools. Even in Lhasa the schools were for the noble familes; there was no opportunity for the general public. Becoming a monk was the only way for ordinary boys to learn to read and write.'

'So when foreigners nowadays say that the destruction of the old Tibet was a tragedy, do you agree? When they say that the life of the simple nomad was one of spiritual fulfilment, that such people, through being in harmony with their environment, knew a kind of happiness unavailable to modern man, what do you say to them?'

Dorje Namgyal sat in silence for at least thirty seconds, as if weighing in the balance the experience of half a lifetime.

'I am rather for a change. Of course many of the

changes that have occurred in Tibet have been for the worse, but I believe that in the end a new society will emerge, better and happier than the one which existed before. I think the education of thousands of ordinary Tibetan children in exile has been a great achievement and that it has laid the foundations of the future Tibet.'

'But what of the life of the nomad? Where there is hardship and ignorance and poverty, can there really be happiness and nobility and spiritual fulfilment? Much of the Western fascination with Tibet is based on the assumption that there can.'

'If the Chinese had never invaded Tibet, I think that I might have been quite happy. I would have known no other life than the one I was born to. I would not have been able to compare my existence with any other. I would not even have envied the lives of the nobility in Lhasa, because I would have known so little about them. I would not have wanted Tibetan society to change, because I would have had no idea of how it might have been changed for the better. But looking back now I am grateful to have escaped such a life. I consider myself to have been very fortunate. It is important for Western people to understand just how hard the life of the nomad was. It was short and often painful. I was the first of my parents' children to survive, but I was their *tenth* child. No, I am sorry for the suffering that the Chinese have brought to the Tibetan people, but I am not sorry that the old Tibet has been swept away.'

'I am sure you know that many foreigners – myself included – consider the Tibetans to be a very balanced and kindly race, with a strong sense of humour and natural capacity for happiness. We generally attribute these racial characteristics to a particular way of life and system of values. If the future Tibet is materially developed with a democratic government and a greatly reduced role for the clergy, won't the character of the

Tibetan people inevitably change? Can the simple good nature of the Tibetans survive in the modern world?'

'Perhaps, I think so. I hope so. But of course Western ideas about the Tibetan national character are often sentimental and oversimplified. Maybe you do not know us well enough yet. Maybe when you come to the end of your travels with Mr Tenzin here you will have come to understand us better.'

Peking has long sought to persuade the world that the only people who fled from the manifest blessings of communist rule were those who had previously oppressed and exploited the masses, the unrepentant nobility, terrified of The People's anger and The Party's just and belated retribution. In fact, the Tibetan exiles in India and Nepal come from every rank and position in society, a large proportion being simple farming or herding people, who, happily for them, lived close enough to the border to be able to escape the terror and the tumbrils.'

'Well, there were a few people in Dharamsala who were more concerned with getting their property back than with the future of the country,' Tenzin conceded as we drove down to the Tarings' house in Rajpur. 'Still are I guess. But nobody takes much notice of them nowadays.'

'The Tibetans were quite keen on their class system though weren't they? Breeding counted for a lot in the old Tibet.'

'I suppose so – in Lhasa anyway – though I don't think even there the situation was as bad as you might suppose. There wasn't a huge gap between nobility and the ordinary people. The nobles were better off, more secure, a bit more comfortable, but Tibet was a hard country for everyone who lived there. The land itself, and the severe climate, prevented people from putting up too many barriers. Perhaps the most powerful Tibetan politician in the first half of this century, a man called Chensal Namgang, came from a peasant family. He was a servant in the Potala who was promoted by the Thirteenth Dalai Lama because of his obvious abilities. Eventually he became both Commander-in-Chief of the Tibetan army and chief minister in the Kashag. Also he was allowed to marry into the nobility and to take the name Tsarong, which is one of the most important in Tibet. He was actually Mary Taring's first husband. She was a Tsarong.

'Mr Taring, the man we're going to see, was her *second* husband. He was a pure-blooded aristocrat and would have been King of Sikkim if his father hadn't refused to accept the crown. He, his father that is, had a Tibetan wife and liked living on his Tibetan estate near Gyantse. So Mr Taring – Jigme, Prince of Taring – is half Tibetan, half Sikkimese.'

When Robert Byron travelled to Tibet in the late 1920s, he was invited for lunch at the Taring country estate: 'Jigme . . .', he wrote, 'wore a robe of maroon silk beneath which showed an undergarment of amber brocade. This magnificence was marred by a tweed hat.' Sixty years later, we found Mr Taring, dressed in an open-necked sports shirt and cotton slacks, sitting on a broken wicker chair in his small Rajpur garden and reading *The Times of India*. He was an elderly man, with a deeply lined face, a full head of grey hair and spectacles. Thin, frail, and slightly deaf, his manner was, however, still animated and affable.

'I'm so sorry that my wife couldn't be with us, but she's on a month's meditation retreat. I'll do my best to fill you in. Come, let's sit down and have some coffee.'

We walked across a lawn behind the house which had a vaguely English appearance. A squat, four or five-bedroom family residence with ugly metal-framed windows, it was a good deal better than the homes most people have to live in, but was certainly no palace either.

We sat around a small, low table. Mr Taring carefully spooned instant coffee powder into three mugs and then filled them up with tepid water from a teapot. As a respite from sweet, milky tea it tasted delicious.

'I imagine you may have seen my wife's book, so you'll know quite a bit about us already,' he began, hesitantly. I said that I had indeed read the book, but that I would still be very interested to hear the story from him. Mr Taring looked pleased. I got the distinct impression that his wife usually dealt with journalists and that her temporary absence was giving him a rare opportunity to reminisce on his own account.

'I come from Gyantse. I expect you know where that is. The Taring estate was a fairly big one: about five miles long by two miles wide. On it there were six small villages where our . . . "subjects" should I say? . . . where our subjects lived. Each village contained around eight familes, so there were probably four or five hundred people in all. These people worked part of the time on their own land and part of the time on ours. We had staff, but mostly the land was worked by the villagers. They made a programme among themselves as to who would work the estate's fields and when the work should be carried out. We then provided the workers with *tsampa* (flour) and either tea or *chang* (barley beer).'

'So do you think it's fair when foreigners use the word "feudal" to describe this arrangement?'

'Insofar as I understand its full meaning, then I suppose so. However, the relationship was not totally one-sided. The villagers paid no taxes; they worked for the estate instead. We had to pay tax to the administration at Gyantse Dzong (castle). We were also obliged to work for the government in Lhasa for almost no financial reward.'

'But am I right in thinking that because of this system, people were tied to one place? If they were born in

Gyantse, they lived and died in Gyantse. Social mobility, in a geographical as well as an hierarchical sense, was impossible.'

'That's true. Of course the situation wasn't the same all over Tibet. In some places there were nomads; in Kham things were organised differently.' He looked across at Tenzin who nodded in agreement. 'But around Gyantse, society was very static.'

'So could it have developed? Could Tibetan society have evolved if the Chinese hadn't turned up?'

Mr Taring sipped his coffee and thought for a minute. 'Well, my family were liberal: they were in favour of adopting new ways and there were others like us. For a year I attended a school in Gyantse which had been started by the British Trade Agent, Mr MacDonald. Later a modern school was set up in Lhasa. But both were closed down because of monastic opposition. All the abbots thought that if foreigners were allowed to live in Tibet, or if foreign languages were taught, then Buddhism would be challenged and Tibetan culture placed in danger. The Thirteenth Dalai Lama had been to India, he had seen the outside world, and as a result he was a force for change. But after his death in 1933 the impetus to modernise was lost. Conservative elements gained the upper hand.'

'So your family decided to send you to school in India.'

'Yes. I went first to Kalimpong: Dr Graham's Homes School. I arrived there in 1918. It's a long time ago now. The only thing I remember vividly is playing hockey with no shoes on. A lot of the boys had been orphaned by the First World War and were very poor. They couldn't afford shoes for games, so the school said everyone had to be the same and play barefoot. Later I went to St Paul's in Darjeeling to join the son of the King of Sikkim. Mary, my wife, was also at school in Darjeeling a few years afterwards. But then you must know all that.'

'During your adult working life in Tibet you were never in any way involved with education?'

'No, not at all. I was a soldier – I was trained as a machine gunner by the British – and for a while an officer in the Treasury. One of my duties used to be to take charge of the finances for the Monlam New Year celebrations. It was traditional for all the monks in the Lhasa monasteries – about twenty thousand of them – to be given a feast. This was very expensive and quite a headache, I can tell you. Then after the Lhasa Uprising I fled to India to be with His Holiness.

'As I was one of the few Tibetans who could speak fluent English I soon found myself at the centre of things again. I'd been in India about six months when the Dalai Lama called me to see him. He was very distressed about the children, many of whom were dying. He told me that he wanted to start residential schools; to get them out of camps and off the road gangs. Mr Nehru had just been up to visit him and had promised that as soon as arrangements could be made, all Tibetan children would be given an education. Afterwards the Indian government was very helpful and extremely kind. His Holiness said to me that he was going to start a school in Mussoorie and that he wanted me to be in charge. I was very surprised and said that I was an army officer, not an educationalist, and that I wasn't sure that I was the right man for the job. But His Holiness just said "You speak English don't you? Teach them what you were taught", so I had to agree.

'In a few weeks the children began to arrive. They were in a terrible condition: suffering from malnutrition and every kind of skin disease. We had no bedding, no cooking utensils, nothing. Meanwhile word spread down to the camps – places like Misamari – that their children would be well cared for in Mussoorie and they began sending them up in such large numbers we could not cope at all.

They had to go on to transit camps in Kangra and Dharamsala, which were far from satisfactory. Things were clearly worse than His Holiness had realised, so he instructed my wife to start a home for orphans and the very needy. She went all over Mussoorie looking for somewhere suitable and eventually she found three dilapidated houses. The children from these homes used to come over to the school for lessons. In those days we had no classrooms; we just used to sit in the shade of the trees as we are doing here this morning. Then after 1961, the Government of India began providing full financial assistance and we soon had buildings, qualified teachers, free clothing and stationery . . . The whole place got going and quickly became what you see today.'

'So do you think the system that has been established over the last thirty years is a good one?'

Mr Taring paused again and began to look slightly fretful. 'The Dalai Lama wants to have modern education combined with traditional Tibetan religious values. His Holiness sees that the Tibetans in exile must be well educated and self-reliant, but also that there is a vital necessity to preserve Tibetan identity and culture.'

'But are such aims necessarily compatible?'

'I think they can be. The system works best in places like South India where there are large settlements, many thousands of people, and where the Tibetans live separately from the local Indian population. Here in Mussoorie it is not like that and I think there are many dangers. Still, you must talk to someone who is up-to-date, someone who understands the present situation. Go to see Mr Karma Kophel. He's the Rector now at the Central School. He'll be able to tell you about such things.'

When the time came to leave, Mr Taring shook me warmly by the hand and said that he hoped we wouldn't hesitate to drop by again if we needed any more information. He struck me as a kindly man, one who –

comparatively speaking – had not been greatly inconvenienced by his years of exile, but who nonetheless had worked hard and done his best to help those less fortunate. From the point of view of a Peking propagandist, he was a thoroughly unsatisfactory specimen. Aristocrat, feudal landowner, army officer, and faithful servant of the *ancien régime*, he belonged to that Tibetan class which the Chinese frequently, scornfully, and inelegantly refer to as 'the Dalai clique'. He ought to have provided perfect material for a diatribe of ideological self-righteousness. Doubtless this makes the reality all the more frustrating.

Mr Dorje Namgyal, who was proving himself to be an extremely assiduous mentor, called to collect us at the guesthouse just after eight-thirty the following morning. He then escorted us all of two hundred yards across to Mussoorie Central School. This was an elegant, two-storey, classically proportioned building, painted a restful shade of pale blue, and set around a large central yard. It seemed to be a harmonious place, in a good state of repair, and financially very well provided for.

'Three types of Tibetan school have been established in India and Nepal,' Mr Namgyal explained helpfully, as we sat on the verandah outside the rector's office. 'There are ones like the Children's Village in Dharamsala which rely on foreign sponsors; then there are schools financed and managed by the Council for Tibetan Education at Gangchen Kyishong – most of which are primary schools – and finally there are the Central Schools, like this one, which are part of the Indian education system and which are funded by the Government of India. These are numerically the most important of the three, and there are around eleven thousand Tibetan children currently enrolled in them.'

The door opened and a strangely etiolated Indian woman, dressed in a pale pink sari, beckoned to us feebly, before collapsing onto a nearby rattan chair, as if the effort expended on this slight gesture had exhausted her entirely. As she neither moved nor spoke, we picked our way carefully past her into the rector's office.

Mr Karma Kophel was sitting behind a desk laid out with the precision of a municipal flowerbed, hemmed in on all sides by closed ranks of gleaming sports trophies. He was in his mid-thirties, with closely cropped, severely parted black hair, and wearing a brown safari suit so sharply and recently pressed that I found myself looking round in vain for the ironing board. Above his head, a picture of the Dalai Lama shared pride of place with one of Mahatma Gandhi, reading a weighty tome held out at arms length. Standing up with military abruptness, he seized my hand and pumped it up and down with tremendous warmth and enthusiasm. Here, then, was a high-ranking member of the Dalai Lama's officer corps, battling to preserve Tibetan culture and identity in an alien land.

Did he, I began, ever feel overawed by his immense responsibility? Education was clearly of such critical importance to the future of the Tibetan cause. No, he replied, not overawed; more depressed.

'Depressed?'

'Look around you. Look at all these fine buildings provided for us by the Indian government. Here we want for nothing. We have enough books, enough equipment, enough teachers . . .'

Nonplussed by this unexpected sarcasm, I merely remarked that these seemed improbable reasons for gloom.

'Really? And what would you say if I told you that standards of education among Tibetans have been falling steadily for the past fifteen years? Look at me. I am thirty-six. I did not begin to learn to read until I was eleven years old. In those days there were no classrooms, and we did not have pencil and paper to write with. But we managed. We learned because we wanted to learn. Tibetan children were desperate for knowledge and they had self-discipline so they acquired it.'

'So where did it all begin to go wrong?'

'This is a complex question, but at least one part of the explanation is simple enough. In 1975 the system of administration in Tibetan Central Schools was changed. Before there had been Tibetan headmasters and Indian principals. The Indian government was paying the bills, so they appointed the figurehead. He dealt with the bureaucracy, while the Tibetan headmaster got on with the job of running the school and supervising the teachers. Everything worked very well.

'Unfortunately, the Indians realised where the real power lay – and they didn't like it – so they decided to alter the rules. From now on, they said, the Tibetan will be known as the Rector. He will have joint responsibility for finance; he will be in charge of the pupils' accomodation; and he will also offer "guidance" to the Indian principal on matters connected with Tibetan language, religion, and culture. But he will have no power. All matters concerning the standards and methods of teaching and the hiring and firing of teachers will come under the sole jurisdiction of the principal.'

'I can see that this arrangement has drawbacks from the Tibetan point of view, but surely it could have been made to work?'

Mr Kophel took a firm grip on the edge of his desk. 'Originally it was decided that no more than 10 per cent of the students in Tibetan schools would be of Indian origin. We explained to the Indian authorities that above all we wanted to preserve our cultural identity and they were very understanding. This school now has one thousand

and fifty-four pupils of whom 18 per cent, nearly one in five, are Indian. Every year we get more and more applications from Indian parents and we are under great pressure to accept them.'

'I'm sorry, I don't understand why they are so keen for their children to come here. Isn't this just another Indian state school? What's so different about it?'

'A good question, to which there are two answers. First, look at the way Indian and Tibetan parents behave towards their children. Indians dote on them – the sons anyway – let them do anything they like, and spoil them completely. Tibetans, generally speaking, are kind but firm and won't put up with any nonsense. Indian parents are horrified by the deterioration in children's behaviour, but collectively they lack the will to do anything about it. So they send them to a Tibetan school and hope we will sort things out for them.

'The second, more important reason, is that the basic medium in North Indian schools is Hindi; in Tibetan Central Schools it is English. Now the Indians have a problem about English. They know it's a world language; they know their businessmen and civil servants must speak it; they know it's the language which unites this country more than any other; but they hate having to perpetuate a reminder of their colonial past. So there is very strong pressure for Hindi to be the language of education and politics and commerce, even though everyone knows this is impossible and self-defeating.

'Indian middle-class parents, who tend to be more pragmatic than the average politician, and who want their children to get on in the world, are frustrated by this ideological obsession, and as they can't in general afford expensive private education they try to get their children into Tibetan schools where they know they will be taught in English.'

'I still don't see why you find this situation so alarming.

Even if 20 per cent of the pupils are Indian, they are still outnumbered four to one.'

Karma Kophel clasped his hands together and leaned foward across the desk for greater emphasis. 'The principal, though by no means the only defect of the Indian education system is that it is designed to turn out good Indians. We are trying to produce good Tibetans. We would like to have more Tibetan teachers, but this is not allowed. Here the majority of teachers are Indian. They teach Indian history, Indian geography and so on.

'Then there is the problem of cheating. Corruption is endemic in India and most exam results can be bought. Tibetan teachers and parents are honest, so our children suffer. More worrying still is the truancy problem. India has changed in the past thirty years. The old idealism is dead. There are now five or six video parlours within ten minutes' walk of this campus. Our children play truant and spend all day looking at Hindi films. These films, which combine sentimentality and violence with the promotion of crude materialist values, are absolutely pernicious. They induce a kind of dream mentality. Children seem to lose all contact with the real world. Of course this is harmful for Indian children, but for Tibetans, the children of refugees, the generation which must recover our country from the Chinese, it is an absolute disaster. You see, we Tibetans should not live a normal life. We should not be comfortable. Our country is occupied and we are at war. We should be disciplined and tough. Instead our children are becoming soft and lazy and ignorant. Very soon, if we are not careful, they will not be Tibetans at all.'

'Quite a firebrand,' I suggested to Tenzin and Dorje Namgyal as we sat outside the guesthouse discussing the morning's encounter. Passionate, intelligent, and articulate, Karma Kophel had impressed me. On the other hand, there had been an uncompromising, Spartan quality in what he had to say which struck me as atypical of Tibetans in general.

Tenzin shook his head. 'No, we need more like him. People like me, busy earning a living, supporting a family, we lose touch with what's going on. He's right, there is a temptation to settle for a comfortable life in India. We must have our best people in education where they can carry on the struggle.'

Dorje Namgyal nodded his head in agreement. 'I'm afraid the pupils *have* changed. Before they used to work much harder. If things go on as they are, the situation will soon be very serious.'

By eleven o'clock the sun had disappeared. Now, in the early afternoon, clouds like ragged coal sacks were being chased across the sky. Dust devils dashed about the playground. A giant, solitary raindrop fell, splat, on the ground in front of us.

Dorje Namgyal, Tenzin and I broke off our conversation to stare at the dark brown stain on the earth, as it spread out to the size of a leaf.

Away to the north, among the great peaks of the Nanda Devi Sanctuary, epic thunder rolled. Every so often the impenetrable gloom was blitzed by a livid, electric flash. Forces of unimaginable violence slugged it out among the glaciers, while an ominous black raft, borne along on a current of cold air, was sucked slowly down towards the burning plains. The afternoon was extinguished, and a kind of proxy night-time fell.

Suddenly, a brief excerpt from the Apocalypse broke over us as a simultaneous detonation of lightning and thunder shattered the air. About a hundred yards away, a fifty-foot pine tree teetered briefly, fought for life, lost the struggle, and then crashed down into the surrounding vegetation. A few moments of silence followed, while we waited, shaken, cringing, for another bolt to strike.

Then, softly at first, accelerating, gaining power, till the gentle patter became a ferocious drumming, the rain began to fall.

'Thank God for that,' said Tenzin. 'The hot season's over.'

Chapter 6

LADAKH

To fly into Ladakh is considered by all who know and love the Himalayas an insult to the splendour of the terrain bordering on blasphemy. We had therefore decided to take a plane up to Kashmir and to drive from Srinagar to the Ladakhi capital of Leh. This depended on the Zoji-la, the most treacherous of the road's three passes, having been cleared of snow by the Indian army. The Delhi newspapers were not altogether encouraging in this respect.

Due to border disputes with the Chinese, Ladakh was closed to foreigners from the Sino – Indian War of 1962 up until 1974. However, after the airfield was opened to passenger flights, visitors flooded in. Tibet itself was still a forbidden land and Ladakh – 'Little Tibet' – was the best available substitute. Nowadays the border squabbles rumble on – with both China and Pakistan – but nobody takes much notice. Tourism is a lucrative business. Every spring campaigning season, the odd platoon is casually slaughtered; the generals try out their new artillery pieces to see if they live up to the manufacturers' claims; and bored reporters file much the same copy as last year. Only the names of the dead, when recorded, are different.

Ladakh's epithet, 'Little Tibet' (from which it is tiresomely inseparable), is fortunately not just a picturesque invention of the tourist trade. Although politically part of India, the region is north of the main Himalayan range and geographically an extension of the Tibetan plateau. Furthermore, its people migrated from Tibet; the Ladakhi language is a junior sibling of Tibetan; its culture is saturated by Tibetan Buddhism; and its monasteries and palaces are all built in the Tibetan style.

Since the destruction of much of the old Tibet and the indoctrination of its people in an alien ideology, it is often said that there are now only two places where a traditional Tibetan society still survives: Bhutan and Ladakh. Bhutan, however, is *south* of the Himalayas and does not therefore have the distinctive Tibetan landscape and climate.

Although it is true that in AD 930 the eldest son of the King of Ngari – a kingdom of western Tibet during a period when the country had no effective central government – became the first King of Ladakh, the Tibetans were not always the dominant people. Over the centuries there has been quite a bit of family bickering and feuding. This culminated in the reign of the Ladakhi King Senge Namgyal (d. 1642), during which the borders of a Ladakhi empire stretched as far as the central Tibetan province of Tsang.

In 1834, the so-called Dogra Invasion dethroned the royal Namgyal dynasty and replaced it with an administration appointed by the Maharaja of Jammu: Jammu being a city and eponymous state in north-western India. Ever since, Ladakh has been under the control of regimes to the south of the Himalayas: hence its incorporation into the new Republic of India in apparent defiance of geographical logic. Today the royal palace in Leh is an empty ruin – the Queen is allowed to live in a smaller one at Stok, a village about ten miles out of town – and Ladakh, much to the continuing fury of the Ladakhis, is part of the predominantly Muslim Indian state of Jammu and Kashmir.

Davinder, the representative of a Srinagar travel and trekking agency, was a lapsed Sikh who had dispensed with a turban, but retained an impressive coal-black beard and an unmistakably martial bearing. We discussed the present condition of the road to Leh and he smiled with the philosophical air of one long accustomed to regarding the pronouncements of Kashmiri officialdom as amusing scraps of fantasy, delicate works of the imagination, rather than as statements usefully approximate to truth.

'They say they're going to open it tomorrow, but they've been saying that every day since this time last week. The trouble is they had even more snow than usual in the Zoji-la last winter – a hundred and sixteen feet to be precise – which took ages to clear. As a result the army was late getting its reinforcements up to Ladakh and at the moment the road is only being used by the military. The buses definitely won't be running for a day or so, but we might be able to get you over in a jeep. I'll come round in the morning if I have anything positive to report.'

At nine-thirty he duly appeared, together with a Kashmiri driver, Farouk, swaddled in a beige shawl that at a distance looked like an enormous brown paper bag. Farouk did not immediately inspire confidence and I had an uncomfortable suspicion that the paint might still be wet on the memory of his sixteenth birthday.

'I can't promise anything,' said Davinder, 'but it's certainly worth going up to Sonamarg. There's talk of letting a few civilians over this afternoon, providing nothing military gets stuck in the meanwhile.'

This being my second trip over the Zoji-la (I had visited Ladakh for the first time five years before), I recalled Sonamarg to be rather a scruffy ski-ing and trekking centre, about three hours' drive away from Srinagar.

We set off along the tarmacked road that leads north-east out of the Kashmir Valley, soon leaving behind its orchards and fertile fields and entering instead a precipitous landscape of pines, rushing waters, and teetering, lorry-sized boulders. High up, the odd patch of discoloured snow, stranded by the approach of summer, hung on grimly, in desperate hope of a cold snap.

There was little traffic on the road and by lunchtime we were in Sonamarg where, in a large, muddy field beside a river, were parked at least a hundred and fifty heavy trucks. Their drivers were sitting about in ragged groups, chatting, smoking, playing cards. Nothing was moving and no one seemed to be expecting anything to happen in the foreseeable future. The way ahead appeared to be blocked by a large snow-covered peak, while just visible on its lower slopes was the thin scar of the road, a mere cat scratch, slanting upwards to the pass.

Farouk went to talk to a soldier who was standing guard on a red-and-white striped pole slung across the road. He returned disconsolate. A military convoy had already left Kargil in Ladakh and would be coming down throughout the afternoon. The road was not wide enough for two-way traffic and we would have to wait. Maybe we would get across tomorrow, he said, without much obvious conviction.

The following morning, after a night spent with my head jammed underneath the steering wheel, I was beginning to weaken, allowing my imagination to dwell on the hot bath and large breakfast that was waiting for me back in Srinagar, when I was distracted by a thump on the roof of the jeep and the appearance of a policeman's head through an open window. If we wanted to get in front of the lorries, the head advised, we had better be quick about it, as the road was opening at six o'clock sharp.

With three or four minutes to spare we reached the front of the queue and as the striped pole swung open, became the first private vehicle that year to travel between Kashmir and Ladakh.

The Zoji-la has the reputation for being one of the most dangerous stretches of road in the world, and its notoriety is by no means ill-founded. Every year an alarming number of people dies crossing a pass no more than 11,600 feet high. It is true that the statistics are slightly inflated by local bus drivers flouting its perils with one hand clutching a bottle, but the responsibility for most of the carnage must go to the road itself. Much of it was blasted out of the hillside and is little more than a steep, narrow, rocky ledge, generally covered in ice. In places it is only about fifteen feet wide, the surface is loose gravel, there are no barriers, and the vertical drop off the side is around 3,000 feet.

One of the disadvantages of crossing the Zoji-la at the height of summer, when theoretically it is at its safest, is said to be the sight of tangled, burnt-out wreckage at the foot of every precipice. At least at the beginning of June, the debris of past disasters is still decently covered by a thick layer of snow.

To my relief and considerable surprise, Farouk turned out to have a healthy instinct for self-preservation. Rather than the classic style of Indian driving – one arm out of the window, one hand clamped on the horn – he preferred to forsake flamboyance for caution, peering earnestly through the windscreen as if his life depended on it. Which it certainly did. I nonetheless kept hold of the door handle just in case, and braced myself to be ready to jump. We struggled up in first gear, gaining height in an interminable series of zig-zags, the wheels spinning occasionally, but fortunately showing little inclination to slip sideways into oblivion.

The pristine snowfields on the adjacent peak grew steadily closer and as the road neared the top and levelled out, we began to pass between ice cliffs, a hundred feet high and twenty feet apart, a kind of Brobdingnagian bobsleigh track. These passages had been dynamited out by the Indian army in places where the snow was too thick for bulldozers to be of the slightest use. It was like travelling between the jaws of a gigantic vice, and I chatted gaily to Farouk in a vain attempt to suppress all speculation about the likely effects of an avalanche.

Having finally reached the summit of the pass, we stopped the jeep and got out. There was nothing much to see: just a wilderness of snow being piled into drifts by a diligent, razor-edged wind; a featureless white world, inimical to life. Overhead the sky was a quilt of pigeon grey. Ahead lay Ladakh, but it might have been Lapland for all that one could tell.

Just an hour later, the landscape had changed to one of gaunt, sienna-coloured mountains, in the folds and clefts of which irrigated terraces were swaying with barley and bright with flowers. Perched on a bleached, leafless branch, a kingfisher searched the frothing stream below. The sun shone from a cloudless sky and the whole landscape was radiant and gleaming.

It is impossible to exaggerate the impact of Tibetan, or in this case Ladakhi, light. Much apparent hyperbole has been written in its praise, but every word is true, and indeed an understatement. Doubtless it is merely the result of the high altitude and thin atmosphere, but its effect is positively metaphysical. The astonishing clarity and radiance make one look at simple objects as if one had never seen their like before. They seem to be purified, redeemed, revealed in their true essence, as they really are without the muddy inadequacies of human perception. Tibetan light is the eye of God, surveying His creation.

I remembered landing at Lhasa airport in 1987, getting out of the plane, and feeling exactly the same sudden surge of joy and freedom, an expansion of consciousness, in which fears are peremptorily dismissed and the mind filled with amazement at the possibilities of the world. Three weeks later, leaving the sunlit uplands of the Tibetan plateau for the forests of Nepal, had seemed like a descent to the underworld.

Few things, however, could be more sobering than Kargil, Ladakh's scrofulous second city (though city is hardly an appropriate term for a town with two parallel streets and around three thousand inhabitants). Nowadays, 90 per cent of Kargil's population are Muslims from either Kashmir or Baltistan and the atmosphere of the place is not really Ladakhi at all.

We arrived at eleven o'clock and stopped for a swift and meagre breakfast. Normally it takes two days to drive from Srinagar to Leh – Kargil being the overnight stop – but having lost an entire afternoon already, Farouk was anxious to push on. We had been driving for five hours (including two hours in atrocious conditions on the Zoji-la) and Leh was still ten hours distant (without allowing time for punctures or minor mishaps). Nonetheless, he seemed unalarmed by this excruciating schedule. He got paid by the journey, not by the day, he explained, and hanging around in Kargil was for him an expensive business.

At eleven-fifteen we were back on the road and by late afternoon had crossed two further high passes, neither encumbered by so much as a snowflake. Pausing for only a few moments at Lamayuru, one of the most spectacular of Ladakh's large Buddhist monasteries, we pressed on relentlessly, and as darkness fell caught our first glimpse of the lights of Leh, twenty miles off, where the savage gorge cut by the Indus abruptly opens out into a wide valley, flanked by stark and barren mountains.

A century ago, Leh was on a major trade artery and in its bazaar merchants from India, China, Tibet, Russia, and Central Asia bargained, quarrelled, and spied on one another. Once, the narrow path through the mountains, barely wide enough for pack animals, had been an important branch line of the Silk Route.

Nowadays Leh is an army camp with a small town attached, and in summer soldiers outnumber its 10,000 civilians by more than five to one. Throughout the day, enormous Antonov transport planes lumber, growling, into the sky, while pairs of silver Mig fighters can be seen practising their low-flying manoeuvres, flirting with oblivion, daring the hills to reach out and grab them. About three hundred yards from the end of the runway stands Spituk, one of Ladakh's more important monasteries.

We had not, the manager of my hotel informed us, arrived at a particularly propitious moment. The underground river of anti-military, anti-Indian, anti-Kashmiri, anti-Muslim feeling had burst into the open and was at present inundating the valley. There had been riots, windows had been broken and houses set on fire. Someone had let off a home-made bomb, and a number of Ladakhis were now languishing in gaol. He was not sure what had been the precise cause of the trouble, but frankly it was immaterial. The Ladakhis bitterly resented being turned into a minority in their own country, both by the army and by the Kashmiris who had followed the army in search of a shrewd deal and a quick profit. Did we realise there were now more Muslims in Ladakh than Buddhists? And that the Kashmiris controlled 90 per cent of the local economy? Furthermore, the place was governed by bureaucrats in Srinagar, who ensured that public funds never made it across the Zoji-la, and that money intended for Ladakh found its way chiefly into the back pockets of their immediate relatives.

'Ladakh . . . ,' he said, melodramatically casting his eyes to the ceiling, '. . . is finished.'

Tenzin said that he was distressed to hear it, but that as we had only a few days before being due back to Delhi, our immediate concern was getting out to the Tibetan refugee centre at Choglamsar on the city's outskirts.

'Impossible. The buses are not running and the taxis are on strike.'

I suggested that perhaps, for a small surcharge, the strike might be suspended. Not broken, heaven forbid, merely circumvented.

No, he replied, this was quite out of the question. Any taxi venturing out would be certain to have its windscreen smashed and the driver would probably be beaten up into the bargain. To say nothing, he added darkly, of any passengers.

Flummoxed by the unprecedented failure of bribery, I decided that the only thing to do was to enlist his sympathy as widely as possible. We were writing a book about Tibetan exiles, I explained, and had a letter from the Dalai Lama's Information Office in Dharamsala to prove it.

No sooner had the magic words 'Dalai Lama' been uttered than the expression on his face changed from hardened unconcern to one of profound and earnest solicitude. Seizing the letter, he inspected it minutely, paying particular attention to the notepaper's printed crest to see if it was an obvious forgery. Satisfied it was genuine, he smiled indulgently, said that now there was clearly no problem at all, and that if I would just be kind enough to wait a moment he would go to see about a car.

'What about the rioters?'

Rioters? If I was on business sanctioned by the Dalai Lama, then no Ladakhi would raise a finger to stop me. The letter would, of course, have to be Sellotaped to the windscreen and then I (and just as important, the taxi) would be perfectly safe.

The taxi-driver, when he arrived about ten minutes later, was rather less sanguine than the hotel manager, but he too was inclined to believe that the letter would have soothing properties. Had I, he enquired nervously, got a press card as well, just in case? I replied that indeed I did, but that in my limited experience, its effect in India was akin to that of petrol on a smouldering bonfire. If anything could be guaranteed to get you into trouble it was the unforced admission that you were a journalist. He shrugged and advised me to keep it handy just in case.

Leh itself is on a slight incline, with the crumbling royal palace – a mini Potala, perched on a crag – a forlorn reminder of past glories, rising from a jumble of broken roofs, grubby streets, and open drains. Choglamsar, the centre of all things Tibetan in Ladakh, is a dusty sprawl of buildings on the floor of the valley, five or six miles away to the south-east, not far from the banks of the Indus.

We drove along roads teeming with armed soldiers, none of whom seemed at all interested in a couple of demented tourists out for a ride, and then freewheeled gently down towards the river. Unfortunately, just when everything seemed to be going well and we were less than a mile from our destination, trouble appeared, precisely as the hotel manager had foreseen. A mob of about thirty

Ladakhi youths had gathered to waylay vehicles coming into town and piled by the roadside were ominous little cairns of rocks. In the ditch lay an Ambassador car on its side, windows smashed, bodywork dented, and one wheel missing.

The driver slowed carefully to a halt and instantly the windows were filled with hostile, shouting faces. Someone thumped his fist on the roof. We got out and at the unexpected sight of a foreigner the crowd backed off two or three feet. A vigorous conversation then ensued between one of the youths and the driver in which the words 'Dalai Lama' and 'Dharamsala' cropped up with metronomic regularity. My letter was produced, flourished, and scrutinised.

Suddenly everyone was smiling. One man patted me on the shoulder, and the encircling faces melted away.

Lobsang Tenzin, the Director of the Children's Village was wearing a brown tweed jacket on top of his monk's robes and had a custard-yellow bobble hat pulled down hard over his ears. His face had a grizzled and battle-toughened appearance. How, he wanted to know, had we managed to get out to Choglamsar when all forms of transport were on strike? He seemed to think it probable that we had been given a lift by our employers: the Chinese secret service. After briefly recounting the morning's events, Tenzin presented our letter of introduction.

This provoked a tight huddle round the director's desk, while the assembled officials tried to work out what it would be best to do with us. Eventually a middle-aged man in a sage-green anorak broke from the group, having appeared to tire of its interminable deliberations, and unilaterally elected himself its spokesman. His name, he said, was Mr Tsangpo, and he was the local headmaster. Regrettably we had come at a bad time as the Dalai

Lama's Representative was out of town and would not be back for the rest of the week. He was in Changtang, not far from the Tibetan border, where a large group of nomads had been settled.

As innocently as possible, and knowing full well what answer I was likely to get, I suggested that I might be able to hire a jeep and drive out to meet him.

Mr Tsangpo gave a hollow laugh. 'The place is swarming with soldiers and as they tend to shoot anyone they don't know and find out who he was afterwards, I wouldn't advise it. You could apply for permission of course, but you won't get it; not even if you take out Indian citizenship *and* live to be a hundred. Now, why don't you go for a tour around Choglamsar with Sonam here and then come back for lunch.'

A man with a rather threatening expression stepped forward a pace. At first I couldn't think what to say, his appearance was at the same time so alarming and so unexpected. Dressed from head to foot in faded blue denim, he was wearing two-tone cowboy boots with winkle-picker toes and a belt fastened by a silver buckle the size of a hubcap. In addition to this sartorial flamboyance, he had a pugilist's physique, and a bullet-shaped head that looked distinctly more Turkish than Tibetan. In other circumstances, I decided, I might well have taken him for a disc-jockey from Ankara.

Outside, Sonam soon proved to be a man whose opinions, for a Tibetan, were as unorthodox as his clothing. We had wandered across to one of the settlements down by the Indus and were searching for the person in charge, when he remarked, entirely unprompted, that the Chinese invasion of his country had not, in some ways, been such a bad thing after all.

Tenzin looked scandalised.

'Before 1959 the monasteries and the aristocracy had all the wealth and power and they wanted things to stay that way. Even the Dalai Lama couldn't get anywhere with them. Tibet would never have become a modern country.'

I was about to ask whether he thought blue jeans one of the more significant benefits of modernity, but thought better of it.

'Surely you can't be happy to see your people living like this? It's not their fault they now have to live in such poverty. It was the Chinese invasion which reduced them to this.'

No, he agreed, Choglamsar was not ideal. It was a very poor settlement. And in general the people were not happy there.

'There are about three thousand people living down in the Leh Valley, nearly all of whom used to be nomads. They don't like being confined in one place. It doesn't feel natural to them. Unfortunately, in Tibet all their wealth was in livestock. Some of them were actually quite well off and maybe owned several hundred sheep and yaks. Then the Chinese arrived. They managed to get themselves across the border, but not their animals. So they ended up here, living in tents, virtually destitute. It wasn't until 1972 that the Indian government built these little houses.'

'So how do they earn a living?'

'Oh, some of them work on the roads; some of them take tourists trekking in the hills. But during the winter, after the Zoji-la has closed, no one in Ladakh does anything. There are no foreigners and the ground is too hard to dig. Most of the soldiers go back to the plains. It's unbelievably cold. Anyone who can afford a plane ticket gets out and goes south: to Delhi, Dharamsala, Kathmandu . . . Anywhere that's a bit warmer.'

The camp leader proving elusive, Sonam suggested a visit to the Tibetan Medical Centre, explaining that it had only been opened a couple of years before. We stepped inside a large, light, ground-floor room, the walls of which were lined with racks full of innumerable glass, screw-topped jars, the sort that I remembered fondly from my childhood as containers for toffees and humbugs and chocolate drops. On closer inspection, however, the contents of these looked distinctly less alluring. At a desk in one corner sat the doctor, a monk, talking to a pallid girl with lank blonde hair and an expression of unqualified misery. On the other side of the room a Tibetan lady in a starched blouse and striped apron was waiting patiently to dispense his prescription.

'The doctor is a Ladakhi, from Thikse monastery, but he was trained in Dharamsala.'

'So he's a practitioner of traditional Tibetan medicine?'

'Yes, of course. You can see all of the various herbs and flowers and so forth in these jars. There are certain types of plant which can only be found in Tibet, here in Ladakh, and in Spiti, the area to the north-east of the Kulu Valley. When His Holiness the Dalai Lama visits Leh he sometimes goes out collecting with the doctors from Dharamsala. Despite the army and the arrival of the modern world, the air and the water in Ladakh are both still very pure.'

'So what do people suffer from mostly?' Tenzin enquired.

'Arthritis in the winter; stomach complaints in the summer. However, there is not so much sickness here, Ladakh is very healthy for Tibetans. It's the kind of place we are used to; not at all like the hill stations to the south of the Himalayas where everyone gets TB and dysentery.'

'So do these people ever consult a doctor trained in the Western, scientific tradition or are they happier with the herbal remedies?'

'Very often they go to both kinds and see which treatment works best. Here in Ladakh people are caught in the middle: half in the modern world, half in the old one. They see planes, and tanks, and buses full of foreigners, and at the same time Ladakh is just like Tibet with the same climate, the same landscape, and of course the big monasteries. Ideally they would like to have both – a bit of the old world, a bit of the new – but I'm not sure that is possible. I think in the end you probably have to take sides.'

'And which side are you on?'

'Me, I prefer the modern world. Anyway, I think before long there won't be a choice. The old world's dying fast. It won't be around for much longer.'

We continued our trudge around the camp's dusty alleyways. I was beginning to find Choglamsar a bit dispiriting. The people standing about, mutely watching our tour of inspection, were ragged, grubby, and if not exactly cowed, then certainly downtrodden. The buildings were adequate, but they had been put up on rough ground, softened by neither a blade of grass nor a glint of water. It seemed a safe assumption the Tibetans had been given the land in the first place because it was a site that nobody else had wanted.

Sonam, perhaps sensing my change of mood, suggested that we might like to see the Dalai Lama's new house, which had been built for him a few miles further down the valley.

'We won't get into any trouble with the demonstrators if we go that way.'

Fortunately, on an early summer day the Leh Valley is a swift and infallible antidote to depression. White-washed monasteries overlook the milky-green waters of the Indus as they have for a thousand years; men and women labour in the fields with teams of *dzos* (a cross between a yak and a cow), singing and laughing in the benevolent sunshine. It seems a vision of a better world, a snippet of the Golden Age, rather than the last redoubt of a culture on the edge of an abyss.

The Dalai Lama's residence – a large detached house rather than a mansion – was set a hundred yards from the road, behind brightly painted wrought-iron gates. After hooting the car horn and shouting for a couple of minutes, an extremely resentful security guard, who showed every sign of having recently been asleep, shuffled down the path to let us in. The building itself was gleaming and new, but the gardens, hurriedly planted out for the inaugural visit, had since been left to wither and die. As well as being a pitiful sight, the parched and trampled flowerbeds seemed an uncomfortable premonition of future neglect.

'It seems a pity they couldn't have cared for these,' I observed to Sonam. 'After all, the Dalai Lama is well known for his love of gardening.' Sonam shrugged. He obviously hadn't the faintest idea what I was making such a fuss about.

'His Holiness comes here for his health; to escape the monsoon. Also, in Dharamsala he gets exhausted. He comes to Ladakh to reflect, to meditate, to recharge his batteries.'

Inside all the furniture was covered with dust-sheets and the carpets were rolled back up against the walls. I gingerly lifted up one corner of a cloth covering the Dalai Lama's throne and instantly had it snatched away from me by the guard, evidently still sulking about the interruption of his snooze. In front of a large colour photograph of the Dalai Lama lay a pile of white *khatas*, offerings of veneration and allegiance, well over two feet high.

'I daresay . . . ,' I suggested to Lobsang Tenzin, between mouthfuls of rice and cabbage, '. . . that the Dalai Lama's recent visits have done a lot for the monasteries in Ladakh. He's always keen to raise standards of scholarship and to weed out the backsliders.'

The director smiled benignly. 'His Holiness has been here six times. His mere presence brings sunshine to a dark valley.'

'But have standards improved do you think? When I was here five years ago, it was common talk that many of the monks were lazy and ignorant and that they had been corrupted by the influx of tourist money. The Hemis Festival, for example. I went to it: there were more camera crews than ordinary Ladakhis, and the monks were charging admission.'

Lobsang Tenzin pondered and chewed his cabbage thoroughly before replying.

'What you have asked is not a simple question. If we are speaking only of Hemis then I would say that its young rinpoche has recently done much to raise standards there. However, there is a wider problem. Before the Chinese invasion, the monks from Ladakh would go to study in Tibet. In particular, they went to Tashilhunpo in my home town of Shigatse; but also to Lhasa: to Sera, Drepung, and Ganden. Now, of course, they cannot. The monasteries are still standing and they have more money than before, but the number of monks is falling and standards are generally in decline. Buddhism in Ladakh is dying, there is no doubt of that. His Holiness is aware of the problem, but there is a limit to what even he can achieve. You have seen for yourself, there is fighting in the streets, the Ladakhis are being overrun, their identity suppressed, their culture destroyed. They have become a minority in their own country; Leh now belongs to the Kashmiris; there are soldiers everywhere.'

'So for entirely different reasons, "Little Tibet" is suffering much the same fate as Tibet itself?'

'As a Tibetan I certainly have much sympathy for these

people. We live in a dark age in which much that is precious has been destroyed. I myself asked the Dalai Lama's permission to become a hermit, but he said that in such a time, we all had to consider our wider responsibility and carry on with our work in the world.'

During lunch I had noticed that the headmaster, Tenzin Tsangpo, who had sat in silence for the most of the time, was becoming increasingly restive. He seemed to be seething with energy; a small reactor in immediate danger of meltdown.

The meal over, pleasantries exchanged, and the director having returned to his duties, the headmaster suggested a stroll round his school, which occupied a site immediately behind the administrative complex. After a brief period of desultory, noncommittal conversation, we stopped on a hillock overlooking the school recreation ground, where a couple of dozen Tibetan children were happily at play.

'Bah!' the headmaster suddenly exclaimed. 'Cricket!'

'I beg your pardon?'

'Cricket. Twenty-two people idling about for a whole day. What an appalling waste of human resources! Pure decadence. The British invented cricket. You know why? Because at the time they had an empire. They had nothing to do, I think. Lots of colonies doing all the work for them.'

'But surely . . .', I protested, annoyed by this sudden and unprovoked attack on one of my favourite pastimes, '. . . if cricket is played properly it can teach you concentration, patience, the importance of fair play. It's generally thought to be a very civilised game.'

'Civilised? All this body-line bowling is civilised? Throwing balls at people's heads is civilised?' (He seemed uncomfortably well informed.) 'Civilisations weren't built by mindless violence, or by people standing around doing nothing.'

'I still can't believe you seriously object to a few Tibetan children playing cricket for an hour or so.'

'I object to it chiefly because it indicates that there is a much wider problem. At lunch today you were talking about declining standards in the monasteries, about the effects of tourism, about the destruction of Ladakhi culture. But what nobody said is that the Ladakhis like it that way. You disagree? Oh they dislike all these Indian soldiers and they dislike the Kashmiris: chiefly because the Kashmiris are much better businessmen than they are. But they like all the other things: they like the transistor radios, the disco music, the cars, the Western clothes. They want everything to stay just the same as it was – Ladakh for the Ladakhis – but now they've become consumers and they're hooked. They can't see there's a contradiction there.'

'I still don't see what this has to do with Tibetan children playing cricket.'

'The fact that they're playing cricket means they're becoming Indianised. They're going soft, just like the Ladakhis. They're forgetting how to be Tibetans.'

'Are you sure?'

Mr Tsangpo looked exasperated. 'All right, forget cricket; forget the Ladakhis; forget what's happening to their society. Look around you. Look at the landscape; look at the mountains. It's a hard country; just like Tibet. This is the best place in the whole of India to educate Tibetans. Frankly, it's the *only* place. The ones that can survive here will survive when they go home. You tell me you've been to Mussoorie and that the Rector there, Mr Kophel, is unhappy about what he sees happening to his pupils. He's right. He's right to be unhappy. The Tibetans in India have all gone soft. They all say they want to go back to Tibet, if only the Chinese would leave. I tell you it's a dream; pure sentimentality. They are comfortable in exile; they won't want a hard life back there. Imagine what would happen if they did go back. Do you suppose that the five million Tibetans who have endured thirty years of hardship, who have been tortured and starved, will be pleased to see the softies from Dharamsala when they turn up and say, "Don't worry; we're back; everything's going to be all right now. Don't worry about a thing. We're going to take charge." Of course they won't. They'll say: "You've had it easy all this time, with your freedom, your videos, your fancy clothes. Now, if you want to call yourselves Tibetans, you'd better get down to some work. Hard work."'

Mr Tsangpo having relieved his feelings, we continued our walk up the hill to his office. A smallish room with books and papers piled up all over the place, it was like the rooms of academics everywhere. It might have been Delhi, or Oxford for that matter, except for the Ladakhi light that flooded in through the window, and the wild, bare Zanskar Mountains visible over the top of a classroom block.

'You see . . . ,' he began in a more moderate and conciliatory tone, '. . . with each generation we are further from our culture and we lose a little more of our Tibetan identity. Here in Ladakh, despite the problems, we at least have a chance to produce good Tibetans. The environment and the cultural background are suitable. Most important of all, this is an autonomous school: we find our own sponsors and are therefore largely independent of the Indian education authorities. As a result, the medium of instruction up to Class Five is Tibetan. We have translated the textbooks into Tibetan. Only after Class Five do we teach in English. This is because our children still have to sit examinations set by the Indian boards and Tibetan is not an approved language.

'Our people in other parts of India are inevitably

affected by their physical surroundings. Gradually, little by little, they cease to be Tibetans: they're just immigrants. In many places the medium of instruction in the schools is the regional Indian language. Tibetan is spoken less and less, written less and less. If this continues for a couple more generations, then it will be foreigners teaching us Tibetan, foreigners teaching Tibetan history, foreigners teaching us about Tibetan Buddism. Language is the soul of a nation and a Tibetan who cannot speak and write his own language is a non-Tibetan. Once the education system set up for us by the Indians served our needs very well. Mussoorie Central School used to have a very high academic standard – half the people now in the government in Dharamsala were educated there – but not any more. From now on we must have schools run for and by Tibetans.'

'But how will you pay for them?'

'We will manage. We will *have* to manage. Some Tibetans in exile have become quite prosperous. They can well afford to pay fees. For the rest, we will somehow find sponsors.'

He paused and stared across to the bare mountains, so similar to those which surround and protect the Lhasa Valley. 'In the end there is only one point to Tibetan education and that is to instil in the hearts and minds of every Tibetan child that they are refugees, that they are living only for the day when they will return to reclaim what is rightfully theirs.'

Chapter 7

NEPAL

The monsoon was over, the sky had cleared, and the Kathmandu Valley was freshly washed and in flower. It was October and the rice harvest was just beginning. As the plane took off, I could see people with wooden rakes tossing straw onto ox-carts in the stubble-fields. Winter with its damp, mist-smothered mornings was only a few weeks away, but for the moment an autumn of warmth and golden plenitude was cheerfully in full swing.

Tenzin leant across to point out his carpet factory as it slid rapidly beneath the starboard wing. Clustered around the nearby stupa at Bodhnath were the shining roofs of new Tibetan temples, built by exiled lamas with the help of their Western admirers (and, according to cynics, with the proceeds of a disreputable trade in religious artefacts). Tibetans and Tibetan Buddhism being suddenly fashionable, Kathmandu had recovered its role as the global capital of ready-to-wear spirituality.

After a leisurely circuit of the valley, gaining height, the plane headed for a gap in the green surrounding hills. Once over the saddle, a hundred and fifty miles of the

Nepal Himalaya were revealed in all their incomparable splendour. As the dazzling peaks of the Ganesh Himal drifted slowly past, even Tenzin, who has lived in the Himalayas for most of his life, forsook his newspaper, tipped his glasses onto the end of his nose, and craned foward for a better look.

We had decided to continue our travels with an undemanding long weekend in Pokhara. Due to business commitments, Tenzin could only spare a few days and as the rains had temporarily washed out the Kathmandu – Pokhara road, we had opted to take the plane. It being the height of the tourist season, this was full of mountaineers and trekkers, dressed in every conceivable shade of fluorescent pink and orange, stroking nascent beards, and chattering in a babel of languages with ill-suppressed excitement.

'Frankly . . .' said Tenzin, '. . . I'm not sure there's anyone down there these days who can tell us very much. I think most of the Mustang guerrillas have left, but I could be wrong.'

'Someone in Kathmandu told me that the only people left in the Pokhara camps were the halt and the lame. "Deadbeats" was the word he actually used.'

'Deadbeats? Who said that?' asked Tenzin sharply, much scandalised. 'A Tibetan?'

'Yes, some young chap I met down in Bodhnath. You know, one of the new sort: T-Shirt, jeans, black leather jacket, film star shades . . .' Tenzin tut-tutted and muttered something about the lack of moral fibre among contemporary Tibetan youth.

'These youngsters who wander round Kathmandu looking like something out of a recording studio weren't even born when the "deadbeats" were being shot to bits by the Chinese,' he observed with asperity, before returning to the soothingly anodyne columns of *The Rising Nepal*.

After about half an hour, the plane banked steeply round, giving us a brief view of Dhaulagiri – nearly 27,000 feet high and about the size of an English minor county tipped on its side – before descending rapidly and landing on Pokhara's grass airstrip with a thump, a rattle, and a cloud of dust.

The Pokhara Valley is a smaller version of the Kathmandu Valley – both being anomalous puddles of flat land set down among the corrugations of the Himalayan foothills – and it lies about a hundred miles to the west of the Nepalese capital, at an altitude of little more than two thousand feet. Historically, the reason for its existence was a trade route from India to Tibet; nowadays, it is the trekking capital of the world.

It had been cloudy the first time I had landed there, and the famous mountain panorama had been revealed a window at a time like a gigantic Advent calendar. On this occasion, however, the Annapurna massif was naked in a cloudless sky; a stupendous wall of rock, rising almost vertically to over 24,000 feet. The actual summit of Annapurna only becomes visible after about a week's walk, but the view from the airstrip is still sufficiently spectacular to awe most people into respectful silence.

Being unencumbered by luggage. Tenzin and I walked straight out through the terminal building, past people struggling into rucksacks, rolling up sleeping bags, counting out tent pegs, and applying thick layers of zinc cream to every exposed square inch of flesh, and strolled a hundred yards down the road, parallel to the runway, to one of the world's more unusual airport hotels.

A simple, two-storey concrete structure painted yellow and blue, the Hotel Annapurna might perhaps be described as Tibetan post-modern in style. We found its manager, Bawa Wangyal, sitting in the garden with his back firmly to the scenery, reading a weighty political tome, with a picture of the Dalai Lama on the front cover. He seemed a friendly man, getting on for fifty, with receding black hair, a check shirt, gold teeth, and the usual, enormous, Rolex-inspired, Bangkok-made, wrist-spraining virility symbol of a watch. Tenzin and he chatted away happily, while I gazed at the mountains and dreamed.

After a while, their conversation turned to a man with an Anglo-Saxon name, with whom, it seemed, many years ago, they had spent countless happy hours playing mah-jong in this very garden.

'Oh, he was an American guy,' Tenzin explained. 'He got chucked out by the Nepalese because they thought he worked for the CIA. I doubt he did actually.'

Bawa Wangyal disappeared indoors to rearrange his hotel (which was 'full'), on our behalf and to fetch some cold beers.

'This place was built with money from the CIA,' Tenzin went on in a matter-of-fact, nothing-could-be-more-normal sort of voice.

'Say again?'

'When the Americans stopped helping the guerrillas in Mustang – at the time Nixon and Kissinger first went to Peking in the 70s – they gave them a farewell present of five million Indian rupees. One of the things they did with the money was to build this hotel: to provide themselves with a regular income. Also they were still bringing weapons up from India and it was a useful staging post.'

Sitting in a peaceful garden, surrounded by cheerful, suntanned trekkers, I found it rather difficult to take this explanation seriously. It all seemed so remote and improbable – even though I was sure it was true – so I resumed my careful scrutiny of the Annapurna massif.

'What you have to remember. . .', said Tenzin, '. . . is that even twenty years ago Nepal was a very different country. It was much wilder then. There weren't all these tourists wandering about.'

The story of the Tibetans' struggle to resist the invasion and occupation of their country properly begins in the seventh century. At that time, in the reign of King Songtsen Gampo, the Tibetans were a martial people, much given to raiding and looting and annoying the undeserving Chinese. A Tibetan empire extended from the Hindu Kush to the gates of the Chinese capital, Xian. Gradually, however, the Tibetan national character underwent a remarkable and mysterious transformation, one which is generally ascribed to the growing influence of Buddhism.

In 1950, when the communist PLA was turning its attention to the 'liberation' of Tibet, having already disposed of the American-backed armies of Chiang Kai-shek, the Tibetan military establishment was small, ill-equipped, and badly trained. This was mainly due to a profound disinclination on the part of both clerical and secular authority to have anything to do with warfare (or even preparation for it), which was perceived to be inherently sinful and irreligious. Ever since the invasions of the rapacious Chinese General Chao-Erh-feng in the first decade of the twentieth century, Tibet's eastern region of Kham had been in a state of continuing confusion and upheaval. The Chinese had managed to hang on to some areas west of the historical border town of Dartsedo, and elsewhere the authority of the Lhasa government tended to wax and wane with almost lunar regularity.

The capital of Kham was the town of Chamdo: 375 miles east of Lhasa; and 280 miles west of Dartsedo. There the governor of the region appointed by Lhasa had his official residence and a detachment of central government troops to protect him from his enemies: whoever they might prove to be at any given moment.

A number of factors combined to make the governor's life uneasy, not least of which was the incipient nationalism of the Khampas, who felt little affection or affinity for their brother Tibetans in Lhasa and who strongly disliked paying central government taxes (needed, among other things, to maintain a standing army), for which they saw precious little tangible return.

Khampa nationalism was, however, moderated by their blind and unqualified devotion to the person of the Dalai Lama. This loyalty extended to the Tibetan Buddhist religion as a whole, although the Khampas tended to admire the institution *per se*, rather than showing any great enthusiasm for the values which it was in business to promote. Unlike their more docile compatriots in central Tibet, the Khampas had little time for any namby-pamby pacifist nonsense and lived robust, masculine lives in which rifles and horses featured prominently. For their part, the central Tibetans regarded all Khampas as thugs and bandits, an opinion which was not entirely ill-founded.

So great was Khampa dissatisfaction with the authorities in Lhasa, that when, in October 1950, the PLA took Chamdo and captured its governor – the cowardly Ngapo Shape, who ever since has been Tibetan quisling-in-chief – quite a number of Khampas were found to have been fighting on the Chinese side, some perhaps for money, and others in the naive and misguided belief that this was likely to further their nationalist ambitions.

Having taken Kham, the area which in different circumstances might have proved almost impregnable, the PLA then proceeded without great difficulty to Lhasa, and Tibet was an occupied country. At first an uneasy peace prevailed. The Chinese army was scrupulous about paying for food, its soldiers were well disciplined, and their officers constantly stressed, to anyone prepared to listen, that they had only come to help their brothers to turn Tibet into an Elysium of freedom and plenty. No attempt was made to interfere with Tibetan society and culture: the monasteries continued just as before, and the aristocracy in Lhasa, having been confirmed in its position of civil authority, concluded that communists were quite nice people really and not nearly so black – or red – as they had often been painted.

Meanwhile, the Chinese built roads where previously there had only been packways, and made sure that in the event of Tibet changing its mind about being liberated, the country could be massively and speedily reinforced.

By 1955, the Chinese were feeling a good deal more secure and they began to consider measures – long since introduced back home in the Great Motherland – that would transform Tibet into a fully communist society. Aware that such developments might not prove entirely popular, they decided that at first these changes would only be introduced in Kham, and that furthermore it would be prudent to disarm the local population first.

Unfortunately for the Chinese, they had reckoned without the Khampas' independence of spirit and their long-standing attachment to firearms.

First the large estates were confiscated, the landowners publicly humiliated, and a few of them shot. Then the system of taxation was revised so as to include monastic property, dissenting monks being arrested and beaten. Nomads were rounded up and made to live where the Chinese could keep an eye on them, while at the same time a programme of political indoctrination was intensified – the clergy being singled out for particular vilification – with anyone suspected of ideological backwardness being violently 'criticised': a euphemism for a variety of forms of torture, both mental and physical.

Resentment mounted and opposition soon became more

organised, particularly in response to Chinese efforts to confiscate weaponry. Now, the Khampas realised, was their last chance: soon they would be helpless. The Chinese reacted to this defiance with predictable savagery – summary execution, including decapitation, was commonplace – and Kham slipped into bloody turmoil.

Meanwhile in Lhasa the government was still trying to find a *modus vivendi* with the Chinese military authorities, vainly advocating reason, tolerance, compromise, and the peaceful resolution of all their differences, much to the disgust of the Khampa leaders who saw little need for saintly forbearance while their way of life was being dismantled, their homes destroyed, and their families slaughtered.

In response to the government's failure to appreciate the dire reality of their position, a group of prominent individuals from both Kham and the north-eastern province of Amdo – pre-eminently a Khampa businessman called Gompo Tashi – met in March 1956 to form a resistance movement, the Chushi Gangdruk, dedicated to opposing the Chinese by all available means.

For the following eighteen years, the guerrillas struggled against suicidal odds, during which time they received remarkably little support – either moral or practical – from Tibetan higher officialdom, which often seemed to regard their activities as something of an embarrassment. As a result, Tibetan armed resistance to the invader was principally Khampa resistance, a fact which reverberates to this day.

As the spring of 1956 turned to summer, the Chinese pressed on with their 'reforms' in Kham, particularly the hasty establishment of agricultural cooperatives. Their efforts were, nonetheless, considerably impeded by the guerrillas who blew up bridges and cut the fragile road links to China with increasing regularity. In response, the Chinese brought in 40,000 reinforcements and began to employ heavy artillery and air power. The town of Lithang was bombed and its monastery destroyed with unspeakable carnage. Atrocious reprisals followed each guerrilla success and for the next three or four years the region was almost wholly devoted to sadism and killing.

In consequence, distraught and despairing civilians began to make their ragged way to Lhasa, where they hoped the presence of the Dalai Lama might afford them sanctuary. Many were later to die in the crowds outside his summer palace, the Norbulingka, when stalemate turned to suppression at the outset of the Lhasa Revolt. The Khampa guerrillas meanwhile fought on, but eventually, underequipped and hopelessly outnumbered, they too were driven progressively westward towards the Tibetan capital.

Though grim, the military situation was not entirely hopeless – not in a country ideal for guerrilla warfare – and for a while the Chushi Gangdruk managed to regroup in the wild Lhoka region immediately to the south of Lhasa. There they began to receive a trickle of covert support from the CIA; weapons and supplies being flown across the Himalayas and dropped by parachute; at first entirely undetected by the Chinese. Having been thwarted in their efforts to keep the nationalists in power in China, the Americans were now able to enjoy a little short-lived revenge. Tibet was only a minor sideshow, however, not least because of the weakness of the Lhasa administration, and its inability to make clear decisions about whether to fight (officially), and if so, where and when and how. Still, American weapons and ammunition enabled the guerrillas to hold Lhoka for a year or so, long enough for the Dalai Lama to make his escape to India through territory still out of bounds to the PLA.

With the Dalai Lama gone the will to fight soon began to ebb away. Gompo Tashi was now critically wounded and although other leaders had emerged, some trained in Guam and Colorado, the battle was drawing to its inevitable conclusion. The Chinese began to intercept the parachute drops and, scrap by scrap, they took and held territory through sheer weight of numbers. With no choice but to retreat, the Khampas headed south, many of them eventually reaching Mustang, a tiny, isolated, vassal state, nominally attached to Nepal, but in more settled times completely ignored by the authorities in Kathmandu. There they set up camp, and there, with considerable difficulty, the CIA continued, intermittently, to equip them.

Mustang had the advantage of being close to home – though a treacherous pass separated it from the Tibetan plateau – but it was extremely remote, and supplies had to be trekked in from Pokhara, up the long Kali Gandaki Valley (the deepest gorge in the world, between the Dhaulagiri and Annapurna massifs). For over a decade, resistance to the Chinese, mostly of a token variety, was carried on with increasing difficulty and decreasing effect, until the *rapprochement* between the United States and the People's Republic finally put an end to hostilities.

The Nepalese, forever fearful of Indian domination, took the opportunity to improve relations with their other giant neighbour, China, the price of this conviviality being, unsurprisingly, the expulsion of the Khampas from Mustang. Despite tape-recorded orders, sent to the guerrilla leaders by the Dalai Lama (by now established in Dharamsala), telling them on no account to resist the Nepalese, with whom the Tibetans had no quarrel whatever, a few of the Khampas refused to surrender and were hunted down and killed. Their flight was, to an extent, justified by subsequent events, as the Nepalese, anxious to impress their new-found friends in Peking, behaved with considerable ruthlessness, and a number of Tibetan commanders, who had laid down their arms peacefully as instructed, spent several subsequent years rotting in Kathmandu gaol. Most of the Khampas, however, trudged down the Kali Gandaki to a tedious life in Pokhara's resettlement camps, the forlorn remnants of a defeated army.

Having watched the plane take off and head back to Kathmandu, Tenzin and I thanked Bawa Wangyal for his hospitality, and hitched a lift into town.

Mr Norbu Dorje, the Welfare Officer at Penjor Ling, the Tibetan camp closest to the centre of Pokhara, greeted our arrival with undisguised dismay. A middle-aged man with round, almost Caucasian features, he sat dolefully at a bare, metal desk, clutching in both hands an enormous blue-and-white enamelled mug, which he squeezed periodically in order to relieve a little of his anxiety and frustration. Even behind dark glasses I could see his eyes flicking nervously around the room, alighting briefly on Tenzin or me before darting away in embarrassment.

At the first opportunity, he quickly explained that there were no longer any ex-guerrillas at Penjor Ling, and that furthermore, even if there had been, they definitely wouldn't have wanted to talk to us. He then let his gaze settle reproachfully on Tenzin. How could he, a fellow Tibetan, have been so insensitive as to be the author of this calamity? Foreigners were one thing, but foreign journalists quite another.

'You must understand that the whole Tibetan question – and especially what happened in *Mustang*' (heavy emphasis, long pause) – 'remains a sensitive subject in Nepal.'

I felt very sorry for him. His insecurity was palpable. He clearly lived in constant fear that some trifling misdemeanour would release a deluge of pent-up official animosity and spite. We were no longer in India – which despite its routine calamities and slaughters still has a strong vein of humanity running through its public life – and here, in Pokhara, the Tibetans found themselves barely tolerated, an unwelcome and potentially embarrassing presence, to be kept at all times under careful observation and control.

To thaw out the conversation, I decided to elicit some harmless biographical information. Where, I wondered, had he come from in Tibet? Scenting a trap, Norbu Dorje at first said nothing and then, as the pressure of the silence mounted, and no obliging chasm appeared to swallow him up, he conceded, with extreme reluctance, that he had come from Kham. Some mental Rubicon had evidently been bridged, however, as after a short pause he went on:

'My family were farmers. We were dispossessed by the Chinese.'

Tenzin smiled encouragingly and innocently enquired whether, as he was a Khampa, he himself had been in the Chushi Gangdruk.

Norbu Dorje stared miserably at the summit of Annapurna 2, framed neatly in his office window. 'I was based at Gyantse, under the command of Gompo Tashi. Also I took part in the Lhasa Revolt. I was outside the Norbulingka when it was shelled.' He paused for a moment and then continued with great bitterness. 'Afterwards the Chinese said that nothing had happened, that reports of a massacre were untrue. Well, I myself was hit by a machine-gun bullet – here in the shoulder – and in the morning there were so many bodies on the ground there was nowhere to put your feet. You know what the Chinese did when they discovered I had been involved with the resistance and that I had escaped? They arrested my mother. They threw her in gaol and beat her up. Eventually she went mad with grief and fear, but they didn't let her out. She died in prison. So many people suffered so much in Tibet, you can't just sit here now and talk calmly of such things.'

'Never mind,' said Tenzin philosophically, as we wandered back to the hotel. 'These people have had a wretched time. It's no wonder they're a bit cagey. In the beginning the camps here were absolute hell-holes: just a lot of tents, mostly by the side of the runway. In the monsoon, Pokhara is the wettest place in Nepal. Up in the mountains you get a sudden thunderstorm; down here you have a flash flood. It was hot and humid: just about the worst possible climate for Tibetans. After three, four, five years, people became acclimatised, but many were dead by then. Half of the ones the Chinese had left alive, got finished off by the bugs in Pokhara. The Swiss Red Cross saved a lot of people, but there've always been problems about foreign aid for Tibetans in Nepal. The Nepalese government doesn't see why the Tibetans should get what they call "special treatment".'

We turned in at the gate of the Annapurna Hotel and flopped down in a couple of deck chairs that had been abandoned in the middle of the lawn.

'And then, of course, he's right about the political problems. The Nepalese are always quarrelling with the Indians, so they need to stay friends with the Chinese, which makes having Tibetans all over the place very inconvenient for them. Here in Pokhara, there are Chinese engineers building a road up into the mountains which goes right past one of the Tibetan camps. And then there's the road from Kathmandu up to Kodari on the Tibetan border: the Friendship Highway. The Chinese built that to encourage trans-Himalayan trade, or at least, so they say. But on Indian army maps it looks a bit different. To the generals in Delhi it seems like a nice broad road for tanks to drive down. Maybe it does to the generals in Peking as well, I don't know.'

In the afternoon we hired a taxi to take us out to Chambaling, a Tibetan settlement about an hour's drive away on the Kathmandu road. We arrived at a very inopportune moment as a local Hindu festival of some kind (no one seemed able to give me precise information about it) was reaching a climax and between five and ten thousand people were jammed together on the narrow path which led down into the gorge of the Seti Khola River.

'That's where the Tibetans live: down there,' the taxi-driver explained helpfully, pointing at the heart of the pullulating throng a couple of hundred feet below. Tenzin and I picked our way to the edge of the gorge through drifts of litter and a small minefield of excrement and peered over. Five seconds were sufficient for us to conclude that the situation was quite hopeless.

We had just informed the taxi-driver – to his great joy and satisfaction – that there was nothing to be done but to return to Pokhara, when we were accosted by a Tibetan in a grubby denim jacket, who said his name was Jamyang Nima and that he was the official in charge. Perhaps, he said, peering out from underneath a tousled mop of greying hair, we'd care for some tea in his house which was little more than a hundred yards up the road?

Evading the outstretched arms of the driver who in despair tried to shoo us back into his taxi rather like a shepherd at a sheepdog trials, we followed our host into his darkened living room, where he flopped down onto a filthy strip of old blue carpet, crossed his legs and beamed up at us.

'What a place, eh?' he remarked cheerfully and with no apparent resentment. 'Just about the worst spot in the whole of Nepal, I'd say.' It occurred to me that I'd seldom seen a man further removed from melancholy, let alone despair.

'Where exactly is this camp?' Tenzin enquired in a bemused voice. 'I can't see it anywhere.'

'I'm not surprised,' replied Jamyang Nima. 'It's down in the gorge, on an island in the river.' He jerked a thumb dismissively in the direction of the sunlit doorway. 'We were given the land in 1974. Of course, no one else wanted it. The whole place is a bit like a practical joke really. In summer it's hot as hell down there. Then when the monsoon comes we get flooded out. The rest of the year we sit, surrounded by millions of gallons of water, trying to work out ways of irrigating our rice crop. The island is far enough above the water level for us to need an electric pump you see, but we can't afford to buy one and even if we could, we couldn't afford the fuel to keep it running. People from the Dalai Lama's office came down here and conducted a survey. They said to irrigate this site effectively would cost over two million Nepalese rupees [£50,000].' He rocked back against the wall, rendered temporarily speechless with mirth. 'Imagine! If we had that kind of money, we could all retire and go and live in Kathmandu.'

'So what do you do?'

'Well, at the moment we're trying to raise the money for some plastic tubing. If we can pipe water from far enough upstream, then obviously we don't need a pump. The Seti Khola falls very rapidly and flows very fast. Actually, one big problem I'm told will be to slow our water down. If it comes shooting out of the pipe at thirty miles an hour then we'll all get washed away.' Jamyang Nima was once more convulsed with laughter. His stoicism in the circumstances seemed extraordinary. I asked him how he managed it.

'Well, actually, we're quite a lot better off than we used

to be. We manage to grow some vegetables all right, so we don't starve. Most of the people who live here were up in Mustang, and in those days sometimes we had no food at all. On one occasion I had to cut my boots into strips and boil them until they were soft enough to eat. At first, you see, in the early 60s, it was just fifteen hundred fighters up there. Nothing was properly organised. Eventually we got sorted out and the place became more like a settlement than a guerrilla base. There were even Nepalese officials. We were all very friendly then.'

'So what was it like when the Nepalese turned you out? Were you glad to come down?'

Jamyang Nima looked suddenly morose. 'No we were not. Mustang might have been uncomfortable, but at least we had hope. Tibet was just a day's journey away by horse. There you could believe that before too long we would all be going home. And then it was so humiliating to be disarmed. I won't ever forget the eight days it took us to walk to Pokhara down the Kali Gandaki. To this. Fifteen years rotting in these camps.'

For a moment I thought his good mood, which had seemed so invulnerable before, had been abruptly dispelled by these melancholy reflections, but after only a few seconds his face once again broke into a cheerful smile.

'I'm sorry you can't see our camp at the moment. With all these people on the path, it would take hours to get down into the gorge. And then you probably wouldn't get up again. You'll just have to come to see us again when the festival's over.'

Back in Pokhara, that evening, I found myself in conversation (on the lawn of the Hotel Annapurna, which was rapidly becoming a kind of outdoor salon), with Samdup Lhatse, a young history teacher at a local Tibetan school.

I said how surprised I had been by the atmosphere of the Pokhara camps: how different they were from those I had so far visited in India.

'That's because our position here is much more precarious. In India the Tibetans have been given land; they have been made welcome. In Nepal we all feel insecure. I see the results of this every day in my classroom. In India, Tibetan children gain high marks, go to university, study academic disciplines, join the professions . . . Here in Nepal the Tibetans have no respect for education. They see it only as a way to earn more money; not at all valuable in itself. In the main, they regard teachers like me as idle chatterboxes, out of touch with the real world. They feel frightened and the only way they can have peace of mind is to buy it. They want cash. They see the easy money – much of it dishonest – to be made in Kathmandu, and they say to themselves, "That's the way to feel safe in this country".

'I teach teenagers Tibetan history. I tell them everything that has happened since the Chinese invasion. And then I ask them what they'd like to do with their lives. In India, the bright ones would say that they hoped to serve the government and His Holiness the Dalai Lama; that they didn't care about the small salary; that there would be plenty of time to make money when the struggle was over and they were back in Tibet. Naive maybe, but admirable don't you think? Here in Pokhara they all say they want to do a degree in business administration, to study accountancy, eventually to work for themselves, perhaps to be successful entrepreneurs like Mr Tenzin here.'

'Eh?' said Tenzin, not looking too happy about the direction the discussion was taking. He evidently thought I was about to urge him to abandon wife and family and to take up a Dharamsala desk job on a pauper's wage.

Above us the vast shadowy peaks of the Annapurna massif were painted on a violet evening sky, which turned first mauve then purple with the steady approach of night. Slowly, moonlight strengthened on their distant snowfields. Suddenly inconsequential, the conversation ebbed away into silence.

From the flat roof of my rented house in Kathmandu I was able to watch the daily progress of the rice harvest. Most of the work had been done by now, and small groups of people sat around in the golden fields, enjoying a brief holiday, chatting, picnicking, and playing with their children in the seemingly eternal sunshine. From my vantage point I could also see, away in the distance, the end of the airport runway, where, twice a week, an elderly 707 belonging to the Chinese airline CAAC, identifiable by a distinctive red flash on its tail, waited to take off on its fifty-minute flight to Lhasa. It was a service that enjoyed some local notoriety, thanks to the quantities of Tibet's artistic heritage said to travel (one-way) in its cargo holds. The jet revved its engines to a demented shriek and vanished. After two or three minutes it reappeared, a silver gnat on the far side of the valley, beginning its tortuous spiral to an altitude higher than the peaks of the Everest region that lay uncompromisingly across its flight path. Tibet suddenly seemed very close.

The telephone rang. 'I've found out where Athar's living,' Tenzin announced with obvious pride in his intelligence network. 'He's in Thamel. We'll go and see him this afternoon.'

Fifty years ago, Kathmandu must have been an extraordinary place. Forbidden to foreigners, there was no airstrip, there were no motor roads to speak of, and only a mountain path connected the valley with the distant

Indian plains. The architecture of the city remained mostly of the traditional kind – constructed in wood and red brick – despite the eccentric passion of the ruling Rana family for immense neo-classical mansions smothered in stucco.

Today, however, Kathmandu is a city out of control, a catalogue of Third World woes, spreading, seemingly unplanned, across the most fertile and productive land in Nepal, its population swelled by Indian immigrants and an influx of the rural poor, its air poisoned by traffic fumes, its infrastructure bankrupt and collapsing.

After lunch I walked with Tenzin through the narrow, rutted streets of Thamel, the district which has become the centre of Nepal's economic salvation and cultural nemesis; its tourist industry. Every third shop sells sleeping bags and rucksacks; every third person is a young Westerner of university age. There are signs for cheap rooms and pizza; chocolate cake and yeti treks; while every fifty yards someone sidles up with little plastic bags of one or another narcotic. It was with some relief therefore that we turned abruptly into an obscure, narrow passage, coming out in a quiet paved area where an elderly Tibetan woman was stringing washing from a telegraph post to the balcony railing of her apartment.

Athar? Certainly she knew where he lived. Up on the third floor.

Athar's room was simply furnished, light, airy, neat, and respectable. Although modest, it felt very comfortable and secure. He himself was a burly man in his mid-fifties, not much more than five feet ten inches in height, but broad, with the build of a middle-weight boxer. He looked to be in good shape, had a full head of black hair, and could still have been a soldier on active duty. He seemed an affable man, pleased to see us, and not at all reluctant to talk about his clandestine past.

I said that I'd heard he was the present leader of the

Chushi Gangdruk, to which he replied with considerable humility that there were actually three people in charge, of whom, certainly, he was one. Furthermore, he insisted, I must understand at the outset that the Chushi Gangdruk nowadays was a political organisation – representing the people of Kham – and one which presently had no military role or capability whatever. Ever since 1974, when the Americans had withdrawn their support, it had, of necessity, concerned itself solely with politics.

'Does that mean you never consider military options nowadays? Never even toy with the idea?' It seemed impossible that having fought for so long, the desire for action could ever be completely repressed.

'Well, looking at recent events in Tibet, the demonstrations and so on in Lhasa, I wouldn't say that the military avenue was *completely* closed. Of course there are many problems. Clearly, the Indians would not permit us to conduct operations from their territory. And at the moment we have no backers, no arms, and no money.'

'That certainly doesn't sound very promising.'

'Maybe, but then we haven't tried to find any. And on the positive side there are around two hundred Tibetans like me, thoroughly experienced in guerrilla warfare. In addition, you may have heard of the Indian army's 22nd Battalion, based in Dehra Dun, which since 1962 has trained over twenty thousand Tibetan professional soldiers. From the very beginning, the Chushi Gangdruk was involved with recruitment for this unit. So I think there *could* be some military possibilities should suitable circumstances ever arise. But for now His Holiness wishes to try political initiatives, so we mustn't jeopardise anything.'

Athar looked across at Tenzin and grinned as though he, another Khampa, could be expected to know pretty much what he, Athar, thought of political initiatives, and the probability of their success as long as the Chinese had anything to do with them.

'Besides . . .', he continued in a doubtful, distinctly half-hearted sort of way, '. . .the Dalai Lama's stress on non-violence must also be taken into consideration.'

'But not necessarily heeded?'

Feigning incomprehension with the skill of a practised diplomat, Athar went on: 'In Kham in the 1950s, I myself saw monasteries being bombed, and during those raids thousands of people were killed: men women, children monks . . . And yet the outside world never heard of these things. There was no publicity at all and the Chinese simply denied that they had ever happened. Much of Tibet is still closed to foreigners, so if we started a guerrilla war, exactly the same would happen all over again. It would be simple stupidity to risk this kind of slaughter. But I repeat, a time may come when things will be different. We still have our contacts in Tibet. We know what goes on there and what people are thinking.'

'Which part of Kham do you yourself come from?'

'From Lithang. Not all that far from China actually. I was born on a farm and from our land it was only five days to ride to the border.'

'So did you see many Chinese people when you were growing up?'

'Quite a few, especially at the time of the Long March. Then, later on, Chiang Kai-shek's lot were around for a bit. So when the communist army arrived in 1950, no one was particularly surprised. The soldiers camped outside of town and at first were very friendly and bothered no one. I remember my father saying they were a nice change, not at all like the Long Marchers, who stole everything and made themselves a terrible nuisance. But of course the Khampa business people were trading with China and they used to tell us what was happening there and the kind of treatment that was being handed out to the ex-Kuomintang. So we had a vague idea of what might happen to us.'

'Do you remember how the fighting began?'

'Well, I certainly remember the Chinese ordering us to give up our weapons. They must have known that we would never do so peacefully. Not the Khampas. In Kham virtually every household had a rifle and even the poorest of the poor had swords. It was a tough place.'

'And so were you immediately involved?'

'No. I had two elder brothers. They were in the resistance from the beginning. One was killed. The other was put in gaol for twenty-two years. He's still in Tibet. But I was told to escort my mother and younger brother to Lhasa. This meant that I was there when Gompo Tashi – who was from Lithang himself – decided to form the Chushi Gangdruk. Up until then the fighting had been very disorganised. We were badly in need of a strong leader and a command structure.

'A meeting was called at Gompo Tashi's house and representatives of the leading Khampa families attended. They were all very annoyed with the Lhasa people, especially the politicians, who seemed quite willing to accept defeat. "Maybe these fancy Lhasa people are cleverer than us Khampas . . .', they said, ". . .or maybe they're just cowards".

'Gompo Tashi admitted that it might be hopeless to try to fight the Chinese, but said that he, for one, wasn't going to give in, and that if he had to die he was going to take a few of them with him. The other Khampas agreed. Khampas are very good businessmen – they're all born capitalists, enjoy nothing more than making money, and don't like having their livelihood interfered with – but they said that from that day forward all business would be suspended. Getting rid of the Chinese was the only thing that mattered now. "Fine . . .", Gompo Tashi said, ". . . but we'll never get anywhere without outside help.

The best people to try first are the Taiwanese, so someone will have to go to India to contact them.'

'I was twenty-five years old and wanted to play a part, so I volunteered to go. Gompo Tashi agreed. There was a well-known Taiwanese agent in Kalimpong, near Darjeeling, and I went down there with a small group of people, mostly about my own age. We went to see this man and told him that we wanted to fight and needed his help. He seemed delighted, took photographs of us, wrote down details, and then went away. Nothing happened. Months passed, but he didn't come back.

'Then one day Gyalo Thondup – one of the Dalai Lama's brothers – came to see us, and said that the Taiwanese weren't in a position to help – they had too many problems of their own – but that he had contacted the Americans, and things were looking a bit more hopeful. He selected six of us and said that he was going to arrange for us to be trained as guerrilla leaders.

'One morning he turned up in a jeep and drove us down to Siliguri on the plains. Eventually we came to a big tea garden, where he left us with another guide whom none of us knew. We started to walk – for about six hours in all – until we came to a river, on the other side of which we were met by a man who had worked for Takster Rinpoche, another of the Dalai Lama's four brothers, and an American. They said we were in East Pakistan.

'First of all we went in a bus, then on a train, and finally we came to an airport, which I assume was Dhaka. There we were put on a military plane. The first stop was Thailand; then Taiwan. I remember looking out of the window of the plane at the Chinese characters on the airport building. Finally we came to Okinawa where we were met by Takster Rinpoche himself.'

'I didn't realise that two of the Dalai Lama's brothers had been so heavily involved. Do you think they had the authority of the Lhasa government?'

'No, I think they were just acting on their own initiative. You see Gyalo Thondup had spent a lot of time in China, so he understood the communist mentality: their aims, and the methods that they would be likely to employ. He knew that what they wanted was totally incompatible with the Tibetan way of life. Whether or not they discussed these things with their brother I don't know, but I doubt it. Given the Dalai Lama's religious responsibilities, it might not have been appropriate.'

'It must have been very strange suddenly to find yourself on an American base in Japan after a childhood on a farm in Lithang.'

'Well, we were certainly very innocent. For example, I remember being extremely disappointed at first. We had expected the Americans to train us to use fabulously sophisticated weaponry. Instead they told us that we would be flying on to Guam where we would spend seven months learning map reading and how to transmit coded messages by wireless. I had no idea that radios were so complicated. Of course none of us had any knowledge of electronics. Actually after a while I really enjoyed it, but Wangdu. . .'

'The same Wangdu who refused to surrender Mustang to the Nepalese and got killed for his trouble?'

'Yes. Wangdu could never get the hang of it. He much preferred the weapons training. He was like that.'

'So what else did they teach you?'

'We were told how to set up underground organisations which would be difficult for the Chinese to break, and then were flown back to Okinawa – the Seventh Fleet navy base – for parachute training. Sometimes they took us very high: as high as you can go without oxygen. On other occasions they made us do low-level jumps in a high wind. It was quite tough.

'After about a year, we had another meeting with Takster Rinpoche and the Americans about where we should be dropped into Tibet. Of course we all wanted to go back to Kham, but the Americans said that three of us, including me, should be parachuted into Lhoka, south of Lhasa. They wanted a reliable means of communication with the Tibetan government.'

'So where did you fly from?'

'From East Pakistan. Not Dhaka this time though. From somewhere further north. There was just an airstrip; no buildings at all. But when I was back there a year later, the Americans had built a big military complex. They were obviously giving themselves the option of mounting a full-scale operation in Tibet.'

I did my best to imagine being flown over the Himalayas, presumably in some rickety old DC3, and then dropped from a great height, heavily armed, into an occupied country.'

'You must have been very frightened.'

Athar shrugged phlegmatically. 'It was quite frustrating because the first time we took off it was too cloudy to jump over the drop area. Anyway, to get something out of the trip, the pilot flew right round to the north of Lhasa – towards Nagchuka – to see if we could find out anything useful.'

'What nationality was the pilot?'

'He was an American. They were all Americans. We were attached to the parachute hooks on the roof of the plane by a huge, fat American man. Years later I met him again in Washington.'

'So when was this flight?'

'Autumn 1957. After the monsoon. The fifteenth of the eighth Tibetan month. We tried again on the twentieth and this time we succeeded. We must have jumped from high up, as I remember taking a very long time to fall. Fortunately we all landed safely. Straight away we buried our equipment – guns, ammunition, explosives, radios, and so on – wrapped up in the parachutes, and then climbed the nearest hill. All the next day we sat on top with binoculars, looking out for the Chinese, but there was no one around. The fighting in the east was very intense at that time and probably they were concentrating their forces there. Unfortunately the other team who had trained with us was not being much help in Kham. Tashi, the wireless operator, passed out in the plane from lack of oxygen and could not be dropped. So during the critical phase of the battle there was no contact with the Americans, and the Khampas didn't get any military equipment or supplies. About a year later I met the Americans in India and they were very annoyed about it.

'Anyway, the next day we came down from the hilltop and went into the nearest village, where we bought a horse and food supplies. We told the villagers we were going on a pilgrimage, and for the next month that is exactly what we did. The Americans had told us to do nothing for a month, just in case the Chinese had heard the noise of the airplane.'

'So at this time in Lhoka it was easy enough to travel around? The Chinese hadn't imposed any restrictions?'

'There was no problem. At this stage I don't think the Chinese had any idea the Tibetans were receiving direct assistance from an outside power. And although they probably expected the Khampas to try to reorganise the resistance around Lhasa at some point, they were not worried about the local U-Tsang people. So after a month, we decided it was time to get to work. This time we dressed up as monks: partly as a disguise and partly because it's very easy to hide weapons under a monk's robes.'

Athar paused and grinned even more broadly at Tenzin. He appeared to be teetering on the verge of a wink. Suppressing the urge with obvious difficulty he set his face in an expression of great solemnity.

'We each had a Sten gun, a 9mm pistol and a belt of hand grenades. We soon reached the outskirts of Lhasa, where we sent a message to Gompo Tashi, who came out to see us. We told him that the Americans wanted a direct link to the administration and if possible to the Dalai Lama himself. They couldn't understand why the Khampas seemed to be fighting an independent war, apparently without the help of the Tibetan government. The Americans had asked us specifically to find out if the government wanted to fight and if so, whether they wanted any help. Gompo Tashi was not very optimistic. He said all the government officials were scared silly and that it was impossible to get them to make a decision about anything. He said that the only one who was worth talking to was the Dalai Lama's Private Secretary.

'A few days later Gompo Tashi arranged for us to see him: at the Norbulingka. He seemed very pleased to see us, interested in what we had to say, and apologised for not being able to give us a definite answer. Part of the problem, he explained, was that each time they held a meeting of the Kashag, the Chinese seemed to know everything that had been discussed. They had tried to find the leak, but with no success. This was one reason why the Tibetan ministers were all so frightened.

'In reply, we told him that it would be impossible for us to stay in Lhasa, but that we would be in the mountains nearby and in constant contact with the Americans. Our job from now on, we said, was to radio back information about Chinese troop movements and to find out if they had any fighter jets in central Tibet.

'So that was how we left it, and for the next year we lived in the hills, spying on the Chinese. All the time, the Americans kept calling us to ask whether the government had made up its mind what it wanted to do. Of course we could tell them nothing. It was very frustrating. And all this time the Khampas were fighting and dying with no support at all, when the Americans were only too happy to help them.'

The flow of Athar's narrative was broken briefly by an exasperated sign from Tenzin, who abandoned his duties as a translator and shook his head slowly in sorrow and disbelief.

'Eventually the Khampas began to lose the war in the east. Without ammunition and supplies, without even the help of their own government, it was inevitable. And as a result the Chinese began to turn their attention to central Tibet. Things began to get much more difficult for us in and around Lhasa. Finally Gompo Tashi realised that if we stayed any longer we were bound to be caught, so he decided to reorganise the resistance in Lhoka. He told me that he had completely given up on the government and that from now on we were going to act independently. He asked me to send a message to the Americans to explain the position: to say that he was no longer in contact with the Lhasa authorities, but that he still had more than two thousand men and he was going to fight his own war. He wanted to know if they would be prepared to supply him.

'The Americans immediately came back and said they were happy to help, but that first they wanted to see his military plans. They said that someone should make contact with Gyalo Thondup, the Dalai Lama's brother in Kalimpong, and that he would arrange a meeting with an American representative. Gompo Tashi then asked me to go to India.

'I immediately went down to Kalimpong to meet Gyalo Thondup. He told me to go to a particular hotel in Calcutta, where I would be contacted by the CIA. Sure enough, there was an American staying there.'

'What did he look like? What was he called?'

'He was a middle-aged man; in his forties; medium build; black hair. He never told me a name. Even if he had, I don't suppose it would have been his real one. Anyway, I handed over Gompo Tashi's plan, but he said, "Forget about the plan for a bit. I want to hear about your year in Tibet." He didn't know much Tibetan and my English was not very good, but he spoke perfect Chinese and Gyalo Thondup had arranged for a Chinese-speaking Tibetan to go with me. I told him absolutely everything that had happened to me and he went into incredible detail, even though he seemed extremely well informed already. We didn't leave the hotel for a week and during that time we talked all day and half the night.

'Eventually he came to Gompo Tashi's proposals. He studied these and said that although they were promising, he thought they were a bit overambitious, given the nature of the terrain and the fact that we had no vehicles. We discussed a modified version and managed to reach agreement. I then said that we needed help in two ways. First we needed military equipment, but second, and just as important, the Chushi Gandruk should have an inner core of men, around five hundred, thoroughly trained in guerrilla warfare. He replied that he didn't think this would be a problem, but that he would have to talk to headquarters first. He told me to stay in the hotel until he came back. Five days later he returned and said, "Okay, you've got the lot. Now we can work together." In addition he said that Tibetan fighters would now be trained in America itself, in Colorado, and that he would take the first group back with him. Gompo Tashi had already chosen fifteen people and they were in Kalimpong waiting for orders.'

The idea of the PLA's legions quailing at the onslaught of fifteen lightly armed Tibetans seemed rather improbable and I tentatively suggested as much to Athar. He responded quite brusquely.

'Altogether the Americans trained about two hundred Khampas. Anyway in a guerrilla war, numbers are not so important. We gave the Chinese plenty of problems, I can promise you that.'

'So did you go straight back to Tibet?'

'Yes. I went back to Lhoka to explain what we had agreed. Almost immediately, the Americans dropped two big loads of arms and ammunition for us. Then, just as we were planning our next move, we received a message that the Dalai Lama was planning to leave Lhasa. We were asked to bring up sufficient forces to ensure his safety. I then got in touch with the Americans to tell them where we were and what was going on. They wanted to know whether or not the Dalai Lama was planning to stay in Tibet, if so where, and what kind of help we might need. His Private Secretary asked me to tell them that His Holiness intended to go to southern Tibet, to stay there for a couple of months, and then to reassess the situation. He himself was very pessimistic and on one occasion he asked me whether I thought, if the worst came to the worst, the Americans would be prepared to come in with a rescue team to get the Dalai Lama out. I said that they might, but that they hated our indecision, and not being told what was going on, and that unless we had a definite plan and were willing to stick to it, they wouldn't be prepared to move.'

'So where do you think you were speaking to at this point? To the American base in East Pakistan?

'No, no. The Americans were in Okinawa. To synchronise our transmissions, we used the time signal of Japanese radio.

'Up to this point things had gone fairly smoothly. Then one evening a messenger came from Lhasa to say that the Norbulingka had been shelled and that the monasteries had all been smashed. Actually his report was a bit exaggerated, but we weren't to know that at the time.

This altered everything and it was immediately decided that the Dalai Lama should leave Tibet. His Private Secretary told me to get on the radio to the Americans, to ask them to talk to the Indian government on our behalf. It wasn't until we actually reached the Indian border that the Americans came through, in the middle of the night, to say they'd straightened everything out and that the Indians were going to let us in.'

'So how often were you in contact with the Americans during this period?'

'From the moment it was decided that the Dalai Lama should go into exile, at least two or three times a day. During his escape the CIA knew – within a few miles – exactly where he was the whole time.'

'I've listened to this story a hundred times, but I've never heard that bit before,' said Tenzin, looking faintly incredulous. 'You make it sound as though the Americans were pretty much in charge of the whole thing.'

'In a way, yes. But of course they never had to do anything.'

'So you don't think there was ever any danger of the Dalai Lama being captured by the Chinese?'

'No, none whatever. At that time, Lhoka and the route south to the border were completely under Tibetan control. Gompo Tashi had more than two thousand men – who were now extremely well armed because of the American airdrops – and we had now been joined by three hundred regular soldiers of the Tibetan army. The nearest Chinese garrison had one thousand troops, but we kept them surrounded for a whole month and let no one either in or out.'

'How about attack from the air?'

'Impossible. The Chinese had no fighters in Tibet; only transport and passenger aircraft.'

'Paratroops?'

'No, they wouldn't have risked it. Maybe they could

have dropped two or three hundred men, but that would have been pointless against the strength of the Khampas. They would have been cut to pieces.'

'So what happened when you finally reached the border?'

'Nothing very much. We sent two men across and they came back to say that the Indians were expecting us. Then the Dalai Lama made a farewell speech in which he said he was sorry that the Khampas had not been given more support and that he was grateful for all they had done. He left behind a letter giving Gompo Tashi command of all Tibetan forces.'

'What did you feel when you saw him walk away into a foreign country?'

'Oh, at the time we were all very sad, but it was not until later that we started to understand the psychological effect of his departure. People just lost the will to fight: even the Khampas. There suddenly seemed no point anymore. Kham was lost; our homes were gone; His Holiness was in exile; why bother to get killed? I think people have never paid sufficient attention to this factor in our defeat. They always emphasise the vast numbers of Chinese troops; their endless ammunition and equipment, and say that it was a hopeless war that the Tibetans were bound to lose. The fact is, without the Dalai Lama, the Tibetan forces quickly became demoralised.'

'But could it really have been any different? Did the Khampas ever stand the slightest chance of defeating the Chinese? Or at least of making them pay such a price for their occupation that the course of events might have been altered?'

'Well, this is an open question and the people who were involved often disagree. For my part, I doubt whether the Tibetans could have driven the Chinese out, but on the other hand I don't think we should have lost the war.

Things could definitely have been very different. Suppose the Tibetan government had come in with the Khampas from the beginning, given us access to the Tibetan army's equipment, and armed the monks in the monasteries, most of whom were prepared to fight to preserve their religion. Suppose later on the government had accepted American help. If these things had happened, I am sure we could have held onto pockets of territory almost indefinitely.'

'Today there would still be areas of Free Tibet?'

'Why not? You see there were then only two narrow roads from China to Tibet and if they had remained cut the Chinese could never have brought in tanks, artillery, or heavy vehicles. They would then have had to fight on much the same terms as us. For sure they could have held the major towns with huge numbers of infantry, but high up in the mountains they would not have been successful. We would have held out just like the guerrillas in Afghanistan did against the Russians. And the Soviet army had much better soldiers and much better weapons than the Chinese did in the 1950s.'

'So which parts of Tibet would have been defensible? From where would you have been able to wage this guerrilla war?'

'There are many places. But take Kham for instance. There it took the Chinese four years to defeat a handful of men with next to no equipment. This was because the area was very wild and the Khampas were tough and determined. The trouble with Kham is that it is too close to China, which makes it too easy for the Chinese to bring in artillery, to resupply their troops, and if necessary to reinforce them. The Changtang and western Tibet are too flat and the weather is too harsh: in winter there is no grass and animals cannot survive. However, in U-Tsang, central Tibet, there are plenty of mountainous areas which are ideal terrain for guerrillas. The only problem there is the timidity of the local people. They are not like the Khampas. They do not have the same temperament.'

'So what do you suppose makes the central Tibetans more pacific? Could it be that in U-Tsang the influence of Buddhism has been more profound?'

Athar brushed this impertinent suggestion dismissively aside.

'No, of course not. The Khampas are also devout Buddhists. In that respect there is no difference.

'Actually . . .', he continued with serene conviction, '. . . I think it has more to do with the nature of the old Tibetan society. Lhasa and central Tibet were dominated by the nobility. Everyone else worked for them. It wasn't such a terrible system, but people weren't encouraged to be independent and proud. Whereas in Kham there were many small landowners and traders. Families were in business on their own account and didn't have to take orders from anyone.

'In Kham, as soon as a boy was born he was encouraged to be brave and self-reliant. When he was fourteen, his father and his brothers would give him a horse, a rifle, and a knife. There was even a joke that we used to tell against ourselves. It was said that if you wanted to call yourself a proper Khampa you should have fought a hundred battles and committed a hundred robberies by the time of your fifteenth birthday. When I myself was fourteen, my elder brothers put me on an unbroken horse and made me hang onto its mane. Every time I was thrown off they put me back on again until I was half unconscious.'

'So what happened to the great Khampa hero, Gompo Tashi, after the flight of the Dalai Lama?'

'After setting up the resistance in Lhoka, Gompo Tashi took a thousand men and fought the Chinese to the north of Lhasa. In the last battle he was badly wounded in the chest by mortar shrapnel. Still, he recovered enough to carry on fighting in Lhoka. But when the Chinese finally pushed us back to Mustang, then he went to India to try to recover his health.'

'That's when I knew him,' Tenzin remarked unexpectedly.

'You knew him?'

'Yes, when I lived in Kalimpong, Gompo Tashi was there. I was his minder.'

'His minder?'

'Yes. He wasn't at all well and I had to take him down to Calcutta for his operations; to buy his train ticket, get him to the hospital, and fetch him anything he needed when he was convalescing there. Unfortunately, the surgery was not very successful. Eventually he was sent to England for treatment.'

'Who paid for that?'

'I don't know,' Tenzin replied. Athar also shook his head. 'I was in Colorado.'

'The only thing I do know . . .' Tenzin continued, '. . . is that it didn't work very well either, because he died a few years later. That's why he never directly had anything to do with Mustang.'

'It was his idea though,' said Athar. 'He and Gyalo Thondup, the Dalai Lama's brother, planned the base in Mustang. They asked me to go up there to see if it was suitable. At that time Nehru hoped to stay on good terms with the Chinese and the fact that they had accepted thousands of Tibetan refugees wasn't going down very well in Peking. The Indians didn't even want to hear about the Chushi Gangdruk, so Nepal was our best bet. Mustang wasn't too bad – it was close to Tibet – but it was difficult to supply and I knew we'd have problems with food. At first we planned to have two thousand people up there, but that was overambitious. Eventually I think there were about eighteen hundred.

'Anyway after the initial reconnaisance, I didn't have

very much to do with the place. I was more involved with the Americans. They wanted one or two experienced Tibetans to help train the new recruits, so I went to Colorado. I must say it was an ideal place. The Rockies are very like parts of Tibet; certainly a lot more so than Guam! Everything went extremely well, except for a brief period in 1961 when the CIA had its budget frozen during the transition from the Eisenhower to the Kennedy administration.'

'Were you ever allowed off the military base?'

'We were allowed out on exercises in remote areas of the mountains, but otherwise we were separated from the local population. For example, when I was taken to Washington on one occasion, to and from the airport I was put in a closed truck like a prisoner. The Americans went to quite a lot of trouble to keep us a secret. Otherwise they were extremely friendly and helpful. I remember the news coming through that the Mustang guerrillas had conducted an extremely successful raid, on which they had killed the Chinese general in command of western Tibet. The Americans were absolutely delighted and threw a big party for us. We all got very drunk.'

'Was Mustang usually so effective?'

'To be honest, no. At the beginning it was all right. The Americans airdropped a lot of arms and ammunition and we had more and more trained men to send up there. But the big problem was always food. Before long the guerrillas were only going into Tibet a couple of times a year and then with a maximum of a hundred and fifty men. Of course, Mustang was never intended as a base for a major offensive.'

'And eventually it caused a lot of trouble between the Tibetans and the Nepalese.'

'And among the Tibetans themselves. Because Gompo Tashi couldn't resume command of the Khampas, a man called Baba Yeshi was sent up to Mustang to be in charge and to get the place properly organised. . . . There was nothing much wrong with him. He was a Khampa; he was also shrewd, intelligent, and could be very charming and persuasive. However, he was essentially a politician, not a soldier. Khampas who had spent years being shot at didn't like taking orders from him. Soon people started to become dissatisfied with his leadership. Gyalo Thondup, the Dalai Lama's brother, wanted to change him; the Americans didn't think much of him, and neither did the Indians.'

'The Indians?'

'Yes. In 1962, the Chinese and the Indians fought a border war which the Indians lost. As a result their attitude to the Chushi Gangdruk changed completely. I told you that we had originally wanted five hundred trained guerrillas and that altogether the Americans had taken two hundred to Colorado. After 1962 the Indians told the Americans that they could train Tibetans in India and that furthermore they would be prepared to help. This was the beginning of the 22nd Battalion in Dehra Dun.

'Anyway, no one thought that Baba Yeshi was the right man for the Mustang job anymore. Except Baba Yeshi. Gyalo Thondup selected Wangdu to replace him and he was sent for further special training, only this time in India.'

'So what were you doing at the time?'

'Me? I was in Nepal, collecting intelligence about what was going on in Tibet. By now, we had an Intelligence Headquarters in New Delhi. When Wangdu was ready to go up to Mustang, I met him in Pokhara, and we walked together for a day up the Kali Gandaki. Our conversation was mostly about how Baba Yeshi would react to being recalled. Wangdu thought he was very proud and that he would take it badly. Baba Yeshi was a good politician and he was being offered a ministerial job in Dharamsala, but

Wangdu was convinced he would still see it as a demotion. Unfortunately he was right. Baba Yeshi not only refused to obey the order, but set up his own rival guerrilla faction. This, of course, was the beginning of the end for Mustang.'

'Was the appointment of Wangdu part of a wider change of policy?'

'Very much so. We now had many more trained men and we had the co-operation of the Indians. We hoped to become much more active and to make many more raids into Tibet from both Mustang and from Walung in eastern Nepal. About five hundred men from the "22" were sent up to Walung.'

'You mean ex-members of the battalion?'

'No, people on active service.'

'But they were in the Indian army.'

'Well, the "22" was made up of Tibetans trained by the Americans and the Indians. But yes, they were in the Indian army all right.'

'So five hundred Indian army troops set up a base in eastern Nepal without the knowledge or permission of the Nepalese government?'

'Yes. I suppose you could put it like that. The Nepalese eventually found out what was going on, but there wasn't a lot they could do about it.'

'Are you sure about all of this?' Tenzin asked, in open amazement. 'I've never heard any of this before.'

'Well, that's because it's not generally known I suppose,' Athar replied placidly. 'But I promise you I'm not making it up. I myself helped to smuggle their weapons into Nepal from Darjeeling. We went along the snowline on the western flank of Kanchenjunga. Above Walung there's a plateau, inhabited by only a few nomads, where you can hide things easily. The troops later went the same way, but they carried on into Tibet, from where they crossed back into Nepal disguised as refugees. The

Indians particularly liked having them there, because they thought if the Chinese attacked them again, they might try to come down between Nepal and Sikkim. They stayed there in Walung until the Nepalese closed down Mustang. Then the Indians had them discreetly withdrawn.'

'I must say I'm becoming more sympathetic to the Nepalese point of view the whole time.'

'Maybe,' said Athar reluctantly. 'But they wouldn't have managed to close down Mustang without Baba Yeshi's treachery. He wanted to stay in Nepal, so he thought he'd make himself more secure by collaborating with the Nepalese authorities. He took out Nepalese citizenship and then told them everything there was to know about Mustang. Everything. As a result a man called Lhamo Tsering, who was both Gyalo Thondup's private secretary and the head of our intelligence set-up in Delhi, was arrested in Pokhara and thrown in gaol for about eight years. Then the Nepalese decided to seize the opportunity to disarm the guerrillas in Mustang. Dharamsala became very concerned about the situation and to prevent any bloodshed, the Dalai Lama sent the Defence Minister with a tape-recording telling the Khampas to put down their arms peacefully. But Wangdu had heard that the Nepalese planned to arrest him anyway and so he refused to obey the Dalai Lama's instructions. He fled back into Tibet and for fifteen days managed to evade both the Chinese and the Nepalese. Then, trying to cross back into India, he strayed into the far north-western part of Nepal, where he was ambushed and killed. All the leading Khampas who had surrendered peacefully were arrested and gaoled for seven or eight years. It was a bad time.'

'What happened to Baba Yeshi?'

'Oh, he still lives here, in Kathmandu. I see him quite often in Thamel. Of course, he cannot associate with the

Tibetans these days. He is no longer a Tibetan. But even though he was responsible for the death of Wangdu, we don't try to kill him. Revenge would not further the Tibetan cause. It would merely annoy the Nepalese. When I see him in the street, I say hello, but that's it.'

Athar paused and looked out of the window. Clear evening light was bathing the rooftops of Thamel with a golden autumnal glow.

'You see,' he said, turning back to Tenzin and me, 'I still remember the time when we were in Lhoka together: twenty-five years ago now. In those days we were friends.'

Chapter 8

KALIMPONG

The Indian Embassy in Kathmandu sits in the middle of an enormous compound, the size of which seems to exert an almost proprietorial influence on the surrounding district. It is more like visiting a major government department than a foreign legation. Indians sometimes find little to distinguish the small Himalayan kingdoms from their own princely states, which in 1948 were swiftly absorbed – one or two under military compulsion – by the newly independent republic. This uncomprehending and dismissive attitude was seen at its most naked in 1975 when, taking advantage of a local ethnic conflict, Sikkim was annexed and its ruling family deposed. India's chief interest in Sikkim was strategic. Politically and culturally, the country had always looked over the mountains to Tibet; not down to Bengal on the plains. However, it was a vulnerable chink in India's defences, through which, in the event of further hostilities between the two regional superpowers, Chinese troops might reasonably have been expected to pour.

At the time there were those who made indignant comparisons between Chinese imperialism in Tibet and the Indian's disregard for the territorial integrity of the Sikkimese. Of course such comparisons take one only so far, as presumably India would not have felt obliged to annex Sikkim if China hadn't invaded Tibet in the first place. Furthermore, the Indians haven't subsequently made a habit of murdering people, and have sought to conquer resentment more by largesse than by repression. Still, northern Sikkim, bordering the salient of Tibet's Chumbi Valley, remains one of the most heavily militarised areas of the subcontinent, completely out of bounds to all foreign (and most Indian) nationals. A limited amount of group tourism is allowed in southern Sikkim and capital Gangtok, but permission for individuals to wander around unsupervised requires a three-month wrestling match with the Indian bureaucracy, at the end of which success is by no means guaranteed.

Mr Asok Diwan was not a particularly important official at the Indian Embassy, but within the relatively narrow bounds of his authority lay the capacity to issue certain 'Restricted Area' travel permits. This ability was of considerable interest to the Choegyal family as Tenzin's 'junior father' – in fact his uncle, polyandry having failed to obscure his paternity – lived in Kalimpong, and to visit him required regular official permission. Furthermore, two of Tenzin's brothers, who lived in Kathmandu, had children at boarding school there.

It was a pleasant morning, warm and sunny, and I sat comfortably on the embassy lawn, dividing my attention between a John Masters novel and a huge colony of fruit bats suspended from a nearby tree. After about an hour and half, and just as I was beginning to think about coming back in the afternoon, an elegant figure in an obviously expensive tweed sports jacket, grey flannel trousers, club tie, and brogues, sauntered across the lawn, the very embodiment of ease, leisure, and moneyed self-confidence. Suppressing a qualm that this might be the ambassador himself, I asked whether he knew the whereabouts of Mr Asok Diwan, an enquiry which was greeted with a smile of immense warmth and benevolence.

'Follow me,' he said.

So as to fulfil an existing contract, Tenzin had asked me to buy a large bottle of Ysatis – a perfume of which Mrs Diwan was said to be particularly fond – from the Duty Free Shop in Bahrain on my flight out from England. This I now placed on the desk in front of me. Mr Diwan picked it up absent-mindedly and without a word stowed it away in a drawer, as if it were a stapler or some other piece of office equipment that he had previously neglected to return to its proper place. He then began to examine my passport in minute detail.

'You are having only one further permitted entry to India,' he observed, stating the obvious limitations of my visa with Vedic sagacity. 'And you are desirous to go to Kalimpong? Why not to Delhi? Or Bombay? Or Calcutta perhaps, which is closer?'

I explained that as I had already visited these cities and tasted their cosmopolitan delights, I had developed an ardent interest in obscure and neglected hill stations.

Mr Diwan ignored me. 'Tell Lobsang . . .' (one of Tenzin's brothers), he said, holding my passport close to my left ear and comparing its picture with my present appearance, '. . . that the aftershave is almost finished.'

'I beg your pardon?'

'English Leather. A big bottle with a wooden top. This big. It has finished and in Kathmandu these aftershaves are being adulterated.'

I replied that I would pass on this information and that I was sure Lobsang would take his sartorial requirements very much to heart. Mr Diwan looked at me severely as if he suspected I was not approaching such an important matter with an appropriate degree of seriousness.

'I think you are working for some government agency,' he said with abrupt ferocity. 'What can you want in Kalimpong? Or Sikkim? Perhaps you are a spy.'

'No, no,' I protested, hurriedly trying to bring the conversation back to aftershave. Mr Diwan acquiesced magnanimously.

'English Leather is a very good make; very expensive. In India they are making also, but mostly water I think.'

A slight, nervous, ragged, little man, hair greying at the temples, dressed in a sleeveless pullover much in need of a wash, scuttled into the room with an aluminium tea tray. Having put it on the desk, he stood at attention waiting for further orders. Mr Diwan stared at him indignantly and then waved him away with a gesture which clearly implied that he was a mean, vulgar fellow whose impertinence could only be overlooked just this once.

'As to Darjeeling . . .' said Mr Diwan, helping himself to a sixth sugar lump, '. . . there is no problem. Kalimpong also is permitted. But as to Sikkim, this is very difficult. In this case could be encountered many obstructions.'

He stirred his tea and stared out of the window, his eyes acquiring a faraway look. 'Have you seen Tenzin's new car?' he enquired at length. I said that indeed I had. 'In Delhi I have a car – not such a fine one of course – but here in Kathmandu it is impossible. So inconvenient. You cannot imagine. Take next week for example. I have promised to take my wife shopping, but I am not having any vehicle. So inconvenient.'

I arrived at Tenzin's house about an hour later.

'Asok Diwan says we can have permits for Sikkim if

you lend him your car for two or three days next week.'

Tenzin, who was in the process of pouring out a drink, seemed struck to stone by this unexpected remark. He stood for some moments quite rigid, one arm (he was holding a bottle of soda water) stiff and outstretched. Fortunately, a friend of his, Wangchuk Tsering, who was sitting on a low sofa, was so convulsed with laughter at the suggestion that he slid onto the floor and had to be helped to his feet still spluttering.

'Does he,' said Tenzin grimly, before stalking off to the kitchen.

'I used to live in Kalimpong,' Wangchuk Tsering remarked, having finally regained his composure. 'I went there in 1956. My uncle was the official Tibetan trade agent. It's a nice place, but very quiet nowadays. Not at all like it used to be. Much of the trade between India and China, as well as that between India and Tibet, used to go through Kalimpong. But with the border closed, the town doesn't really have much point to it.'

Kalimpong may once have been the chief entrepôt of the Himalayas, but today, if anywhere can lay exclusive claim to this distinction, it is probably Kathmandu. Nepal is one of the poorest countries on earth, but in its capital there never seems to be any great shortage of cash. Much of this comes from (diverted) international relief aid; some from smuggling; some from tourism; and some from legitimate trade and manufacture.

So successful have a few exiled Tibetans been in this bubbling entrepreneurial cauldron that they are now dollar millionaires, with business connections in Bangkok and Singapore, Western Europe and the United States. Such Tibetans see themselves (and potentially their country) as part of the Asian economic miracle and nowadays their dislike of the Chinese is stimulated still further by ideological contempt for the economic failures of communism. The Dalai Lama's Dharamsala administration may have been set up in imitation of Nehru's paternalistic socialism, but many of his subjects – the Khampas in particular – are instinctive and enthusiastic capitalists. Ask a bureaucrat in Dharamsala about a future free Tibet and he will talk of rebuilding the monasteries, or of public provision for education and health. Ask a Tibetan businessman from Kathmandu and he will emphasise his country's untapped natural resources, intelligent and industrious people, and its vast potential for economic growth. On one occasion I encouraged a leading Tibetan entrepreneur to set out his vision of the future. 'Ten years after the Chinese leave . . .', he insisted, '. . . Tibet will be like Taiwan. We have a big country and a small population: it will be easy to develop. We can easily create a modern industrial base with the help of the Japanese or the Koreans, and before too long we should have quite a high standard of living. Historically Tibet was isolated by its geographical position, but its people were not by nature isolationist. There were always traders. Today there are jet airplanes. A direct flight from Lhasa to Delhi would take an hour and a half; to Bangkok would be only three hours.'

I retailed this opinion to Wangchuk Tsering, himself a successful businessman, and, along with Tenzin, one of the so-called 'Kathmandu carpet barons', a group much mythologised and greatly envied by less affluent Tibetans elsewhere in the subcontinent. He smiled. He didn't disagree, he said, but perhaps my interlocutor had been just a little over-optimistic.

'He's right in saying that the Tibetans are very good at business. Foreigners like to think of us as very spiritual and unworldly people. Actually we're quite materialistic – certainly more so than the Europeans I've met – though not as much as the Indians, who in general think about almost nothing but money.'

'But why did this talent for business flourish here in particular?'

'Well, for a start, the Nepalese economy is not as tightly regulated as the Indian. In India there have always been import restrictions and currency controls to protect their domestic industry and to prevent unemployment. Of course there are rules in Nepal as well, but in general there are fewer of them. However, as far as the Tibetans are concerned, I think their entrepreneurial spirit here was born out of simple necessity. You see, unlike the refugees in India, the Tibetans in Nepal *had* to depend entirely on their own efforts. We got very little aid from international relief organisations. The Nepalese government only allowed the Swiss Red Cross to help us; no one else. People must work and eat, so something *had* to be started.

'With the help of the Swiss we set up an export enterprise called CTC – the Carpet Trading Company. This provided small workshops with a market for their products and slowly the business got going. I was actually sent from Dharamsala to help out. I worked for the Tibetan government until 1982.'

'So what exactly were the Tibetans making in those days?'

'They were weaving traditional woollen carpets, with complex patterns, in bright colours. In other words, ones precisely the same as those we'd always made in Tibet: for the monasteries, for our homes, for saddlebags. . . .'

'And who bought them?'

'One of the principal markets was the tourist industry. This grew steadily in Nepal during the 1960s and '70s, the foreigners liked to take home a Tibetan carpet as a souvenir. But there was also a small export trade. I decided that we should try to expand this part of the business, so I got in touch with a large company in London – OCM – that imports all kinds of oriental carpets and distributes them throughout Western Europe. To our surprise, they started to do an extremely good job. The big breakthrough came when we began to understand this new market and to make the sort of carpets that Europeans would buy in large quantities. We realised that we could produce high-quality woollen carpets far more cheaply than anyone else.'

'So did traditional Tibetan designs become much less important?'

'Oh yes, there is only a very limited market for them. Nowadays our carpets are nearly all in European styles – art deco even – but they are hand woven with Ladakhi wool and coloured with vegetable dyes. It is the quality of the materials and the workmanship that are important.'

'So how big is this industry? People say that Tibetan millionaires are quite common in Kathmandu these days.'

'Well, I'm certainly not a millionaire and I don't think Tenzin is either. But a few people have done very well. The carpet business has been booming for over ten years now and last year the total export turnover was around seventy million US dollars. In international terms this may not be very much, but it is increasingly important to the economy of Nepal: not just because of the foreign exchange we earn, but because carpet weaving is very labour intensive. We employ thousands of people: washers, dyers, spinners, weavers. . . . You see, so many of the other industries that the Nepalese would like to get going – electronics, for example – require foreign expertise, foreign capital. . . . Whereas the carpet business just imports a little wool. This is why we are so popular with the government at the moment; even though we are Tibetans.'

'This business is dominated by the Tibetans?'

'Yes, completely. Most of the workers are Nepalese, but the vast majority of people working in managerial positions – the people who got it going in the first place – are Tibetan.'

'So how much do the Nepalese workers get paid?'

Wangchuk Tsering hesitated and looked rather defensive before replying. 'It depends, but around two hundred and fifty Nepalese rupees a square metre [£6.25]. A skilled weaver can make about four square metres a month. In addition he would probably be provided with living quarters because he comes from another part of Nepal. You see, no one from Kathmandu wants to work in a carpet factory: there are far too many ways to make fast, easy money here. So we send recruiting scouts out into the countryside, where there is a lot of unemployment and a thousand rupees [£25] a month is a very good wage. In Kathmandu it may not buy very much, but in the hill villages it's enough to feed and house a family.'

'So what suddenly prompted you to go into business on your own account?'

'Well, the Tibetan government could only afford to pay me a very small salary. My wife set up a shop on Kantipath, in the centre of town, which fortunately was quite successful, so we were just about able to live. But then in 1979, the situation in Tibet became more relaxed and I was able to get in touch with the rest of my family for the first time in twenty years. I discovered that although my mother had died, my brothers in Lhasa were alive, and that they had young families. Although they were very poor, they were desperate to get their children out to be educated in India. I could not refuse them, even though this would involve a great deal of expense on my part. So I talked the situation over with my wife and resigned from the government service.'

'But how could you know you were going to do well in the carpet business? There must have been a considerable element of risk. And what I really don't understand is why you people in Nepal aren't put out of business by your compatriots in India. After all, virtually every Tibetan settlement in the subcontinent tries to support itself with a carpet factory.'

'The first part of your question is easy. In 1982 the carpet business here was booming, so starting my own company was not particularly risky. But as far as the competition is concerned, you are right. In theory there is no way we can compete with the Tibetans in India. They get huge tax incentives from the Indian government, and things like transport are much cheaper there. For example, air freight to Europe from Delhi is almost 50 per cent less than it is from Kathmandu. However, most of the Tibetan carpet factories in India are mixed up with Dharamsala in some way. There is some element of central planning or marketing. For some reason this means they don't place sufficient emphasis on export and also makes them slow to react to changes in demand. In general they take much less trouble to understand what the customers actually want. They just go on producing traditional Tibetan carpets and somehow expect to be able to sell them. Their emphasis is on the producer not the consumer. This is a socialist not a capitalist attitude and so they don't make nearly as much money as they ought to. Nowadays they are trying to copy us, because they see how well we are doing, but so far we have managed to stay at least one jump ahead of them.'

On the flight from Kathmandu to Biratnagar there was not a tourist to be seen. At least half of the plane's passengers seemed to be Gurkha soldiers, returning to the British army's recruitment centre at Dharan, and in place of red and orange rucksacks, the overhead lockers were jammed with khaki kitbags and bulging bedrolls. Having secured a window seat, I was once again able to indulge in my favourite pastime: gawping at the mountains. For the armchair mountaineer, it was a particularly satisfactory view. Everest, Lhotse, Makalu, and the more distant Kanchenjunga – four of the five highest peaks on earth – were all neatly framed by my porthole. Tenzin, on whom mountains were, unsurprisingly, beginning to pall, doggedly read the in-flight magazine and tried to forget about the responsibilities of his business life, which he was once more obliged to abandon for some weeks. It wasn't, he had explained to me in the departure lounge, that he didn't trust his brothers to look after things in his absence. It was just that . . . well . . . just that he didn't trust them really.

On the starboard side of the plane, green foothills gave way to the flat, dusty Terai, a strip of land, invariably the colour of a digestive biscuit, that lies along the Indian border. It rose up gracefully to meet us.

In the arrivals hall the temperature was about ninety degrees Fahrenheit, but one young Sherpa, presumably on his way home to the Everest region, steadfastly refused to take off a scarlet down jacket that would have been more than adequate in a blizzard on the Khumbu Icefall. It was clearly his most treasured possession.

To cheer himself up, and to forget about the potential incompetence of his brothers, Tenzin began to haggle with one of the taxi-drivers, who in response strove, unsuccessfully, to display only the most peripheral interest in the prospect of gainful employment. Having finally agreed a price ten rupees short of a punch-up, we piled into his rickety car, tied the door shut with a piece of string, and set off on a five-hour drive to the south-easternmost tip of Nepal.

Biritnagar is an apology for a town, a ghastly, disorganised mess of black puddles, one-eyed three-legged dogs, putrefying refuse, naked children, and scrawny, malnourished cows, their shipwrecked ribs protruding through grey flanks caked with malodorous mud. Fortunately, 200 yards beyond the municipal boundary begins some of the loveliest countryside imaginable: yellow mustard fields, so brilliant as to seem electrically charged, dark green tea plantations in which to bathe one's frazzled eyes, and steep forested hills, behind which the snowfields and summit ridges of either Makalu or Kanchenjunga can occasionally be glimpsed, floating, disembodied, above a layer of pastel haze.

It was three o'clock when we got to the border and there seemed every chance of reaching Kalimpong that same evening. It would only take four hours more, Tenzin explained, when formalities had been completed and we were firmly on Indian soil.

The Nepalese customs official was evidently feeling the heat and could barely summon up enough energy to stamp our passports before waving us weakly through. Alas, his Indian counterpart was a man for whom the clearest and simplest explanation was proof positive of incorrigible villainy and intrigue. He seemed in particular to take an instant dislike to me. What, he demanded to know, was an Englishman doing in the company of a Tibetan, at an obscure Nepalese border post, attempting to cross in broad daylight? Clearly I was up to no good. There could be little doubt that I was a smuggler; of precisely what was the only question to be answered. It was at this point that he discovered, while rummaging through our luggage, my laptop computer. Eyes glowing with triumph, he summoned two guards, gleefully announced that we were under arrest, and then hustled us over to the main administrative building to be interrogated by his superior and afterwards, so far as he was concerned, incarcerated.

Tenzin, whose courtesy is fathomless, looked at me for a moment with an expression tinged with reproach.

'What on earth did you have to bring that wretched thing for?' seemed to be what politeness forbade him to ask.

We found the senior customs official sitting cross-legged in a swivel chair, scratching himself and spitting into a wastepaper bin. He stared at us morosely. For three or four minutes no one said anything, and the silence was broken only by the official delving inside his shirt in search of some particularly excruciating itch. Eventually he seemed to decide that the psychological offensive had gone on long enough and beckoned to the lackey in possession of our passports. Every single entry and exit stamp was then discussed in exhaustive and repetitive detail – a process which took about an hour an a half – before he reluctantly turned his attention to my computer. This he shook vigorously for some seconds, before lifting it up to his ear and listening intently. Reaching into a drawer he next produced a large, rusty penknife and handed it to me.

'He wants you to take the back off so he can look inside,' said Tenzin without emotion.

'With a penknife!?'

'Yes.'

'But if I do that I'll lose all the memory. Tell him it's impossible.'

Tenzin sighed and began a long apologetic explanation in the most soothing voice he could manage under such invidious circumstances.

'He says in that case he's going to have to ring the security people in Kathmandu to see if we're known criminals. I hope you realise just how long it will take him to get through on the phone – hours, possibly days – to say nothing of how long it will take the police in Kathmandu to work out that they've never heard of us?'

'How about bribery?'

'Not a good idea,' Tenzin replied. 'He might take it, but

on the other hand he might take it and then turn nasty, in which case we could be in serious trouble.'

It was a few minutes short of midnight when we were grudgingly released into the inhospitable blackness. Fortunately, just beyond the check-post were several taxis, their drivers stretched out on blankets underneath some nearby trees. Most were disinclined to stir, but one man, when prodded, sleepily agreed to take us into the nearby town of Siliguri. Providing, he said, we didn't mind push-starting the car, its ignition being temporarily out of service.

Siliguri, although scarcely a place of great cultural interest or architectural splendour, is at a major road and railway junction, where traffic from Bihar and Bengal converges, before heading off to India's eastern states of Assam and Arunachal Pradesh. Even in the middle of the night the road was thunderous with heavy lorries, while from a marshalling yard came the sound of steam engines snuffling and whistling and crashing into lines of recalcitrant trucks.

Tenzin had by now recovered his composure and ceased to inveigh against uniformed despots in general and Indian customs officials in particular. 'Let's see if they'll let us in at Sinclair's,' he suggested. 'It's not the sort of place I could afford when I used to live round here, but frankly I've had more than enough cheap hotels for one lifetime.'

In colonial days, Sinclair's Hotel – to which a drowsy night watchman finally admitted us – chiefly accommodated travellers switching from the national broad-gauge railway to the narrow-gauge line up to Darjeeling. Nowadays it caters for Indian businessmen and boasts air conditioning, a Chinese restaurant, and lobby with marble floor. All traces of the past have been thoroughly expunged and only the name survives as a reminder of the time when Calcutta was the seat of the viceroy and Darjeeling was the 'Queen of the Hills'.

The following morning, a lengthy inspection of all available transport at last revealed a vehicle that looked capable of getting us up to Kalimpong and we set off again, rested, and in restored good humour. It soon became apparent, however, that we were unlikely to enjoy a particularly tranquil drive, as the road was crowded with Indian army traffic – mostly lorries, but also artillery and light armour – heading up to the Sikkimese frontier with Tibet. As in Ladakh, I was forcibly reminded of the large Chinese forces still poised on the border and the understandable apprehension that this arouses in Indian military minds.

Three hours' drive brought us to the bridge over the Tista where the road from Siliguri to the Sikkimese capital, Gangtok, intersects with that from Darjeeling to Kalimpong. Several dozen Indian troops were standing guard, albeit rather listlessly, and we were instructed to present our area permits to a Sikh sergeant-major of Falstaffian girth, who entered our particulars in his ledger with the solemnity of a recording angel.

Such elaborate security precautions were due chiefly not to the threat of imminent Chinese invasion, but to the 'Gorkhaland' guerrillas, who had been making themselves a nuisance to the Indian authorities, sporadically, for some years past. Since the mid-nineteenth century, there has been a large-scale influx of Nepalese settlers into both Sikkim and the Darjeeling–Kalimpong area – a movement originally encouraged by British planters who needed additional labour for their tea plantations – and of late this has resulted in sustained and violent agitation for some form of regional autonomy. The Indian government, not unreasonably, points out that there is already a Gorkha homeland – called Nepal – and that if the guerrillas and their supporters feel so strongly about being governed by Bengali bureaucrats in Calcutta, they might consider returning whence they came as a possible solution to their dilemma.

The valley of the Tista River is hot, humid, and equally famous for its orchids and its leeches. Having crossed the bridge, however, we immediately began to climb, and within ten minutes the air had freshened and the jungly vegetation given way to deciduous woodland stained with scarlet poinsettias.

At a mere 4,000 feet above sea level, Kalimpong only just qualifies as a hill station. Nonetheless, in the main street, most of the traders were wearing coats or heavy pullovers, and one or two small clouds with a deficient sense of altitude could be seen hanging around the gothic church tower that immodestly dominates the town. The Foreigners' Registration Office, to which we were obliged to pay a cursory visit, was heavily sandbagged, and it was impossible to avoid the accusing fingers of heavy machine guns, set up to cover every conceivable angle of attack.

'Kalimpong's got worse,' opined Rinchen Tsewang, Tenzin's junior father. We were sitting in the front room of his small hotel, looking out through double doors onto a busy thoroughfare. On the wall, sedate, framed pictures of the Dalai Lama and Mrs Indira Gandhi were separated by a lurid poster of Sylvester Stallone festooned with an entire arsenal of automatic weaponry. A man of about sixty-five with a lean, deeply lined face, neatly trimmed hair, and a somewhat lugubrious expression, he obviously couldn't for the life of him understand why Tenzin – normally such a sensible, responsible person – was wasting his time wandering around India in the company of a vulgarly inquisitive foreigner.

'The streets are filthy, the government offices are always shut, and there are soldiers everywhere with rifles, looking for someone to use them on. If these Gorkhaland people feel so hard done by, they should try being Tibetan for a bit.'

His wife, a matronly woman, smiled indulgently and said nothing, while a sturdy girl, her daughter by a previous marriage, jumped up from behind the reception desk to prevent a toddler in a sky-blue romper-suit from beheading the hotel's cat.

As was the custom in Kham, Tenzin's mother had married two brothers, both of whom later served in the resistance and escaped to India in the early 1960s. In 1982, when she was finally able to rejoin her family, she opted to live with the elder brother, her first husband, Tenzin's father, in Kathmandu. This was as much from necessity as from choice, as her younger husband – Rinchen Tsewang – had remarried some years before, Tibetan marital arrangements being rather lightly policed compared with the Western variety.

'My mother was not all that pleased to find that he'd married again,' Tenzin remarked, as we strolled through the town after a lunch of *thukpa* – Tibetan noodle soup – and cold mutton. 'A lot of the Tibetans who went through the bad years after the Uprising and during the Cultural Revolution are quite resentful of those people who made it out to India. They think we had a pretty easy time. To be honest, I think my mother feels that we all deserted her. She was left in Tibet with just my sisters for company. Her two husbands and four sons were all in India. Of course no one planned it that way – my fathers were fighting in the Chushi Gangdruk and could easily have been killed – but unfortunately there's still some deep sense of betrayal. If she blames anyone in particular, it's my junior father. She finds it difficult to accept that he remarried and had another family at the same time as she was being harassed and humiliated by the Chinese. Of course, from my point of view it's different. I have a great deal of admiration for the way that he supported us all at the beginning. In the early '60s, he was responsible for keeping twelve people housed, clothed, and fed. After the border was closed, there was absolutely no work here in Kalimpong; or in Darjeeling for that matter. All the traders – both Indians and Tibetans – were sitting around with nothing to do, so my junior father set up a mah-jong house.'

'A what?'

'A mah-jong house. Every day people would come to our home to play mah-jong. We used to provide them with food and drink free of charge and in return, at the beginning of each new game, one rupee would be set aside for the house. We survived on the proceeds from gambling for quite a few years. My father was himself an extremely skilful mah-jong player and his winnings provided a very reliable income. Considering that we were refugees and had no money at all to begin with, we lived quite well. We certainly never went hungry. Anyway, my brothers and I are very grateful for what he did for us and nowadays we are happy to be able to return the favour.'

'How do you mean? Doesn't the hotel support your father and his family?'

'The hotel makes only a small profit, so we send a little extra money. My father is in his late sixties, and we want him to be able to buy good-quality clothes; to eat and drink what he likes; to be free from financial worry. Also my brothers and I paid for the education of his three children, which he could not otherwise have afforded. After school the boy came to work with us in Kathmandu, but the two girls have both been to university. One is still training to be a doctor; the other has a BA in English and now works as an air hostess for Pan Am. Actually, she flies on the Delhi–Frankfurt–New York route, so quite often she looks after the Dalai Lama when he travels to Europe or America.'

I said that the extended family system obviously worked very well, but that in general Tibetans didn't seem to feel much sense of obligation to a wider society.

'For example, if the Dharamsala administration were to ask the more affluent Tibetans to pay income tax at a higher rate so as to help poor people like the ones we met in Simla or Manali, I don't get the impression that the idea would go down very well in Kathmandu.'

'Well . . .', Tenzin replied, '. . . if the British government were to raise the level of income tax, I don't imagine it would be a very popular measure either. People always think it would be a good idea for the government to spend more money, just as long as they don't have to contribute anything personally. I should imagine that the British and the Tibetans are much the same in this respect. Still, you're right in a way. Most Tibetans feel a strong responsibility to their own relations, but they expect other people to look after themselves. Of course, if we were to return to Tibet, then there would have to be a centralised system of taxation. We'd all have to get used to the idea. But I don't think it would affect our attitude to the family. That would remain the primary social institution; just as it is here in India. The family is the basic structure within which Asian people seek security. It insures them against unemployment, sickness, old age, and so on. Even if a future Tibet were able to afford a welfare state, which contrary to what some people in Dharamsala would have you believe, is fairly unlikely, I still think that allegiance to the family would be more enduring than it has proved to be in Europe and America. Anyway . . .', he concluded, '. . . here we are. These are the godowns I was telling you about.'

In front of us on the hillside were several extremely large warehouses. Still in a reasonable state of preservation, their walls and roofs appeared to be completely intact, though a number of the windows were broken, providing a convenient means of access for dozens of nesting swallows. We walked up to one about the size of an aircraft hangar and Tenzin leant on the unlocked door, which creaked slowly open.

'You'll have to get my father to tell you about these. He knows far more about them than I do. But in here I think is where they used to store the Tibetan wool and the yaks' tails and so on.'

'Yaks' tails?'

'Yes, I think they were used chiefly for fly whisks. Now, as you can see, there's nothing. At least you can see how big these godowns are and get some idea of the volume of trade that used to come through here.'

'No, no, not just yak tails.' Richen Tsewang looked at me severely over the froth on the top of his beer. We had returned to the hotel and were discussing the state of the world before dinner. 'It was quite a complex system of trade. But then if you're really interested . . . .' – he stared at me dubiously – '. . . I'd better start at the beginning.

'I myself was about fifteen years old when I first started trading in Tibet. I would go away for up to two months, sometimes with other people; sometimes by myself. I went on horseback and carried a rifle. This was quite normal in Kham: young boys had to grow up quickly in those days. I used to go to a town on the Chinese border, Dartsedo, where I would buy brick tea – the leaves are compressed into small blocks which I would then take up to where the nomads were grazing their animals. There I would barter for skins, wool, butter, herbs, musk, deer horn . . . and yak tails. Some of these things could be sold back to the Chinese, but much of the trade was with central Tibet and with India. Before long I was sent off on my first seven-month trip to Lhasa with a team of twenty mules. (Mules are actually a bit of a nuisance and it's quite difficult for one person to control more than ten. Whereas twenty yaks are no problem at all, because they're so docile. The big trouble with yaks, however, is that they're slow. You've no idea how slow they are. Mules may be bad-tempered, but they're much quicker.)

'When I was nineteen, my father announced that he was going to go on a pilgrimage to Lhasa and that afterwards he would spend three years there, visiting sacred sites and improving his spiritual understanding. It was decided, therefore, that the family business should go with him and I was sent down to Kalimpong to get things started. Trading between Lhasa and Kalimpong was relatively easy because a one-way trip is only eighteen days and, furthermore, the Jelap-la, the pass between Sikkim and the Chumbi Valley in Tibet, is usually open in winter.'

'But there must have been lots of people already in business on the route.'

'Yes, of course, but there was still room for a newcomer. There was consistent demand in Lhasa for both basic commodities and luxury goods. Many small traders operated just between Kalimpong and Lhasa, while the big families would go right across to China; a trip which took about a year, there and back. Actually, the big problem was not the excessive competition, but getting permission to trade in the first place. To do business in India, you needed a permit, the issue of which was controlled by three large Tibetan families: the Reting; the Sadutsang; and the Pomdatsang. They had a kind of semi-monopoly and consequently were extremely rich. These three families had people working for them everywhere; all over Tibet. If you were friends with them, they helped you out. If they didn't like you, you got nowhere. Fortunately, we were given a permit and were able to start up in business. We decided to import luxury goods into Tibet – watches, toothpaste, finished textiles – and to take wool, pig bristles, and yaks' tails down to Kalimpong. These we obtained from the nomads to the north of Lhasa. The Western goods we bought from syndicates controlled by the British.'

'So was this trade only barter? Was there no cash involved at all?'

'It was a combination of both. All the traders would use Tibetan banknotes – the currency was called the *sang* – whenever they needed to.'

'And could you make an adequate living?'

'Oh yes. Certainly. Providing you were careful about which merchandise you bought and sold, you could easily make 200 per cent return on your capital. It was a good business: everyone made money and everyone was happy. After his three years in Lhasa my father returned to Kham, but I still came down to Kalimpong. We were doing so well. Then the Chinese turned up, and within a few years the trade was dead. In 1959 the border was closed and Kalimpong became what you see today: a small market town; some flower growing – orchids, poinsettias, that kind of thing – a few schools; a very quiet place.'

'So what happened to the big three families?'

'Well, the Retings were already in decline. As you probably know, they provided one of the regents of Tibet after the death of the Thirteenth Dalai Lama. But then we had a period of political upheaval – in fact a small civil war – and in 1947 Reting Rinpoche was murdered. His family suffered as a result of their fall from power. As far as the Sadutsang are concerned, I don't know what happened to them; they certainly don't have any business interests around here any more. The Pomdatsangs also went away. I'm told there's only one of the family left alive: a woman who lives in Seattle.'

Chapter 9

DARJEELING

'It's a shame really,' Tenzin remarked the following morning, as we drove back down to the Tista bridge.

'Kalimpong's fairly boring nowadays. It used to be very different when the Dalai Lama's brother, Gyalo Thondup, was here. In those days there were Chinese spies, Taiwanese spies, the Chushi Gangdruk, the Indian security people. . . . Also, until recently, Tsepon Shakabpa, the famous Tibetan historian, lived here. He would have been an interesting man for you to have talked to, but sadly he died not long ago.'

Just before the bridge a pale green bus with 'Siliguri–Gangtok' painted on the side was letting off passengers at the security check-post.

'It's such a pity we haven't got permits for Sikkim,' Tenzin continued dolefully.

I agreed that it was, but Mr Asok Diwan having proved so unreasonably demanding, there was nothing else we could have done in the time available, and consequently not much point in getting depressed.

'I suppose not,' he replied, evidently unconvinced. Brightening up he went on: 'We'll see if they've got room for us at The Windermere. It's much the best hotel in Darjeeling and it's owned by Tibetans.'

At nearly eight thousand feet, Darjeeling (originally in Tibetan Dorje-ling, 'Place of the Thunderbolt') is one of the higher Indian hill stations, and so the road on the three-hour journey from Kalimpong is uphill most of the way. It is by any standards a beautiful drive, particularly when you have reached a sufficient altitude for the view of Kanchenjunga – at 28,210 feet the world's third highest mountain – to be unimpeded by subordinate ridges. The town itself is a motley collection of buildings, home to around fifty thousand people, stacked up above elegantly contoured tea terraces and, like most hill stations, in imminent danger of crashing down among them at the mere suggestion of an earth tremor. A recent dearth of foreign tourists – thanks to the Gorkhaland disturbances – has allowed it to remain the hill station most sympathetic to the requirements of Raj nostalgia; the one in which you feel most confident of encountering Dame Peggy Ashcroft in memsahib persona.

Many of the steep and narrow streets are inaccessible to cars, so Tenzin and I paid off the driver and panted up the hill to the Windermere, well known in India as the best-preserved and most genteel of the old colonial establishments.

I had been expecting to like it very much and was extremely put out to receive only the most perfunctory acknowledgement of my existence from an elegantly attired Tibetan behind the reception desk. At least I assumed he was Tibetan; though dressed in a Harris tweed jacket, grey flannels, and a silk Paisley neck-scarf it was hard to tell. I looked at Tenzin for reassurance: Tenzin looked back at me, equally mystified. Suddenly, with sinking heart I recognised the origin of the pernicious influences that had been at work on this charmless individual. He had evidently attended one of the numerous public schools, founded in Darjeeling during the last century in imitation of English models, and which have continued to thrive in a time capsule to the present day.

Tenzin enquired politely, in Tibetan, as to the availability and cost of accommodation. The receptionist replied, in English, his voice filled with ennui, and languor, and self-esteem.

'Our rooms are seven hundred rupees a night. Meals are compulsory.'

'How do you mean "compulsory"? Suppose neither of us feels hungry?'

'I mean that three meals a day will be charged for. Our guests always eat in the hotel.'

'But suppose we prefer to eat out?'

'If our prices are too expensive, I suggest you try the Planters' Club.'

'I should have known it would be like that,' said Tenzin resignedly as we stumbled back down the hill towards the bazaar. 'Darjeeling is a sanitorium for old Bengalis: or at least for *rich* old Bengalis. The Windermere must be full of long-term guests, which is why they can't be bothered with passing trade like us.'

Having descended a couple of hundred feet and then clambered back up a flight of steep steps that led to the verandah of the Planters' Club, we slumped down in fragmenting wicker armchairs surrounded by pots of geraniums, solaced ourselves with the sublime view of Kanchenjunga, and waited for someone to appear. The whole place seemed to be a kind of terrestrial *Marie Celeste*. Eventually, every available bell having been vigorously and persistently rung, an ancient retainer in a bottle-green jacket shuffled out of the gloom at the back of the snooker hall.

'Yes, sir, we are having rooms, but we are not having hot water. Plumbing is on blink, sir. Maybe tomorrow we are having.'

A hundred rupees turned out to purchase an extensive suite with three beds, polished boards, a cast-iron fire-place, and a bath on legs big enough for two substantial Victorians to have lain full-length facing each other.

'One coal bucket is in room charge, sir. Extra bucket is six rupees. Room boy is lighting fire at teatime.'

On my way downstairs again I decided to drop in at the club library to investigate the literary tastes of expatriate tea planters, but the door was padlocked and pinned to it was a yellowing cardboard notice: 'Closed Mondays'. Why Mondays? Clearly, on Sundays reading and such-like frivolity would be inappropriate. But Mon-days? Puzzled, I wandered out onto the terrace where I found one of the club's officials, a retired Indian military man with a drastically clipped moustache and a haircut of irreproachable pre-war severity, supervising the lubri-cation of a tripod-mounted Maxim gun, already gleaming with Brasso and apparently in full working order. Divorced from the consequences of its use, it was a wonderful piece of machinery, as delicate and ingenious as the sextant or an astronomical telescope.

'May I take this opportunity to welcome you to the Planter's Club on behalf of the whole committee.'

Thanking him for his hospitality, I said that I was sure that I was going to be very comfortable, especially when the hot water came back on. 'Oh, by the way, why is the library closed on Mondays?'

He thought for a moment, as if he had been asked a question of almost unanswerable profundity concerning the essential God-given nature of things, before replying: 'Just tradition old chap. No reason. Just tradition.'

Clearly anxious to redirect the conversation to more familiar and trustworthy ground, and if possible to engage me in a subject dear to his own heart, he went on: 'I'm afraid we can't offer you Scotch, but try the Sikkimese whisky – Red Barrel – I think you'll find it's not too bad at all. Supplies have been a bit of a problem just lately, but we've been making do you know, making do.' His voice faltered as if he had been burdened suddenly with a sobering awareness of the world's inexorable decline.

'Tell me, this Maxim gun, it isn't by any chance one of the ones that went to Tibet with the British Younghusband expedition?'

'Couldn't say. Shouldn't think so. There were thousands of them made you know.'

There was a pause, then, as if to forestall any further disconcerting enquiries, he barked an order to the three servants who had been holding a tin of brass polish, a duster, and an oil can respectively, smiled graciously, said that administrative duties unfortunately called, and disappeared.

On 19 July 1903, Colonel Francis Younghusband set off from Darjeeling – braving the leeches and the monsoon floods – up the Tista Valley into Sikkim. There, to the north of Gangtok, he picked up a military escort, before crossing the Tibetan border and setting up camp at the small settlement of Khamba Dzong. His mission was to negotiate with Tibetan representatives, to provide the then Viceroy, Lord Curzon, with reassurance about the security of India's northern borders from Russian invasion, and if possible to secure trade concessions for British merchants. Unsurprisingly, the Tibetans proved no more amenable to diplomatic conversation after this invasion than they had done beforehand. The representatives of the Manchu Chinese, the Ambans, were contacted in Lhasa, but no help was forthcoming. Younghusband languished in Khamba Dzong: Curzon grew impatient.

Eventually, it was decided that a reinforced British expedition should advance further into Tibet, where it was hoped more senior and more talkative officials might be encountered. Equipped with four artillery pieces and two Maxim guns 1150 soldiers duly set out. They got as far as the small village of Guru, where a Tibetan force of 1500 men was drawn up to oppose them.

The British told the Tibetans that they intended to advance as far as Gyantse, the country's third largest town; the Tibetans told the British to go back to Yatung on the Sikkimese border and to stop making a nuisance of themselves. They had absolutely no intention of conspiring with the Russians, they said, they just wanted to be left in peace. Perhaps the most tragi-comic episode in the whole of British imperial history then ensued.

The Tibetans had elected to defend the road to Gyantse from behind a large stone wall, a defensive measure which, given the state of Western military technology at the beginning of the twentieth century, was truly pathetic in its futility. The British troops advanced; the Tibetans waited. Nobody fired. Reaching the defensive wall, the British were bemused to find the Tibetan general and his staff sitting on the ground in front of it. Cameras were brought out and a few photographs taken. Younghusband wrote a dispatch to the Government of India to say that a bloodless victory had been achieved. The *Daily Mail*'s intrepid reporter penned some copy along similar lines.

Meanwhile, moving round the Tibetan flanks, the British methodically began to disarm the outlying soldiers there. The Tibetans were by now virtually encircled. Unfortunately, it would seem that many of the firearms were not government issue, but the personal property of the troops themselves. Their peremptory confiscation therefore caused considerable resentment. Fist fights broke out and before long the situation deteriorated into a general brawl. Finally, as if he could stand this absurd and ignominous situation no longer, the Tibetan general got up, jumped on his horse, drew a pistol and shot a nearby British soldier in the jaw.

The scuffle suddenly became a battle: the Maxim guns opened up at point blank range and within a few minutes around five hundred Tibetans were dead. The British forces suffered nine casualties, none fatal, and after treating the Tibetan wounded as best they could, the expedition advanced to Gyantse.

Once again, as at Khamba Dzong, Younghusband was obliged to sit and vegetate. His camp was attacked, the local fort was shelled and captured, but still no useful discussions took place, the Tibetans continuing to insist that there was nothing to talk about and that the British should go back to India. Finally, in July 1904, the decision was taken to advance the remaining 150 miles to Lhasa. The Tibetan army had already attempted to defend the highest pass on the road, the 16,548 foot Karo-la, but this had been cleared with the loss of four British dead and the slaughter of a further three hundred or so Tibetans.

On 4 August Younghusband entered Lhasa only to find that the Thirteenth Dalai Lama had fled. This did not, however prove an insurmountable difficulty and an Anglo-Tibetan treaty was swiftly concluded (without any reference to the authorities in Peking).

Two months after they had arrived, the British began to withdraw. For them it had been a minor and irritating excursion on the frontiers of their empire, the sort of bother that, on the whole, they could have well done without. For the Tibetans the affair had been a traumatic initiation into the world of modern realpolitik. But for the Chinese it had been a severe loss of face, yet another humiliating incursion into what they considered their sphere of influence by the rampant and unassailable Western imperial powers. Habituated to assaults on their eastern seaboard, they now found themselves being poked and prodded 1500 miles to the west. Determined to reassemble such fragments of their authority as remained, a diplomatic counter-attack was launched, and the rapacious army of General Chao Erh-feng dispatched. A vanguard of 2000 soldiers finally reached Lhasa in February 1910 – having dallied along the way for some recreational pillage and rapine – and for the second time in a decade, the Dalai Lama was obliged to flee. This time, ironically, to British protection in Darjeeling.

'It's surprising . . .', said Tenzin, '. . . but there's nothing left nowadays. You'd expect to find a shrine or something, but as far as I know there's no memorial of any kind. In fact I think the exact house in which the Thirteenth Dalai Lama lived has been knocked down. There's a small Tibetan settlement nearby, with a carpet factory and a shop, but that's all.'

Despite not having been in Darjeeling for sixteen years, Tenzin was quickly beginning to feel at home. Remarkably little had changed, he said, and to prove the point he led me down a dark flight of steps beneath a Bata shoe shop. We came out in the kitchen of a Chinese family, which owing to the steepness of the terrain was not the basement I had been expecting, but a large sunny room with a balcony. Two elderly ladies were cooking: one stirring a stock pot; the other chopping coriander. They didn't seem at all surprised to see us. Neither did a large tabby cat which, ignoring a caged canary, was vainly trying to grab a string of wind-dried sausages hanging from a hook in the ceiling. On the walls were framed photographs of solemn-faced ancestors, dressed in suits of pre-revolutionary elegance, while open on the kitchen table was the yellowing review section of the Calcutta *Telegraph*, the first two pages of which were devoted to an extract from a book by Paul Theroux, in which he described a visit to Mao's birthplace in Shao-shan.

'I often used to come here for lunch when I lived in Darjeeling,' Tenzin explained. 'You see, this family doesn't really run a restaurant; they just cook for anyone who happens to drop by. The food's excellent and very cheap: at least it was twenty years ago. I daresay it still is.'

'But what are Chinese people doing in Darjeeling? And why is their business being patronised by Tibetans?'

'Well, Tibetans have never had anything against Chinese *people*. Certainly not Tibetans from Kham like me: we're used to them. And you'll see, there are lots of Chinese in Darjeeling. Mostly they're the descendants of the people who got thrown out of Tibet in 1911, when the Manchu Empire was replaced by the Chinese Republic. The Tibetans sent them all back to China by sea from Calcutta, rather then letting them all go overland. Some of them stayed here.'

'So what language do they speak?'

'I speak to them in Nepali, but I guess they also know Mandarin, maybe a bit of Tibetan, perhaps Hindi or Bengali, and certainly some English.'

'Hence the English-language newspaper?'

'I suppose so. The Chinese are a clever race. Tibetans recognise that. We don't feel any instinctive animosity towards them.'

*

After noodle soup and jasmine tea, we walked back up the hill to the offices of *Tibetan Freedom*, the newspaper of which, twenty years before, Tenzin had been the youthful and inexperienced editor.

'It was in Darjeeling that I first began to learn English: in 1963.'

'But *Tibetan Freedom* is a Tibetan-language publication?'

'Oh yes. In those days it was the most important one. Now Darjeeling is more of a backwater and *Sheja*, published in Dharamsala, has a bigger readership and of course tends to get better stories by being at the centre of power. As you know, the principal English-language magazine is the *Tibetan Review*, based in Delhi.'

'I can't really see you as a journalist. Did you enjoy it?'

Tenzin laughed uneasily. 'No, not really. I just wasn't cut out for it. I did the job for three years, but it was not at all easy. For a start, information was hard to come by. There were very few people getting out of Tibet, so, often, to fill the space, we were reduced to translating international press reports. I suppose that served a function at the time. And we also carried news from the various major settlements.'

'So how was it financed?'

'It was subsidised by the administration and also by Gyalo Thondup personally. Not that we needed vast amounts of money. There were only eight pages, printed fortnightly, with three editorial staff and a couple of freelance writers. Let me tell you, we were not highly paid.'

'So was it a government mouthpiece, or did you have editorial freedom?'

'It wasn't just propaganda, but there were certain restrictions. The paper was the Dalai Lama's idea in the first place and he asked his brother to get it going. Controversy was not really what they had in mind. For example, I once ran a story which drew attention to some of the differences which exist between Khampas and the Lhasa Tibetans. I was immediately summoned to Dharamsala to be shouted at. I understand why they were annoyed. The Tibetan refugees were scattered all over India and they wanted to hold everyone together.'

We found the current editor, Mr Tsewang Gyurme Maja, sitting swaddled in a thick woollen wrap, his pencil poised like a dagger over a crisp pile of proofs. He had a smooth, round comfortable face, sleek black hair and large, slightly bulging brown eyes. He beamed at Tenzin and welcomed me to Darjeeling with refined and formal politeness.

His office was on the first floor of a neat wooden building, painted dark green, the windows of which looked north-east across the misty corrugations of Sikkim, to the saw-toothed mountains of Bhutan.

'It's lucky you've come . . .', he said, '. . . as I'll be retiring at the end of the month.'

This seemed suprising as he looked not a day over fifty and in robust good health. 'Retiring? Why's that?'

'Old age. I'm nearly sixty-five. Since 1972 I've combined this newspaper job with that of Welfare Officer for the Darjeeling region. I have responsibility for six thousand people, including more than two thousand chldren at seven different schools. I find I just haven't got the energy any more.'

I expressed my astonishment that he could give up such an agreeable occupation voluntarily: a little newspaper of his own; a warm, bright office in one of the loveliest places in the world; above all the opportunity to live a thoughtful, independent, useful life, free from material want, in dignified moderation and simplicity.

'I would like to read more . . .', Mr Maja continued,

taking very little heed of such objections, '. . . perhaps write a little. But above all I must devote more of my time to religion. Death cannot be so very far away and I must begin to prepare for it. I must study, reflect, meditate. We Tibetans take dying very seriously you know. Not at all like the untidy way you Westerners go about it: pretending it won't happen until the last minute and then getting in a panic.'

'But surely you'll miss all this? Your work? Your colleagues here?'

'I suppose I shall. But then again, perhaps I will be happier. How can I know?'

Had he, I wondered, always been interested in literature and journalism, or was his present occupation an unlooked for gift of fate? Something that exile had thrust upon him and which now could be laid aside with few regrets.

'Well, I have always studied religious literature and philosophy. We do not have much secular writing as you understand it. As for journalism, this is just something I became involved with here in India. In Tibet I was a politician. The members of my family have always been government employees.'

'So what led to an editor's desk in Darjeeling?'

'I escaped from Tibet in '59 and went to Mussoorie, where I asked the administration for employment. The first job they gave me was listening to Radio Lhasa, to find out what the Chinese were broadcasting in Tibetan. This was very fascinating because it enabled me to understand what they really thought of us. It was during the Norbulingka crisis that I had first become aware of a fundamental difference in perception.'

'How do you mean?'

'The Tibetans have always tried to deal with the Chinese rationally, as one human being to another. But I began to realise that the Chinese were simply incapable of treating Tibetans as equals. For example, when the crowds gathered around the Dalai Lama's palace to protect him from abduction, the Chinese wanted to persuade the people to disperse without having to employ their military power. Of course, in the end they used their artillery and many of the demonstrators were killed, but at first they tried more peaceful methods. These were both very funny and very revealing. Around the Norbulingka they had put up loudspeakers, and hour after hour they would broadcast to the people there:

' "If you all go home . . .", they said, ". . . in a couple of days we promise we'll organise an enormous feast with wonderful food: the best you've ever tasted. We'd actually like to have it today, but we're still waiting for the vegetables to arrive. But if you just go home and wait patiently then we'll be able to get on with fixing things up."

'Naturally all the Tibetans were very puzzled. They wondered what the Chinese were talking about and how they could be so stupid. But I began to see that in trying to bribe us like children, they were revealing their complete incomprehension of the Tibetan national character. This has made me very hardline, as far as our dealings with Peking are concerned.'

'So what do you think about attempts to find a compromise solution to the Tibetan problem? Or, more importantly, what does your newspaper have to say about such things?'

'I try to present both sides of the debate, while at the same time trying not to damage Tibetan unity.' (Tenzin snorted and stared briefly at the ceiling.) 'If, for example, there is a disagreement between the Dharamsala establishment and the Tibetan Youth Congress – and as you probably know such disputes are far from infrequent – then I print both points of view. I also, to some extent, present my own opinions in editorials. For example, I feel very strongly that the Dalai Lama is wrong to make concessions over Tibetan sovereignty and in the past I have not hesitated to say so.'

'So you don't feel any necessity to defer to the official line?'

'No, not at all. Of course Dharamsala pays – it costs them about 120,000 rupees [£4,800] a year – and without this subsidy we could not possibly continue as we do now. Part of our task is to smuggle papers into Tibet itself – to let the people there know what is really going on – which is scarcely a good way to make a profit.'

'Do you have much trouble these days?' enquired Tenzin. 'When I was here – during the Cultural Revolution – getting things across the border was all but impossible.'

'It's certainly got harder since the riots in Lhasa. Until a short while ago we were able to send them from Nepal – crossing the border in the normal way at Kodari on the Kathmandu–Lhasa road – but now this is very difficult. Sometimes our carriers chicken out just before they reach the check-post and throw them away. It's very irritating, but I can't say I blame them. The Chinese consider this activity a serious offence and if they get caught they get put in gaol. Probably for a long time.'

He laughed, and putting a pinch of snuff on his thumb nail, inhaled loudly, in each nostril.

'Still, we'll manage. We always have done. In the '70s, the only way in was through Solu-Khumbu; the Everest region. The country is very wild there and the passes are high, around 20,000 feet, but we didn't let such problems stop us.'

Before excusing himself from further conversation and getting back to work on his proofs, Mr Maja had invited us to his house that evening for dinner. There was, he said mysteriously, someone he wanted us to meet; someone who had to remain anonymous, but someone he nonetheless felt sure would be of interest.

It was a murky, moonless night when Tenzin and I set off from the Planters' Club and made our way by feeble torchlight along the narrow, broken paths that led to a distant part of the lower town. Because of the altitude, the temperature drops rapidly in Darjeeling after dark and it was by now very cold. Several guard dogs, approaching their duties with exemplary zeal, came hurtling out barking and snarling, and the warm yellow rectangle of Mr Maja's front door, when Tenzin finally pointed it out, was an extremely reassuring sight; a welcome refuge in the inhospitable blackness.

'His present wife . . .', Tenzin whispered as we stood shivering, waiting for someone to let us in, '. . . was married before and her children by that former marriage are now the Dalai Lama's Representative in Washington and His Holiness's Private Secretary.'

Before I could comment on these intricacies, the door opened and we were ushered into a large, comfortable living room, with sofas, piles of books, old silk *thankas* on the walls, and a small shrine in one corner. The electric lights, which were very dim and flickering, were augmented by the gentle glow of a paraffin lamp on a low table. Mr Maja was nowhere to be seen.

After a few moments he appeared, leading by the arm a frail, bent, grey-haired old gentleman, dressed in smart grey flannels – obviously new – and a starched white shirt. There was a brief kerfuffle while this venerable figure was arranged in an armchair, his slippered feet supported by a footstool, and a pashmina shawl draped tenderly around his stooping shoulders. When he was finally settled, Mr Maja smiled at him benignly and a young girl of nine or ten ran forward and kissed him firmly on the cheek.

'This man is a good friend of mine,' explained Mr Maja. 'For reasons I prefer not to go into, it is better that you should not know his name. Safer. Even today we must be careful. He has a story that I thought you might care to hear. I have explained to him what you are doing and he is happy to talk to you.'

Tenzin replied to this introduction with formal courtesy and the old man leant forward slightly, listening intently to every word, storing them in his memory as if they were things of great and lasting value. After a while he spoke in a subdued voice, looking down at the backs of his battered hands as if he wasn't quite sure whether they belonged to him or not:

'The story of my life is not unusual. Many thousands had similar experiences.'

This self-deprecation drew a murmur of remonstrance and encouragement from Mr Maja. The little girl, leaning on the back of Tenzin's chair, waited with rapt attention.

'My family came from a village not far from Gyantse. I suppose we were a kind of minor local nobility. In all about three hundred people used to work for us.' He smiled wanly at his recollection of a past now so remote and improbable as to seem little more substantial than a dream.

'When the Chinese came to our part of Tibet, we realised we would be in for trouble. We understood enough of their ideology to know what they thought of landowners. So my father called a family meeting to decide what we would do. We discussed trying to escape to Bhutan, but I had very young children, and my father said he certainly had no intention of going without us, so in the end we opted to stay. Surely, we thought, the communists can't be that bad: they're just people after all. If we do what they want and cause no trouble, then probably everything will be all right.

'Anyway, within a few days of their arrival the Chinese

called a meeting, which, they said, all "Class Enemies of the People" were required to attend. We didn't have much doubt that this included us, so my father and I went along of our own free will: we just walked down there. Immediately we were arrested and imprisoned.

'At first the Chinese said they were looking for members of the Tibetan resistance, but after a while they turned their attention to what they called our "crimes". We were criminals, they said, and if we wanted to stay alive we would have to confess. Of course we said we hadn't done anything, but they just kept shouting at us, for hour after hour. "What mistakes have you made? What crimes have you committed against The People?" This went on for about a month.

'One afternoon they told us that we were going to be put on trial. Sure enough the next day we were tied up and dragged in front of a large public meeting. Most of the people there I had never seen before: they certainly didn't come from around Gyantse. The officer in charge of the "trial" stood up and said that thanks to the courage and dedication of his soldiers, The People's Exploiters had been apprehended. "We have done our part . . .", he said, ". . . the rest is up to you." The Chinese would not be able to punish The Exploiters, he explained, unless they had first been denounced by The People.

'Nobody spoke. I don't know how long the silence lasted, but it seemed like a long time. After a while the officer began to get rather cross. Eventually someone, a Tibetan, shouted out that I was a murderer and a liar and that I had been in the resistance. Immediately, before I had a chance to say anything, two soldiers began to hit me in the stomach with their rifle butts.

'After I had been beaten half unconscious, I was dragged away and taken in a truck to the prison in Gyantse: which was actually a few cells in converted stables beneath the post office.

'The following day I began to realise that despite the rough treatment, I had been one of the lucky ones. The other "Class Enemies" from our area had been similarly denounced and beaten up. A few of the younger ones had been selected for "re-education", but the rest had been sent on to the prison in Gyantse. However, rather than bringing them the twenty-two miles by lorry, the Chinese had strapped them across horses, as if they were sacks of vegetables or something, and then driven them over rough country at a gallop. Worse still, they had been tied to Tibetan wooden saddles, so that when they arrived at the prison, they all had broken ribs and some had broken arms. For two days they were left in agony without medical treatment of any kind.

'For the first time we began to understand just what kind of people we were dealing with.

'My father and I spent most of 1960 chained to a wall. We were even left chained up at mealtimes. The guards would just put the food on our knees and to eat we had to bend our heads down like animals. They themselves were hungry most of the time and they talked continuously about the famine in China which had been caused by the policies known as the Great Leap Forward.'

He stopped and looked at Tenzin whose face was quite expressionless. We had both heard plenty of such stories before, but seldom told with such graphic and unemotional simplicity.

'Did you try to make friends with any of the guards? I imagine that in prison one can become desperate to strike up a relationship – however unsatisfactory – with one's gaolers.'

'No, it was not possible. I'm sure they were too frightened. Certainly, if they felt any pity for us, they never showed it. Eventually, towards the end of the year, we were being given only one mug of ground peas a day. This usually had stones and bits of rubbish in it. All the prisoners suffered from stomach problems because of this diet and of course there was no sanitation: just a bucket.

'My father and I became convinced that before long we would either die from disease, or else starve to death. Every day we spent hours discussing how we might possibly escape. In Gyantse there was a building that belonged to the Indian government and which consequently had diplomatic immunity. If only we could get to it, we thought, then maybe we would be safe. Unfortunately, one day when we were talking about this for the thousandth time, we were overheard by a Chinese official who could understand a little Tibetan.

'I spent the next five years in solitary confinement. The other prisoners were by now being taken out to work on labour gangs and it is only thanks to them that I am alive today. Although they themselves were getting very little food, they would find scraps – old cabbage leaves for example – and throw them in through the bars of my cell. The Chinese only gave me a tiny amount of barley flour and I was so thin that by pressing on my stomach I could feel my own backbone.'

'What was your state of mind during these years? As someone who has led a fairly comfortable and secure existence I find it impossible to imagine. Did you think you might go insane? Did the prospect worry you?'

'Well, you feel pain and misery: this goes without saying. But when you have finally accepted your fate, there comes a strange serenity. When life and death are no longer opposites, but merely alternatives between which it is reasonable to choose, then your mind knows a kind of peace. Whether this is sanity, I do not know. Different criteria apply. I clearly remember deciding that I would prefer to die. I asked a guard for a pencil and paper and wrote a letter to the officer in charge of the prison requesting to be shot. This was nothing to do with bravery; it just seemed a sensible way to resolve the situation. Of course all Tibetans believe in reincarnation, so this perhaps makes such situations easier for us to deal with. We are a religious people and although I have never been a monk, never been trained to mediate, I used to repeat various simple mantras while concentrating in my mind's eye on the face of the Dalai Lama. This too, after a while, would bring me a kind of release.

'Anyway, in 1965 I was moved with the other prisoners to Shigatse. There I was no longer alone, and the food was much better. We got *tsampa* (barley flour) and potato soup. Sometimes there was even tea. Eight months passed. One day we were told that we were going to an agricultural commune, a day's ride to the north. Actually it turned out to be a stretch of desert that the Chinese had decided for some reason to cultivate.

'When we got to this place we found that there was nowhere for us to live, so the first thing they made us do was to dig deep holes in the ground. These were then surrounded with barbed wire. At night we had to go down into these pits and the ladder was drawn up. Eventually, of course, huts and proper wooden guard towers were built. In the end I think the camp had about five hundred inmates, of whom we reckoned around eighty used to die each year from overwork and malnutrition. That's nearly 20 per cent, so people could expect to live for only five or six years on average. I myself spent eighteen years in that camp: right through the Cultural Revolution and for nearly a decade afterwards.'

He paused and seemed to shrink back within himself. His eyes, from which the light had been suddenly extinguished, stared vacantly at a point in the middle distance, two feet above the floor. Mr Maja got up and taking off a white woollen scarf wrapped it gently round the old man's neck. This kindness seemed to revive his spirits and he began again with renewed animation.

'After we had built an irrigation scheme – which took

about two months – the ground could be brought under cultivation. We planted pear and apple trees, barley, wheat, and peas. I was put in charge of apples. Believe me, I now know everything there is to know about apples. Although working in the fields probably doesn't sound too bad, I promise you it wasn't very pleasant. We went out before dawn and got back long after dark. We laboured in all weathers and in winter our feet used to freeze. Although we were hungry, we were not allowed to touch any of the food we were growing. Nor were we allowed to talk to one another during the working day. If anyone was caught breaking the rules, the Chinese would make them strip and lie face down on the ground. Two strong men would then push a kind of heavy stick up and down their backbones. It was terribly painful and one man I knew went permanently mad as a result of this punishment. In 1983 I was finally released, after twenty-four years' imprisonment.'

'What on earth did it feel like to be free again? You must have been exultant.'

'Actually I felt very little joy. I walked down the main street in Shigatse and thought "Well, here I am then." But there were Chinese soldiers everywhere. In some respects, the whole of Tibet is one vast prison camp. And what had I to look forward to? I was now an old man. Also I had no money.

'The only thing I wanted to do was to find out what had happened to the rest of my family. I knew that my father had been let out in 1967, but I now discovered that despite his eight years in gaol he had still been treated as a "Class Enemy". It was at the beginning of the Cultural Revolution, so of course he had been shown no mercy. My family had been thrown out of our home and forced to live in the stables. Because they came from the "Exploiter" class, they were not allowed to join the commune, nor were they allowed to speak to anyone, or even to look at them directly. Other local people used to hide food for them, or else they would have starved. Or at least starved sooner. In 1970 my father finally did die from malnutrition. My mother was already dead: just from grief I think. Apparently my two brothers had also been arrested and imprisoned. The elder one was released in 1980, but for two years his hands had been chained behind his back. As a result, his arms are so weak that today he cannot even wash his own hair. My younger brother spent fifteen years in prison. He came out to find that his son had been executed in 1963 for being in the Tibetan Youth Resistance. My sister's son had also been executed at the same time. My own children were alive, but because they came from the "Exploiter" class they had not been allowed to go to school. They were completely illiterate and had had to survive by begging. What's left of my family is still in Gyantse. They have one cow, so I suppose this is some improvement.'

'What really angers me . . .', said Mr Maja after a long silence, '. . . is hearing people claim that the Chinese only behaved badly in Tibet during the Cultural Revolution. "Look what happened in China itself," they say. "Millions of people were killed; the entire professional and intellectual class dismantled; even Deng Xaoping sent to labour on a commune." But the Chinese began to murder Tibetans by the thousand in 1959 – seven years before the Cultural Revolution – and they're still at it, fifteen years after it was supposed to have ended. The Chinese say they want to create a classless society and that's why the remnants of feudalism must be crushed. But in fact their main motive has always been to get rid of educated, strong-minded Tibetans who might try to oppose them. They persuade themselves that everything they've done in Tibet has been for the Tibetans themselves – for the "revolutionary masses" – whereas in fact, from first to last their actions have been governed by national self-interest. They wanted to secure their western borders; they wanted Tibet's natural resources. Every other motive is pure hypocrisy. For thirty years they've treated us with contempt.'

The old man said nothing, but smiled at the little girl, and stretched out his hand. Despite his sufferings, his spirit had remained intact. Even his frail and battered body seemed at that moment strangely delicate and refined.

Chapter 10

BANARAS

'I can't say that I'm looking forward to this next bit,' said Tenzin goomily on the morning of our departure from Darjeeling. The bit in question was a 400-mile journey south-west to Banaras, at the heart of the Gangetic plain.

Around midday we set out on the tortuous road back to Siliguri, turning our backs on Tibet, and pausing only for a final gaze at the snows of Kanchenjunga, before descending into the clammy shadows of the forest. The road and Darjeeling's famous narrow-gauge railway run intertwined down to the plains (there are 132 level crossings in about sixty miles), but landslides during the previous monsoon – chiefly due to indiscriminate felling – had ruptured the track in a dozen places. Gradually the wind gusting into our faces blew warm and I was reminded of the essentially perverse nature of travel in India: when one is stifling on the plains, one dreams of the cool, resinous breeze of the hills; when one is shivering at 8,000 feet, one craves the blood-hot embrace of sea level.

Train travel in India is invariably tedious and uneventful: one talks lethargically to one's fellow passengers; one looks out of the window at an ocean of flat, brown land drifting imperceptibly past; one frets at the length of time spent standing at stations; and one reflects for the fiftieth time that on the next occasion one really will bring an inflatable pillow/longer novel/bottle of whisky/mosquito spray/etc.

The train from Siliguri was certainly no exception as it lumbered for interminable hours – twenty-three to be exact – across an unchanging landscape, stopping at obscure towns teeming with human life, where no one from the outside world ever thinks to go. It was six in the evening by the time we finally reached Mughal Sarai, a junction just outside Banaras, on the main line from Delhi to Calcutta. This being the nearest that Indian Railways was prepared to take us to our destination, we stumbled out resentfully and travelled the final few miles into town by road.

Morning dawned, still and blue and clear: one of those glorious autumn days in India which somehow resist every attempt to discountenance their unblemished serenity; the cacophony of lorries, buses, cars, rickshaws, the hooting and yelling of the streets, all being miraculously assimilated into the prevailing mood of golden calm.

A brief phone call to the Central Institute of Higher Tibetan Studies revealed that its Principal, Samdong Rinpoche, was unable to see us until the late afternoon, so Tenzin and I, having several hours to play at being tourists, decided to take a walk to the banks of the Ganges.

Preparations were in progress for a festival – as they generally are in Banaras – and down the centre of the road leading to the river, stakes were being driven into the tarmac to separate those on their way to bathe in the redeeming waters, from those returning, duly beatified.

Galaxies of fairy lights and festoons of tinsel were being draped across the open shop fronts, while loudspeakers, tied to lampposts by a web of cables abandoned by some Gargantuan tarantula, belted out Hindi film music at a sufficient number of decibels to awaken even the most drowsy and negligent deity.

Assaulted by popular, devotional Hinduism, it is sometimes hard to believe that it is a manifestation of the same religion that for three thousand years has been the cradle of mystics and philosophers.

'Durga Puja,' said Tenzin contemptuously. 'It's terrible this festival. Thousands of animals are slaughtered here in Banaras alone. Imagine how many there must be all over India. The Tibetans here sometimes force themselves to watch these sacrifices as a spiritual exercise; to develop compassion for other creatures. Awful.' He shook his head sorrowfully.

Durga, blood-drenched and skull-garlanded, is the terrifying and wrathful form of India's great mother goddess, Devi, and certainly her annual propitiation is best avoided by the squeamish, or anyone with a fondness for goats. Such deities are of course associated with a vast and complex mythology, an epic of gods and men, by means of which technicolour drama, religious truth may (it is hoped) be indirectly perceived. Down on the streets, however, Durga often seems to be merely a conduit for the violence hidden just beneath India's superficially pacific face; a gruesome icon of pain, providing a focal point for all the rage, misery, and frustration felt by the country's suffering millions.

Fortunately, on the *ghats* by the Ganges all was, as yet, relatively tranquil. The greatest commotion was being caused by gangs of men with high-pressure hoses, clearing several feet of compacted mud – a legacy of the monsoon floods – from the bathing steps down into the river. One or two *saddhus*, or naked holy men, posed happily for photographs, while young boys splashed and laughed in the filthy water, ducking each other beneath the scum and floating detritus. Several pious matrons, saris transparent after their ablutions, got on with the family washing, apparently oblivious to the rumpus. Occasionally a tattered island of marigolds, or splinter of charred sandalwood from Manikarnika, the burning or cremation *ghat*, drifted slowly past on its way to the distant Bay of Bengal.

Banaras, which claims to be the oldest continuously occupied city in the world, is India's supreme centre of pilgrimage, a place where heaven and earth are believed to coincide, a *tirtha*, or ford, across the river of *samsara* – the inexorable round of death and rebirth – to the far shore of spiritual liberation. Even the ground plan of the city is regarded as a mandala, a sacred diagram, representative of all India. At dawn, when the pilgrims wait to pray to the sun god, Surya, symbol of the Divine, worshipped by Hindus under many names and in countless forms, it is a place to move even the most determined atheist to tears.

Yet Banaras today, despite the palaces and temples that line the western bank of the river, is still a city which bears the scars of despoliation. In 1194, the Muslim army of Muhammad Ghuri destroyed a thousand temples – 1,400 camels being needed to carry off the plunder – and for the next five hundred years various *jihad*s afflicted Banaras with intermittent pillage, slaughter, and demolition. As a result, there is no major Hindu complex that predates the seventeenth-century reign of Aurangzeb: Islamic zealot and last of the great Mogul emperors. Not that Hinduism was the only victim: it was the Muslim invasions which finally drove Buddhism from the land of its birth, ending the spiritual commerce between India and Tibet which had been in progress since the seventh century.

*

Samdong Rinpoche had said that he would see us at five o'clock, so partly to kill time and partly because it's an extremely pleasant thing to do in itself, Tenzin and I decided to take an afternoon stroll through the Deer Park at Sarnath. Only four miles north of Banaras, Sarnath is also holy ground, the Deer Park being where Siddhartha Gautama, the Buddha, preached his first sermon and set out the fundamental tenets of his new religion. Once there were monasteries housing perhaps fifteen hundred monks; now the brick foundations of their cells are all that remain, besides a 300 foot high *stupa* – or reliquary monument – that proved substantial enough to defy even the most determined and persistent of vandals.

Two Tibetan pilgrims were circumambulating the *stupa* and Tenzin asked them where they came from. 'From Sera . . .', they said, the new Sera, '. . . near Mysore in South India.' Forty years before they might have replied 'Lhasa' or 'Shigatse'.

Less than half a mile from the Deer Park, in a quiet and leafy avenue, stand the neat, modern buildings of the Central Institute for Higher Tibetan Studies. When Tenzin and I arrived for our appointment, the students seemed to be away on holiday. The whole campus was deserted and it was only with the aid of a venerable Indian watchman, who would not have inspired the slightest misgiving in even the most timid of burglars, that we successfully located the principal's office.

Samdong Rinpoche turned out to be a monk in his early fifties, of medium height, his closely cropped hair greying slightly. He had surprisingly delicate features, but these were belied by a grave and authoritative manner, a suggestion of steel beneath a silken exterior. Holding aside a curtain, he ushered us into a large room, where, eschewing the place of honour behind an imposing desk, he settled himself on a low chair and indicated that we might care to do likewise.

I said that his institute had a great reputation – a pleasantry which was no more than the truth – and that perhaps he could explain how it had come into being. I had been told, I said, that nowhere was doing more to counteract the devastation wrought by the Cultural Revolution.

Samdong Rinpoche left this compliment sail past him unnoticed, and for a moment said nothing.

'Actually . . .', he began, solemnly, '. . . the nature of this institution is not very clear in the mind of the Tibetan authorities. Or the Indian authorities for that matter. It began as an ill-conceived solution to a particular problem. The problem no longer exists, but the institute continues just as before.'

Surely, I protested, he was being too modest. Samdong Rinpoche fixed me with a gimlet stare, as if modesty, as much as pride, were an emotion with which he was mercifully unacquainted.

'It is true that we have a good library and we are doing our best to improve it. This is important as the Chinese have destroyed most of the libraries in Tibet, chiefly, as you say, during the Cultural Revolution. In India there are now three good collections of Tibetan books. Here in Sarnath; the Library of Tibetan Works and Archives in Dharamsala; and the Sikkim Research Institute of Tibetology in Gangtok. We currently have around seven thousand volumes of the traditional Tibetan loose-leaved variety; slightly more than forty thousand bound in the Western style; and around a hundred and twenty thousand on microfilm and microfiche. So we have made a start; we hope to expand.'

'Is there, to your knowledge, a significant library left anywhere in Tibet? It is said that the Chinese have been extremely thorough.'

‘A Hungarian scholar who came here told me the one at Sakya monastery still seemed relatively intact, but I cannot confirm his impression.’

‘So do you think that some Tibetan works may have disappeared for ever?’

‘It is my opinion that around a hundred thousand titles are irretrievably lost.’

A short silence ensued while Tenzin and I digested this appalling statistic. Samdong Rinpoche sat, unmoving and expressionless.

It occurred to me that his list of libraries in India had not included any of those at the large monasteries re-established in exile.

‘You are going to Sera? Well then you will see for yourself. The facilities there are functional: barely adequate. As to your first question: this institute came into being due to the large number – fifteen hundred or so – of monks being housed in deplorable conditions at Buxa Lama Camp, up near the Bhutanese border. There was no opportunity for them to study, or to do anything useful, and many were dying of tuberculosis. Some had followed His Holiness the Dalai Lama into exile; others had fled to India because of violent attacks on their monasteries. I myself left Drepung, near Lhasa, when it was shelled by the communist forces. No one knew what to do with them, so in 1964, as a partial solution to the problem, it was decided that a hundred and fifty would be allowed to study at the Sanskrit University in Banaras. Accommodation was provided here in Sarnath.’

‘But when did this place become an academic institution in its own right?’

‘Samdong Rinpoche held up an admonitory finger. ‘I am coming to that. By 1970 the situation had completely changed. It seemed that the new agricultural settlements in south India were going to prosper and that therefore the Buxa monks could be successfully resettled. The future of Tibetan studies here was very much in doubt. Eventually, however, it was decided that we should try to set up an autonomous institute, entirely independent of the Sanskrit University.'

'Were you yourself instrumental in this decision?'

'The Dalai Lama asked me to take charge in 1971; before that I had been a schoolteacher in Simla and Dalhousie. When I arrived the broad outline had been set out, but nothing further had been achieved.'

'So what precisely did His Holiness ask you to do?'

'I was given four main objectives: to preserve Tibetan culture and tradition by all available means; to restore the lost Indian texts which are nowadays found only in Tibetan (in other words to supervise their translation back into Sanskrit); to provide opportunities for students from Indian areas, who traditionally went to Tibet for their higher education; and finally to experiment with the traditional Tibetan Buddhist education within the format of a modern university degree course. We wanted some of our students to have qualifications that would be recognised elsewhere. His Holiness the Dalai Lama is very anxious that Tibetans should have access to foreign centres of learning: that there should be a reciprocal relationship, and mutual understanding thereby increased.'

'But how was this to be financed? It all sounds very expensive.'

'Oh, this institute has always been paid for by the Indian government. It is very, very, generous of them. We may have had our disagreements with the authorities, but in the end we have always managed to settle our differences.'

'Differences? About what?'

'Well, you have spent some time in this country; you know its strengths and its weaknesses. Intelligent decisions may be taken at the centre in Delhi, but they still have to be implemented by the local bureaucracy. At this lower level we have often met with strong opposition. For example, some people think that Tibetan traditional education is completely out of date; of no use whatever in the modern world. They get very annoyed when they see Indian taxpayers' money being spent on it and do everything they can to frustrate the good intentions of their own government.

'Then you must remember that this is Banaras: the holy city of the Hindu religion. Many Hindus are not at all pleased to see their government subsidising Buddhism. They think that some Buddhist teachings are opposed to Hindu practice – in particular their caste system – which of course they are, though we would never dream of interfering.

'And finally there is corruption. Only last August I had to threaten to resign over the appointment of a person supported by a minister in the state government.'

Samdong Rinpoche stopped for a moment, as if having involuntarily recalled an extremely unpleasant experience. He went on with an expression of immense distaste.

'This minister is himself a very rough and uncultured person, a most uncivilised individual, yet he insisted that his candidate should be appointed to a senior post in this institute, even though he had none of the requisite qualifications. There was a great deal of argument and ill feeling – even threats were issued – but in the end, after very sharp disputes with the highest functionaries, I succeeded in getting this appointment stopped. And I myself am still here, even though there were many times when I thought it most unlikely that I would be able to continue. You see what these people in the end are forced to recognise is that I am very faithful to India. It is still a good country, despite some serious deficiencies. The democratic system is quite strong and even when facing political antagonism at a very high level, upright persons with moral strength still have ground on which to make a stand.'

On the evidence of this short speech, I decided that the rinpoche would make a very formidable enemy indeed and I began to feel slightly sorry for the corrupt and uncultivated minister, who had clearly taken on rather more than he had bargained for.

'What I don't quite understand . . .', said Tenzin, '. . . is how the institute differs from the monastic system of education. What exactly do you teach here that they don't?' As an afterthought he added: 'I was at Sera in the 1950s. Not that I learned very much, I'm afraid.'

Samdong Rinpoche smiled at him approvingly, partly it seemed because he had once been a monk, but mostly because of the self-effacing assessment of his academic achievements.

'We offer a nine-year course to an MA degree. In the monasteries, to reach the level of *geshe* takes a minimum of fifteen years. As far as religious studies are concerned, the monasteries do a much better job. But here we offer a slightly wider syllabus. We teach root and commentary texts in both Tibetan and Sanskrit; then students must study either English or Hindi, plus an additional modern subject. At the moment we offer economics; political science; Tibetan history; and Pali.'

'But you think for the study of religion and philosophy the traditional monastic environment is superior to that of a university?'

'Of that there is no question. At Drepung, I was a very average student. And yet as far as philosophy and logic are concerned, I am now able to debate with all the visting professors from European and American universities, without any hesitation or embarrassment. This is because the grounding I received in Tibet was such a good one. Since the Chinese invasion many people have been highly critical of the Tibetan monastic system. The Chinese themselves have regarded it with great hostility. But what they overlooked, or were not prepared to see, was the very high level of education that it could provide. They claimed that the monks were ignorant and wasteful of the community's resources. Of course, not all monks were brilliant students, but many were very well trained. Tibetan traditional scholarship was of a very high standard and so far, after thirty years in a foreign country, I have not seen it equalled.'

'To what do you attribute this excellence? One of the chief criticisms I have heard levelled at the monastic system is that it involves a huge amount of memorisation – chiefly of sacred texts – and that in consequence there is very little room for original or creative thought. In other words that Tibetan Buddhist education is suffocated by an excessive respect for tradition.'

Samdong Rinpoche stared in horror. Clearly he had not previously encountered such an outrageous level of heresy.

'The most important thing about Tibetan monastic education. . .', he replied with intimidating gravity, '. . . is that it concentrates on developing the mind of the student. It teaches him *how* to think. It tries to awaken the potential of the entire intelligence; to generate sensitivity and receptiveness to any kind of knowledge or situation. Because of this emphasis, information is easily retained. That which I learned in the monastery, I will never forget. Nowadays I learn many things on many subjects, but within a week half of them have vanished.'

Feeling disinclined to venture further down this controversial path, I tried a different tack:

'Working as you do to piece together the fragments of Tibetan culture, do you ever find it difficult to restrain your sense of anger and outrage?'

'Anger is out of the question. It is not a suitable response: not for a Buddhist monk; not for any good Tibetan. From the beginning I have striven to control harsh feelings towards the Chinese: even though my own monastery, in south-eastern Tibet, was destroyed long before the Lhasa Uprising. I come from a remote village, close to where the borders of China, Tibet, Burma, and India all meet. The nearest large town was actually Gauhati in India, about fifteen days away by horse. Our village had only twelve houses and was surrounded by thick forest. It was very isolated: completely cut off from the world.' He paused for a minute, as if unsure whether or not to go on.

'My own personal history is unimportant, but in one sense it is interesting. I was born into a very poor family. We were small farmers and had to struggle to stay alive from one year's end to the next. Of course, in those circumstances there were no educational opportunities for children whatever. Then, when I was three and a half, I was recognised as the reincarnation of Samdong. An oracle had identified our village and accurately described our house, so a search party was sent out. I was one of three brothers and at first it was unclear which one of us was the correct reincarnation. However, I passed a number of tests including the identification of eight or nine objects that had belonged to my predecessor. I was then taken to live in the monastery and enthroned shortly afterwards. Immediately I was provided with a tutor: a very kind man and a great scholar.

'In 1950, at the age of eleven, I was sent to Lhasa and enrolled at Drepung monastery. There I was to begin my higher education. However, when I was only half way through my course of study I was obliged to leave Tibet due to the violent behaviour of the Chinese. This I considered a great personal misfortune, but thanks to the intervention of His Holiness the Dalai Lama, I was able to resume my education in India and in 1968 I was finally awarded the degree of Geshe Lharampa.' Lharampa being the highest category of *geshe* degree, of which only sixteen are awarded each year, I decided to treat any of the rinpoche's further remarks about his meagre academic abilities with a fair degree of scepticism.

'Now, leaving aside the question of whether or not I really was the reincarnation of Samdong. . . .'

'There is some doubt?'

'Well . . . perhaps . . . I am not sure. But leaving aside this question, it is certain that I have been extremely fortunate. I have had the opportunity to live in a great monastery like Drepung and to receive teachings from the highest gurus. If I had not been recognised as a reincarnate lama, I would not even have been a monk. My life would have been very miserable in all respects: material, educational, and spiritual. Quite probably I would have been a fighter and killed many Chinese, or instead, been killed by them.

'Which brings me back to your question about whether I feel angry about what they have done in Tibet: the murders they have committed; the libraries they have burned. My own brother, who had none of my advantages, became a guerrilla in the Chushi Gangdruk. His hatred of the Chinese was extremely passionate and he tells me that he was responsible for the deaths of many Chinese soldiers. Of course both his anger and his motivation were very understandable, but that does not make them correct. After all, killing is killing. Today he grows older and begins to repent. He comes to see me to ask what he must do to avoid the consequences of his sinful past. I have a great deal of sympathy for his position, but I tell him that he must begin by recognising that what he did was wrong. To be a good Buddhist, to be a good Tibetan, one must eliminate anger and strive to feel only compassion for one's enemies.'

'But isn't this to require all men to behave like saints? Your brother was obviously very brave, prepared to sacrifice his life so that others might live in freedom, and in many countries he would be considered a hero. I am sure that many Tibetans would consider his actions heroic.'

'That may be so, but from a religious point of view he was mistaken. Killing is wrong: under *any* circumstances. And now . . .', said Samdong Rinpoche, getting up hurriedly, '. . . let me show you round our library.'

As we left the office, I found myself feeling rather indignant. It was all very well for a scholar in Banaras, his salary paid by the Indian government, to espouse such a noble morality, but my sympathies remained firmly with his brother; the passionate sinner. No wonder the Tibetans had lost their country when those with the courage to fight had been undermined by their political and spiritual leadership. On the other hand, I couldn't help liking the rinpoche: he was undoubtedly a clever and dedicated man, acting in accordance with high principles, which clearly he himself found awkward at times.

Outside in the garden the Indian watchman was waiting for us in the shade of a tree. He must have been standing there for well over an hour. Although he presumably saw Samdong Rinpoche nearly every day, he immediately came shuffling forward, bent down, and touched his sandalled feet. The exiled lama was to him a holy man and the fact that he was a Buddhist – whereas the watchman himself was undoubtedly a Hindu – made not the slightest difference. The recipient of his veneration caressed the old man's head in an absent-minded sort of way. For a moment I glimpsed the instinctive understanding that exists between inhabitants of the same cultural world. At the same time I was acutely aware of being on the far side of the canyon which still separates West from East.

In the late afternoon of the following day, Tenzin and I left Banaras and caught the train to Gaya. (Actually it was the overnight train to Calcutta; Gaya being a stop just five hours down the line.) Like Banaras, Gaya is a place particularly sacred to Hindus and every year it is visited by thousands of pilgrims who come to pray for the spiritual wellbeing of their ancestors. Our destination, however, was Bodh Gaya, a village seven miles to the south of the city, the site of the Buddha's enlightenment, the holiest shrine in the Buddhist world, and for centuries the foremost objective of Tibetan pilgrimage to India.

It was around nine-thirty when the train came to a shuddering and discordant halt and we jumped down onto the darkened platform, just failing to tread on a woman lying full-length in the dust, suckling her frail and diminutive baby. Gaya is in the state of Bihar: the poorest and most overpopulated in India. Although there were a few lights high up in the roof, they were so feeble as to emphasise, rather than to disperse, the diesel and soot-soured gloom.

In contrast, the street outside was a pulsating fairground of coloured bulbs and neon strips.

'Oh no,' said Tenzin. 'It's Durga Puja again. I should have known they'd make a meal of it in Gaya.'

A rickshaw ride in search of a bed for the night quickly turned into a guided tour around one of the more disagreeable circles of hell. Seemingly in every street a temporary shrine had been erected, from which the gruesome image of the goddess, draped with cadavers and annointed with gore, glared out malevolently at the seething throng of her wragged and pitiful admirers. A hundred loudspeakers thumped Hindi love songs into the stale and sticky air, while gangs of youths jostled and punched one another in an atmosphere of simmering sexual aggression.

Needless to say all the hotels were full to overflowing, their lobbies packed with huddled bodies, like mortuaries in a war zone. All except one that is; but after a cursory examination of the offered room, its one sagging bed besmirched with urethral stains and rectal smears, Tenzin and I decided simultaneously that the station floor was incomparably more hygienic and in fact preferable in every respect.

A small bribe pressed into the palm of a railway official actually procured us a wooden bench, which after a couple of hours in Gaya already seemed an unwonted luxury.

'It's not too bad, really,' said Tenzin. 'And . . .', he added approvingly, '. . . there are even some Tibs over there on the floor.'

'Tibs?'

'Tibetans; young ones. Look, a couple, over there in the corner.'

I was awoken at first light by a man who, in order to tell me that my brief tenancy of railway property had expired, jabbed me hard in the ribs with the wooden handle of his mop. The floor was already empty and the young Tibetans had gone, but from a nearby washroom came the sound of hawking and spitting and retching and sloshing – India's dawn chorus – as her inhabitants slough off the pollution of the night and gird themselves for the ordeal of another uncertain day. I went to join them with a toothbrush but quickly returned. By the wall opposite the door, a yellow lake of urine, fully nine inches deep and ten feet across, was lapping against the stained and fractured tiles.

'Buddha said that to live is to suffer,' I observed sententiously to Tenzin as we stood outside in the freshish air. 'If by living he meant living in Bihar I'm bound to say he had a point.'

My more practical companion, who was looking surprisingly spruce, merely nodded and set about trying to find an auto-rickshaw willing and able (at least half of them seemed to have punctures) to run us the seven miles out to Bodh Gaya.

Despite the unrelieved squalor of the town, God – or whatever deity is so fortunate as to own the freehold on this particular patch of the earth – appeared to have been quite busy in the countryside overnight. The entire landscape seemed to have been mist-sprayed assiduously, and a fine and sparkling dew gave flickering highlights to every dusty leaf and blade of sagging grass. After fifteen minutes' chugging along, a cool wind chafing our faces, we were both feeling a good deal better.

'Bihar is a ridiculous place,' said Tenzin good humouredly. 'It's quite out of control of the central government you know. The whole state is run by gangsters – "dacoits" they call them here; or "goondas"; they have lots of words for criminals in Bihar – who are all armed to the teeth and do exactly as they like. Even this road, which looks peaceful enough now, is extremely dangerous after dark. People are always getting held up and Bodh Gaya is effectively cut off until dawn.'

It was at precisely this point that the chain parted company with the drive shaft and the auto-rickshaw came squealing to a halt.

After a shower and a recuperative late breakfast of vegetable curry and chapattis, Tenzin and I set off to walk down to the famous Mahabodhi Temple. This incorporates within its precincts an ancient peepul, or bo tree, under the grandfather of which, in 528 BC, the meditating Buddha is said to have been enlightened as to the true nature of reality and the most effective means of dealing with it. All along the roadside were flimsy stalls, attended by a hundred or so Tibetans, attempting to sell scarves and pullovers to a handful of indifferent pilgrims. It was a warm day and no amount of entrepreneurial zeal seemed likely to be rewarded. We stopped to talk to one man. His summer home was in Mussoorie, he said. Bodh Gaya was a good place: peaceful and at the same time, quite profitable. It was certainly much better than travelling from town to town, being beaten up and robbed: which was an occupational hazard these days, and one becoming less and less easy to avoid. It wasn't that Tibetans were singled out for this treatment; it was just that India was getting progressively more lawless. Why? Well doubtless overpopulation had something to do with it. And then there were all these violent films and videos people watched nowadays. The spread of television also tended to make people aware that others were much better off than they were. And it showed them things they couldn't hope to buy: like cars and air conditioning. To say nothing of corruption in public life, which became everyday more apparent. He seemed a thoughtful kind of shopkeeper.

I then asked him about the merchandise he was selling; or rather attempting to sell. No, he agreed, it was not good quality – it came from Ludhiana in Punjab and was woven from artificial fibre – but then it was cold for only a couple of months a year in northern India and most people preferred to buy a different garment every season. It was a deplorably feckless attitude: enough to break the heart of someone from a cold country where good clothes kept you alive, were made only with the best available wool, and were lovingly repaired whenever occasion demanded. But then, that was India for you.

At the entrance to the temple itself, a Sri Lankan monk in a brilliant orange robe was hosing down the marble pavement. This, as well as much of the gold leaf on the statuary, looked extremely new. Tenzin said he thought it was probably Japanese Buddhists – these days visiting Bodh Gaya in increasing numbers – whose donations had made such improvements possible.

The sun was now high in a whitened sky and from the nearby road came the shrieks of schoolchildren playing football, the rumble of an occasional lorry, and the steady honking of taxis and rickshaws. Perhaps, I suggested, we should return in the evening, when it would be cooler and calmer. Tenzin readily agreed.

We were stopped on our way out by a Tibetan, who politely enquired if either of us could spare a few rupees as, he explained, with the help of eloquent gestures, his wooden hand protectors had been worn through by countless thousands prostrations, and his pilgrimage was in general need of a thorough overhaul and refit. Although he promptly handed over the sum requested, Tenzin seemed to do so with notably little enthusiasm. 'My family gives a lot of money to religion . . .', he grumbled when his compatriot was well out of earshot, '. . . but it's not up to individuals to ask for it. This fellow's been living in India too long. The next thing you know, he'll be begging.'

Crossing the road, we entered the shady porch of the nearby Tibetan monastery: an institution of particular importance as the Dalai Lama's senior tutor, Ling Rinpoche, had been its abbot until his death in 1983. There we found Jigme Jimba, an elderly monk with enormous, translucent, Buddha-like ears, eating a bowl of boiled rice and, between mouthfuls, talking to a young novice in a schoolmasterly sort of way.

'Hmmm . . .' he said, indistinctly, after Tenzin had described the purpose and progress of our travels, but then, putting down his bowl, having apparently decided to give us the benefit of the doubt, he went on: 'In that case you'd better have tea,' and poured himself a large mugful.

His lunch complete, he got up and shuffled off down a darkened corridor. Tenzin and I followed him in the uncertain hope that this was what he had intended.

'The monastery is fairly quiet at the moment,' he called over his shoulder. 'We have sixty rooms for pilgrims, but most of them are empty. When His Holiness the Dalai Lama comes here, if we had six thousand rooms we'd have to put fifty people in each.' Leading us out into the open air, we began to climb an external staircase, eventually coming out on the flat concrete roof of the building. From fifty feet up there was a good view of the Mahabodhi Temple complex and in the opposite direction, of a large grassy field with a brightly painted Tibetan pavilion to one side of it.

'That's where His Holiness gives his teachings. More than a quarter of a million people come to hear him: from Ladakh, Zanskar, Kulu, Manali, Lahul, Spiti, Dolpo, Mustang, Khumbu, as well as for Sikkim, Bhutan . . .'

'The Himalayas must be deserted,' I whispered to Tenzin, as the litany continued.

'They are, very nearly,' he replied.

'Not to mention all the Westerners from America, Canada, Australia, Britain, France, Switzerland, Germany, Italy. . . .'

'It really is amazing: I've been twice.'

'And this is where His Holiness stays,' said Jigme Jimba, reluctantly cutting short his list and struggling to produce a large key from somewhere underneath his robes. He opened the door of a rooftop apartment. Inside there was a modest antechamber; a bedroom containing a hard single bed; and a bathroom with bright pink enamel fittings. The general impression was one of comfortable austerity. 'His Holiness puts a cushion on the floor here . . .', observed Jigme Jimba, pointing, '. . . so that he can meditate looking out of the window at the Mahabodhi Temple.'

Not for the first time I reflected that if power corrupts and absolute power corrupts absolutely, then someone has clearly forgotten to explain this universal truth to the Fourteenth Dalai Lama of Tibet. Literally worshipped by several million people, he continues to live life free from indulgence or ostentation, and in a land where spiritual charlatans are scarcely unknown, to provide a spotless moral example.

'Obviously, the accommodation for His Holiness is very new . . .', said Tenzin, '. . . but how long has this monastery been here at Bodh Gaya?'

'Well, the main building was put up in 1938.'

'And how long have you been here?'

'I came in '47.'

'Before the invasion then?'

'Yes. In those days, when the border was open, many Tibetan monks used to come down to visit the holy places in India and Nepal: Bodh Gaya; Sarnath; Lumbini; Kushinagar. Not all of them remained behind of course. I came as a pilgrim, but then the Chinese arrived in Tibet and it seemed a good idea to stay.'

'Where did you begin your pilgrimage?'

'I set out from my monastery in Amdo. Actually there were two of us. We passed my companion, Lobsang Palden, on our way up the stairs just now. First of all we visited the holy places of Central Tibet. Then, after a year or so, we carried on across the mountains to India.'

'That must be about fifteen hundred miles in all.'

'I suppose so,' replied Jigme Jimba, seemingly unimpressed by his own exertions, 'but you must remember we were on horseback for the first part of the way. We only walked from Lhasa.'

*

Back at our hotel, we found the manager in a state of considerable excitement. He was a nattily dressed young man from Delhi, who having known the euphoria of gaining secure government employment, was now tasting the bitter pill of exile to (as he saw it) one of the more remote, poverty-stricken, and generally benighted spots in the whole of the Indian subcontinent. His kitchen supplies, which had been due that morning, had so far failed to arrive.

'Bihar is run by gangsters,' he fulminated. 'All the officials are corrupt. Sometimes these hoodlums turn up in Gaya, take over the best hotel,' (I refrained from asking exactly which one he meant), 'stay for a week, then leave without paying. What do the police do? Nothing. They are too frightened. They are corrupt also. And these goondas have better guns. I tell you . . .', he went on, jabbing an accusatory finger in my direction, '. . . you British are partly to blame. This democratic system was your fault. When we got independence, we should have become a *fully* socialist country; then we would not have had these dacoits to deal with.'

As gently as I could, I tried to point out that corruption was not exclusive to capitalist countries, certain socialist regimes having proved less than blameless in this respect. He looked deeply unconvinced.

'But the USSR and China . . .', he protested, '. . . look at the great strides they are making.'

Tenzin sighed and wandered off. Such sentiments were a reminder that despite the political animosity between the two countries, many Indians, particularly young educated ones, are still determined to believe that China had succeeded where India has failed: in spite of all evidence to the contrary and all that the Tibetans might tell them were they only prepared to listen. Both nations freed themselves from foreign domination in the late 1940s, both had underdeveloped economies and huge and growing populations. Nowadays, they believe, the Chinese common man is better off than his Indian counterpart: a prosperity which has been achieved by greater righteousness and rigid discipline. The socialist dream was not faulty; it was the Indian devotees who were insufficiently rigorous and pure.

The approach of evening had lent numinous refinement to the atmosphere of the Mahabodhi Temple. The noise of the traffic had died away, the schoolchildren had gone home, and the shadows were slowly lengthening into a soft and timeless twilight. Tenzin and I strolled around the perimeter of the temple gardens, past the pool where the Buddha is said to have bathed after his enlightenment, and stopped simultaneously to breathe in the scent of roses and the mood of immemorial calm. A flock of pigeons clattered off a nearby roof and fell in a silent swoop towards the glassy water, their reflections racing to join them.

Down by the bo tree itself, a group of Tibetan monks, perhaps thirty in all, were seated cross-legged on the grass, quietly chanting and blowing intermittently into conch-shell horns. They had been joined in their devotions by a Japanese, three Sri Lankans, a group of eight white-robed figures whom I took to be Korean, and a small woolly dog: some fraction Lhasa Apso.

The sight of pilgrims from different corners of Asia, briefly united at the birthplace of their religion, was a profoundly satisfactory one. Buddhism took over a thousand years to establish itself as the great pan-Asian creed – and during this prolonged expansion it tended to develop in different ways in different lands, adapting itself to the climate, the terrain, the character of the people, and the pre-existent culture. Unlike Christianity, it had no divinely inspired text, and no pope, patriarch, or centralised authority of any kind. In consequence it grew organically, and after a few centuries the outer branches were well out of sight of the roots and predictably dissimilar in appearance. As a result Buddhists in, say, Japan, tend to know very little about their co-religionists in Sri Lanka or Thailand, and one often hears the same kind of disparaging remarks made about what is perceived to be an aberrant or inferior tradition, as, for example, the Orthodox are apt to level at Catholic Christians, or vice versa.

Owing to both the geographical isolation of its homeland and to the vigour of the animist and shamanistic tradition onto which it was grafted, Tibetan Buddhism was long misunderstood by the outside world. When first encountered by Europeans, it was perceived to be so different from the Buddhism of Sri Lanka and south-east Asia that it became known as 'Lamaism'. This was partly due to the particular importance the Tibetans appeared to place on the role of the lama, or spiritual mentor, and partly because it seemed a tradition so baroque in comparison with austere early schools, that it was assumed to be a corrupt and inferior form of the religion, debased by its borrowings from Hinduism and the Tibetan occult.

This pejorative assessment is no longer fashionable, because it is now understood that Tibetan Buddhism is derived from the late Indian variety and is hence the final phase of an extremely long process of continuous development. Furthermore, it is also appreciated that there is really no such thing as 'pure' Buddhism – there are only different schools with some fundamentals in common and much else about which they profoundly disagree – and therefore there can be no such thing as 'impure' Buddhism either.

For their part, the Tibetans have shown themselves to be no more immune to cultural chauvinism than anyone else, by insisting that their form of Buddhism is the only complete tradition, and that all others are thoroughly second-rate and fragmentary in comparison. This, needless to say, is a point of view which evokes little sympathy in Rangoon or Kyoto.

Still, under the bo tree all such factious sentiments seemed to have been forgotten and, as if to symbolise the prevailing mood of international amity, the Lhasa Apso had fallen asleep in the lap of the Japanese monk. Tenzin was so obviously content just to be there, it seemed unfair to require him to analyse his emotions more precisely, but it struck me that on this tiny patch of Indian soil, the Tibetans were no longer exiles. They were at the epicentre of their cultural world, the descendants of countless generations of pilgrims, and while India's millions might be lapping the temple walls, here at least they were thoroughly at home.

Chapter 11

BYLAKUPPE

It was seven in the morning and the tide of commuters crossing Howrah Bridge into Calcutta looked like a vast migrating herd, impelled by some obscure, atavistic, and probably self-destructive instinct, to fight its way into the heart of the rotting and ramshackle city. Down below, on the Hoogli's strong brown flood, a black barge was being rowed against the current by dozens of oarsmen: small, dark men; their string-like muscles taut.

We had shared a compartment on the overnight train from Gaya with an elderly woman and her middle-aged son: cultivated, articulate Bengalis, returning from a pilgrimage to Banaras. With the approach of the station, however, their affable, confident manner had vanished entirely, as they prepared themselves, mentally and physically, for the ordeal of confronting their city. Indeed, so discomfited did they become by the unwelcome approach of home, that they almost forgot to say goodbye, before collapsing with their cases onto the platform and being swept away in a torrent of jostling and shoving humanity.

As our plane to Bangalore did not leave until six,

Tenzin and I found ourselves with most of the day to waste, so having treated ourselves to the extravagance of an hotel and showered off the railway's grimy patina, we went out for a walk along Chowringhee Road, paid a brief visit to St Paul's Cathedral, crossed the southern end of the Maidan, and ended up, only half by accident, at the colossal white marble pile of the Victoria Memorial. Outside on his plinth, still quite imposing despite the annual attrition of the monsoon, stood the Viceroy, Lord Curzon, at whose instigation the memorial had been built.

If the Raj could melt away like snow in August, I remarked to Tenzin, then perhaps the Chinese colonial empire might also fall victim to the implacable forces of mutability. Curzon could not have imagined that within thirty years of the memorial's completion, the world of which it was so grandiose a symbol would have crumbled away into dust. Perhaps some members of Peking's senescent hierarchy might be similarly deluding themselves. After all, the planners of thousand year Reichs have generally succumbed to the fate of Ozymandias sooner or later.

Inside, underneath the gigantic dome, was a youthful, almost girlish Victoria: Albert's bride. Despite being double life-size, she still seemed rather a frail icon for an empire. I translated the inscription for Tenzin – 'Sic transit gloria mundi' – who remarked that it was very appropriate, indeed prescient, considering what had happened so soon after the statue's completion.

It was dusk when we finally made it out to Dum Dum airport and boarded the decrepit old 737, its paint flaking, its seats sagging and broken-backed.

'This thing's certainly seen life since it left Seattle,' said Tenzin, in a tone of enforced jocularity.

The flight was of course full. All flights in India are. Before sitting down I briefly surveyed my fellow passengers. Most were businessmen and about 10 per cent of them were white. Not so very long ago, Calcutta was the commercial capital of India and the nation's major port. Nowadays most of its 12,000,000 inhabitants scrape a living however best they can. Our destination on the other hand, Bangalore, is a boom town. Until recently an obscure southern city, it is now India's electronics capital, the subcontinent's somewhat muted reply to the roar of the 'Asian Tiger' economies: Japan; Korea; Taiwan; Hong Kong; and Singapore. It is in Bangalore that Indian scientists know about super-computers, nuclear power, ballistic missiles, TV satellites, and aerospace.

We took off and the flickering lights of Calcutta were quickly replaced by the utter blackness of the central Indian night. Down below in the villages, oil lamps hung from the rafters and the women cooked over cow-dung fires.

'Do you know . . .', said Tenzin suddenly, '. . . it's just occurred to me that I'm the only adult member of my family who's never been down to South India. Nearly all the exiled Tibetans make the trip sooner or later.'

'How do they get there?'

'Well, it depends where they're starting from, but from Kathmandu they mostly go by bus to Delhi – which takes twenty-four hours – followed by two or three days on the train down to Bangalore; then another bus to Mysore. It's a long way. And of course that's why no one was very keen to go there. They must be around fifteen hundred miles from the Tibetan boarder. Maybe two thousand miles from Lhasa. Down in Karnataka you really are an exile.'

In the morning we went to see the Dalai Lama's Representative in Bangalore, Mr Tempa Tsering. We eventually found him, after a protracted search, on the ground floor of an unremarkable brick house in the middle of a dusty and labyrinthine residential district. He was a smiling, articulate, forty-year-old, with shiny black hair, wearing a newly pressed blue cotton shirt.

'Come in, come in, come in,' he said affably, ushering us into his shabby but functional office. Flakes of old green paint were peeling off the walls and falling, like some strange form of industrial pollution, onto a long row of battered filing cabinets.

He would have been a farmer back home in Tibet, he informed us without being asked, instead of which, here he was a civil servant. He laughed loudly, as if there were something intrinsically comical about such an occupation. From an adjoining room came the steady clatter of manual typewriters and a subdued hubbub of earnest conversation.

Tea was brought and for a while we sat chatting agreeably about global realpolitik, the United Nations, human rights in China, the present situation in Tibet, the future of Hong Kong, the Asian economic miracle, the probable fate of the Soviet Union, the likely success, or otherwise, of the European Community, in fact a whole gamut of subjects over which one exerts not the faintest zephyr of influence while sitting comfortably in a Bangalore suburb.

'I have to tell you . . .', said Mr Tempa Tsering, when finally we got down to business, '. . . that you have not arrived at a particularly auspicious moment. Last week an offical delegation of American Christian leaders came here hoping to visit our settlements at Bylakuppe, Hunsur, Kollegal, and Mundgod, and because their papers were not "in order" – precisely what was wrong with them I have yet to discover – the Indian authorities sent them all the way back to Delhi. They have not so far reappeared. Now you don't have any papers at all, which may be in some ways an advantage. Of course, for Mr Tenzin there is no problem. But for you. . . . The Indians are not at all keen on foreigners visiting the Tibetans in South India. Without permits it's not allowed, officially that is, and even *with* permits, obstacles somehow tend to arise at the very last minute.'

'Why do you suppose they are so sensitive? After all, there is a constant stream of journalists going up to Dharamsala.'

'Well, I imagine the government would like to prevent that if it thought it could. But doubtless such a blatant policy would attract just the sort of media attention it is trying to avoid. Or perhaps the authorities in Delhi feel they can keep an eye on foreigners in the north, whereas down here, in fairly remote bits of Karnataka, they are much less easy to supervise. I don't know. The Indian bureaucratic mind is frankly rather hard to understand sometimes: for a simple Tibetan like me. Take Mundgod for example. The official reason why you are not allowed to go there is that there is an important naval base nearby. Nearby! Mundgod is over fifty miles from the sea. Everybody knows that India's biggest naval base is at Cochin, a city which I believe is nowadays a major tourist centre, promoted at great expense by the Indian government. Anyway, to be practical, I'm afraid you'll have to forget about Mundgod. The last person who went there without permission was an eminent German anthropologist. He managed to stay for just under an hour before the police arrived to take him away. And not only that: they threw him out of India entirely. No discussion – or at any rate very little of it – they just put him on a plane back to Frankfurt. Extraordinary when you think about it. Quite extraordinary. Then naturally there are repercussions here, if the Indians suspect that we have been aiding and abetting this kind of thing.'

'So what do you suggest?' asked Tenzin, in an exasperated tone of voice.

'Well, I would go to Bylakuppe and stay there as long as you can. If the police start asking questions, then move to Hunsur, which is on the way back to Mysore anyhow.'

'Remind me about Bylakuppe.'

'Bylakuppe is about sixty miles west of Mysore – which in turn is about seventy-five miles south-west of here – and is made up of 6,800 people in the Old Settlement; 4,500 in the New Settlement; plus around 1,200 monks at Sera and Tashilhunpo monasteries.'

'And what about the other Tibetan camps in South India?'

'Hunsur is between Mysore and Bylakuppe. It has 3,500 settlers and the monks at the Lower Tantric College. Then there are another 4,500 people at Kollegal, forty miles to the east of Mysore. And finally there is Mundgod, which is two hundred miles to the north-west of Bangalore, with around nine thousand inhabitants, including the monks at Drepung and Ganden. As you probably know we have re-established all three of the major Lhasa monasteries down here, as well as one of the Tantric Colleges, and Tashilhunpo which was the seat of the Panchen Lama in Shigatse.'

'So altogether there are about thirty thousand Tibetans in South India?'

'About that number I suppose, give or take a couple of thousand. Anyway, to return to Bylakuppe. If you are careful, you should be able to stay there for several days. But as the authorities are being particularly difficult at the moment, I would arrive at night if I were you. Once you are at the settlement, or better still, inside Sera monastery, then no one is going to go running to the police. None of the Tibetans will inform on you. However, on the edge of our land, there is an Indian village – which you have to pass through – and we know for certain that the police pay a number of the local people to keep an eye open for unexpected visitors. Money buys anything in India. Anyway, I can't say I really blame them. It's a harmless enough way of earning a few extra rupees.'

An hour or so later, finally weary of conversation, and doubtless mindful of work clamouring for his attention, Tempa Tsering handed me a letter of introduction to one of Bylakuppe's welfare officers, and then came out into the street to see us off. 'I wish you luck,' he shouted after us, standing in the middle of the road, waving and still smiling.

The Chinese invasion has produced a whole new stratum in Tibetan society, I reflected as we drove away. People who would have worked on the land, generation after generation, growing barley, raising yaks, have of necessity become an educated middle class. And very impressive they are too: amid the corruption and cynicism of India, their honesty, selflessness, and hard work are little short of miraculous. Tempa Tsering had struck me as a model of probity, a man living for an ideal, nourished by a cause.

'Yes, well, they're not *all* like that you know,' said Tenzin, after I had regaled him with such sentiments. 'I agree that *some* of these people in government service are very, very good. And they get paid next to nothing, which makes their attitude even more admirable. But there have been a few cases of . . . well . . . misappropriation of public funds.'

At one-fifteen, when Tenzin and I turned up at the bus station, the two o'clock 'Luxury Express' to Mysore was already quite full, and by the time our bags had been strapped to the roof and we were both reasonably satisfied that they are likely to remain that way, there were only two remaining seats. 'Oh dear,' muttered Tenzin, as he picked his way with difficulty towards the back of the coach, 'Some luxury. Perhaps we should have taken the train after all.' At this point, when the passengers were without exception packed tightly into the central aisle, the driver arrived, started the engine, crashed the gears, and we set off with a lurch, a roar, and a blast of imperious klaxon.

Things sorted themselves out after a while, though not before Bangalore's less desirable suburbs had been left behind and we were well out into the South Indian countryside. A landscape more different from Tibet would be almost impossible to imagine. In a pale blue hazy sky, meringues of cloud drifted listlessly at the behest of a light tropical breeze, while from the heavy red soil, bananas and mangoes grew with Edenic luxuriance and profusion. Shining rice paddies stretched away to an insubstantial horizon, against which were silhouetted bizarre outcrops of rock, like fossilised mammoths, petrified on the hoof by some sudden and violent cataclysm. The road was lined with coconut palms, and in slow muddy rivers, dark-skinned women in scarlet saris scrubbed down their buffaloes with long-handled brooms.

After a little more than three hours the bus thundered into Mysore, horn blaring, braking only for cows, and scattering the routed citizens in the accepted Indian manner. As dusk was already beginning to settle and thicken in the tree-lined streets, we immediately hired a taxi to carry us the remaining miles to Bylakuppe, and within twenty minutes were on our way once more.

Leaving behind the local Maharajah's palace – a preposterous jumble of pillars and domes resembling a less inhibited version of the Brighton Pavilion – we were soon back out in a wide, rolling landscape, where red-tiled villages hid themselves among folds in the land, often betraying their existence only by the thin scarf of bluish smoke that hung above the rooftops in the still and humid air. Along the grassy verge, sand-coloured cows ambled home, escorted in a desultory way by dreamy herdsmen, lost in reflection, and serenely confident that their animals were in little need of either directions or intrusive supervision.

In such a setting, the tribulations of the world can seem at times to be no more than ripples on the surface of a profound impersonal calm. There is an overwhelming sense of an inexorable continuum, indifferent to individual passion and despair, a stately flow of time out of an unimaginably distant past into an inconceivably remote and equally mysterious future. A glow of rusty gold floodlit the cloud castles of the western sky. Darkness fell.

I awoke to discover a startled Tibetan face peering in at me through the taxi window. Tenzin, it seemed, was already negotiating for that night's bed and board.

'We're here. . .', he said superfluously, '. . . at Bylakuppe New Settlement. This lady says she'll take us in.'

'Are you sure? She looks a bit unwilling to me.'

'Oh, it's all right. She's a bit wary of foreigners that's all. Apparently the day before yesterday, some Japanese people got flung out by the police.'

We followed the woman across some rough ground until we came to a long, low outbuilding. There she stopped before a battered door which looked, in the light of her torch, as though it might once have been used in an advertisement for a firm of locksmiths. When the final bolt had been wrestled from its socket, we stepped inside to find a bare concrete room with two rusty beds and an upturned packing case.

'Well, I can see why there's a need for security.'

The walls which had once been painted a vibrant

buttercup yellow were now smeared from floor to ceiling with the limb fragments and dried blood of a thousand pulverised mosquitoes. The fluorescent tube in the ceiling buzzed angrily, while just outside a tap relentlessly dripped.

'I'll toss you for the best bed.' Tenzin won, but despite his victory looked anything but exultant.

'All I can say . . .', he said, bouncing on the protesting springs, '. . . is that so far I'm glad I don't have to live here.'

The morning sunshine revealed a dusty road, lined with small, squat, white-washed houses, and a *chorten* from the top of which prayer flags had been strung, via a power line, to the front of a general store. Forty or fifty Tibetan children, in blue and white uniforms, were making their way slowly and noisily to school.

'Well, it looks fairly Tibetan,' observed Tenzin in a tone of qualified approval.

This was more than could be said for the surrounding landscape, or as much as one could see of it, which was flattish and divided by hedges into stubbled fields. Away in the distance, I could just make out what appeared to be a forest.

The woman of the night before, who still seemed less than overjoyed to find herself with visitors, said that if we were going to see the welfare officer at the Old Settlement, then she would arrange a jeep to take us there. It was, she explained, two or three miles away and we might get lost. Her solicitude was for me marred by near certainty that she was prepared to go to almost any lengths to get rid of us.

*

Namgyal Wangdu, the Welfare Officer, was a powerfully built man, in his early fifties, with thick black hair, a voice which suggested energy and decisiveness, and a simply colossal stainless steel wristwatch. Until quite recently, he wanted us to know, he had been the Political Officer with the Indian army's Tibetan Battalion, up in Dehra Dun. 'I was a brigadier . . .', he explained with considerable pride. He seemed delighted to see us, and anxious to be helpful, though happier on the whole to discuss matters military, than anything more prosaic. Tenzin gently tried to broach the subject of permits and the Indian authorities, but Namgyal Wangdu cut him short with a deafening salvo of laughter.

'Hah! Maybe they won't find out,' he spluttered with the confidence of a man who clearly didn't care very much one way or the other, and who certainly wasn't going to be intimidated by a handful of scrawny policemen. 'I shouldn't worry about it too much if I were you. We'll sort something out.' This plainly being the end of the matter as far as he was concerned, he went on: 'I was in Colorado, you know, to be trained by the Americans. I was supposed to stay there six months, but it ended up being two years as the Chinese were all over Tibet by that time and parachuting in was a pretty good way to commit suicide.'

'Perhaps . . .', said Tenzin with studied politeness, '. . . it would be possible for someone to show us round the settlement here – if that's not too much trouble.' Namgyal Wangdu looked at him blankly, as if, just for a moment, he had forgotten where he was.

I decided to try a conversational compromise; one in which humdrum parochialism could be spiced with a stimulating frisson of violence. 'Do you still have a lot of wild animals around here? I understand that when you were first clearing the land they were a real hazard.'

'Wild animals? You mean elephants, tigers, that kind

of thing. Oh yes, plenty. At least in the forest – which is only five kilometres from here – there are still a lot of elephant. Right now we're building another ditch to try to keep them out. Tigers? I'm not so sure. I don't think there are so many of them nowadays. But it was always the elephant who did the damage. They killed dozens of people back in the '60s. You see, when Nehru wanted to get the Tibetans out of northern India and the Karnataka state government offered him this land, around here was nothing but jungle. Now, of course, that we've cleared it and ploughed it and planted it, one or two of the locals would quite like to have it back. But that's another story.'

'Is it very good land then?'

'No, not particularly. The soil is all right – so long as you fertilise it – and the climate here is not too bad: we're two thousand six hundred feet above sea level, which means that the temperature never goes much above ninety-five degrees Fahrenheit. It never gets *really* hot here, like it does on the northern plains. But the big problem is water. We're supposed to have thirty-five inches of rain, but it's very unreliable. If the monsoon fails, which it quite often does, then we lose most of the maize crop. Of course if we could afford irrigation, it would be another matter, but that's out of the question. Anyway . . .', concluded Namgyal Wangdu with a self-deprecating chortle, '. . . I don't know so much about all of this. You'd better go over the road and talk to a real hero.'

'Who's that?'

'The milkman. He's been the saviour of us all in the last couple of years.'

We found Dawa Gyalpo – a small, quiet, unassuming man, about thirty years of age, with curly hair and a knobbly face – bending over a steaming aluminium vat marked 'Minnesota Valley Engineering, New Prague,

Minnesota, U.S.A.' Behind him on the wall was a large blackboard covered with dense columns of figures. Those for previous years had been recorded permanently with white paint, while contemporary statistics had to make do with a more precarious existence in chalk. Dawa Gyalpo smiled at us wanly.

'Liquid nitrogen,' he said. 'Take a look.'

Peering into the vat through ascending wreaths of mist, I could just make out an evil-looking yellow crust.

'Semen,' he explained without emotion. 'Jersey semen. Actually it comes from Bangalore.' So saying he produced a kind of gigantic hypodermic and jabbed the air with it a couple of times, rather like a fencer practising thrusts. 'It's quite amazingly effective: last year we got 194 calves.'

'You mean you farm Jersey cows here? Don't they all die?'

'Oh no, on the contrary, they're particularly resilient. Of course, it's a long time since they came from Europe; they're fully acclimatised by now. But as a breed, they do very well in South India and the milk yield is exceptionally good: about seventeen litres a day.' He glanced at the blackboard as if for confirmation. 'They're expensive to buy in the first place – about eight thousand rupees – but believe me, they're worth it once you get them established.'

'It must be rather different from yak herding in the Himalayas.'

'Yes and no. In Tibet the nomads had only yaks, but quite a lot of the farmers kept cows.'

'Did your family?'

'No. At least I don't think so. We were farmers all right, but we used to grow barley near Shigatse. Anyway, I can't be certain. I was less than three years old when my parents left. Everything I know about cows and farming I've learned here in India.'

'The Welfare Officer, Namgyal Wandu, says you're the saviour of the settlement.'

Dawa Gyalpo looked taken aback. 'Oh, I don't think it's quite like that,' he said hurriedly. 'Certainly the dairy is quite successful and when we have crop failures due to lack of rain then it seems doubly important.'

'So is this some kind of communal system?' Tenzin enquired.

'No, not really. Bylakuppe does have an agricultural cooperative – of a sort – but the dairy is run more on capitalist lines. You see the cows are owned by individuals who bring the milk daily to one of two collection points. Then we sell it for them: mostly to Indian manufacturers of yoghurt and cheese. The people who own the cows are also shareholders: each share costs ten rupees. For each cow we pay out a regular income of sixty rupees a week. Then at the end of the year the shareholders get a dividend dependent on our profits. Last year, for example . . .' (he consulted his blackboard for the precise information) '. . . we sold 474,496 kilos of milk, from which, as you see, we gave a dividend of 1,440,000 rupees. In addition we were able to donate 70,000 rupees to the general funds of the settlement.'

'No wonder you're popular.'

A modest man, Dawa Gyalpo allowed himself another brief and hesitant smile. 'Well, the scheme *is* successful; people are very keen to participate; and it is expanding, especially due to the success of artificial insemination. But you mustn't forget it's only one enterprise among many. If you want to know more about the whole settlement, then you'll have to talk to Lobsang Tendar. He's the secretary of the Cooperative Society. I'll take you to see him if you like.'

*

Lobsang Tendar's office turned out to be next to that of Namgyal Wangdu, and through the open door, like the sound of distant artillery, the brigadier could be heard booming impatiently at his subordinates. Lobsang Tendar himself was a solid, open-faced man of about forty-five, wearing a red check shirt which, like the insemination equipment, seemed to have begun life somewhere in the American Mid-West.

'Before you make any assessment of the success or failure of this place . . .', he began earnestly, while sweet milky tea was being poured into a heterodox assortment of cups, '. . . you have to understand precisely what we are trying to do. If the Tibetans had been given a choice, I daresay that most of them would have settled around Darjeeling, Gangtok, or maybe in Bhutan. These are the areas where, south of the Himalaya, they instinctively feel at home. This would not have been at all practical, and of course the Indians were determined to prevent it. So here we are down in Karnataka. In some ways, however, this is not such a bad thing. We are very isolated – the nearest city, Mysore, is sixty miles away – but as a result we have an opportunity to preserve our identity in a tightly knit community. So far, for example, we have had almost no intermarriage with other races. From this point of view, it doesn't matter that we are a long way from Tibet, or that we are quite poor. What is important is that we should be able to support ourselves, to be self sufficient, so that we can remain fully Tibetan. Unfortunately . . .', he stared across to his colleague and sighed, '. . . despite the efforts of people like Mr Dawa Gyalpo here, we are not being entirely successful.'

'Why is that? Everything seems very well organised and quite prosperous.'

'I wish that were indeed the case,' said Lobsang Tendar, stirring his tea rather too vigorously and then, to compound his frustration, having to mop up a small puddle with his handkerchief. 'The basic problem is that we have a finite amount of land and an expanding population. Of course in some ways we're pleased that people should have a lot of children – we need more Tibetans to make up for all the ones that have been killed by the Chinese – but when your resources are limited, things are never straightforward. Originally we were given three thousand acres of land, for which we had to pay a small lease to the Karnataka state government. This was increased by a further two thousand when we began the New Settlement. The original idea was that there should be one acre for every individual. Now we have many more than five thousand people. But this shortfall is by no means the end of it. If each person had just one acre and nothing more, then I'm afraid he would starve to death. The land is not irrigated, which means that we can get only one crop a year – despite being in the tropics – and if the rain fails then we get nothing at all.'

'So what do you grow here now? At the beginning you must have had very little idea of what to plant.'

'That's true. The first group of settlers came very close to despair. They found it an extremely hostile place and couldn't see how they could possibly make their living. They tried growing cotton and tobacco, but both failed. Fortunately they were still being helped by the Red Cross, who arranged for a Swiss agricultural expert to come out here and give them some advice. He tested the soil, looked up all the weather statistics, and finally decided that maize was the crop most likely to succeed. He was right. However, maize needs water: no water; no maize. And after a while, if you just grow maize, it doesn't matter how much fertiliser you use, the soil becomes impoverished and completely dried out. After twenty-five years, we are at that stage now. We have to experiment with other things, but of course the older people remember the initial failures and are very resistant to change. Some experts tell us we could farm silkworms. At the moment we are giving out sunflower seeds free to anyone who will plant them.'

'But I thought this was a cooperative.'

'Well, it is and it isn't. We buy the produce from the farmers, order sufficient fertiliser, and negotiate an annual bank loan of 2,500,000 rupees: for the cooperative's working capital. We own sixteen tractors, which the people can rent off us at sixty rupees an hour, and we also have nine thousand hens, two flour mills, and a seven-acre vegetable garden. However, the bulk of the land is divided up into individual plots and people's income is therefore dependent on what they can grow for themselves. Until 1966, we tried farming the land communally, but it just didn't work. As soon as we divided up the land, productivity shot up. As a result people had enough money to buy cows and were able to participate in Mr Gyalpo's milk scheme.'

'I still don't see why you claim to be so unsuccessful.'

'Well, in the last two or three years we've had a couple of very bad dry summers. Even in a good year, however, planting, growing, and harvesting takes only about four months. Because we can only get one crop, there is no employment for our people during the remainder of the year. As a result, all the able-bodied men and women go off selling woollen goods, just as they do in the north. Some of the young boys and girls – often the better educated, more articulate ones – get jobs in Bangalore: working in hotels and restaurants; that kind of thing. Sometimes they find they can earn quite a lot of money – a lot compared with what they can earn growing maize – so they are reluctant to return. This is precisely the situation which we were anxious to avoid. Little by little our young people come to accept different social values, speak less and less Tibetan, become more and more

Indianised. And the core of the problem is economic: we cannot hope to keep them here unless we can make this settlement more economically successful. Please don't misundertand me . . .', said Lobsang Tendar, as if suddenly aware that he had painted an excessively gloomy picture, '. . . in many ways I think the Tibetans have done very well in exile. To a large extent we have preserved our identity and our culture – so far. But as the years go by, then new pressures build up and we have to try even harder than before.'

That evening, at the brigadier's insistence, we transferred our belongings to the official guesthouse, over at the New Settlement. It was an uncomplicated, single-storey building with spartan accommodation, but by virtue of its position on the brow of a low hill, pleasantly breezy, with noticeably fewer mosquitoes than elsewhere in Bylakuppe. Outside, large clumps of scarlet poinsettias were ostentatiously in bloom. The land sloped gently down to the maize fields, while away in the distance, the dark bulk of the elephant-ridden forest was now plainly visible.

Needless to say, the following morning Authority turned up, demanding to know who we were and what we thought we were doing there. Fortunately, it was Authority in the relatively congenial form of a young, bespectacled Tibetan who explained, rather sheepishly it seemed to me, that he was working for the Indian police. Tenzin immediately adopted his most emollient manner and smilingly protested our total ignorance of the required permit, indeed went so far as to suggest that surely the official must be mistaken, worrying himself needlessly, and in general taking his commendable conscientiousness to quite unnecessary extremes. The young Tibetan looked doubtful, insisted on writing down our passport numbers and then, *sotto voce*, promised to deny all knowledge of us in the short term, just as long as we agreed to be extremely discreet. 'Whatever you do . . .' he said, '. . . don't go near the Indian village. Otherwise you'll be arrested and blackmailed.' He seemed to have few illusions about the probity of his employers.

The previous afternoon, we had expressed a wish to meet one of Bylakuppe's original settlers and the brigadier, ever anxious to be helpful, had said that a carefully selected individual would be waiting for us at the offices of the New Settlement at ten o'clock sharp. No excuse would be brooked. Our man would be there. We could depend upon it.

Nima Woche was a small, slight figure, apparently in his early sixties, with grey receding hair, a farmer's deeply tanned complexion, and square, steel-rimmed spectacles. He was dressed simply in a white open-necked shirt and baggy cotton trousers. Over his shoulder was slung a battered canvas bag – similar to the ones used to carry gas masks in the Second World War – which looked as though it might well contain all the worldly goods he had managed to amass during thirty years of toil. He was evidently bewildered at having been summoned to talk to us, his own inclination clearly being for discretion, reticence, and peaceful anonymity.

We sat outside on a wooden bench, under the shady roof of a wide verandah. Yes, he admitted, he had been in Bylakuppe from the beginning. He stared hard at Tenzin and seemed to find his appearance somewhat reassuring.

'I was working on the roads, close to the border of Sikkim, when an official from the Tibetan government came and asked us if we wanted to be resettled down in South India. He had eight hundred places to fill. We would be given land, he said, and would be able to farm for ourselves and our families. It sounded a good idea. Life at that time was very hard: we were paid very little; there was not enough food; many people were dying; and there was no prospect of any real improvement. So I said yes. Most people did. We were all put on a train, which took three days to get to Bangalore, and from there we were taken by bus. I don't know what we had expected. Agricultural land I suppose: fields. Instead all we found was a small clearing in the forest, with just a few tents. Nowadays . . .', he said, looking round at the neatly white-washed buildings, while in the background type-writers clattered and a neglected phone obstinately declined to be silent, '. . . nowadays it all seems so solid and peaceful here, but then it was very different. It was hot – not like in northern India, but humid, so you couldn't breathe – we were more than a thousand miles from Tibet, and the forest was all around us. We felt imprisoned by it. It seemed impossible for us to push it back. We had no tractors then. If we cut down a tree, it would take three or four men days to dig out the stump and the roots. Then there were the wild animals: elephants, tigers, panthers, wild boar. . . . It was very dangerous. Three men in my work group were killed in the first few months. After a while we built huts out of bamboo and mud, but they were very uncomfortable. The temperature never dropped. It was always hot, even at night. And at night you could hear the animals in the forest calling. All around us. Then when the rain came, there were snakes everywhere. Huge things: some of them four, five metres long. Actually there still are in the monsoon; that hasn't changed.'

'What kind of snakes?'

'I don't really know the names. Cobras: you can recognise them easily enough. I suppose the really big ones are some kind of python. Anyway, after about six months I think we'd all have gone back to the road-gangs if we'd been given the chance. Of course the Indians were very keen for us to stay. They gave us some farming equipment, but until we'd cleared the land there wasn't much use for it. At least we got enough to eat. That was the only thing to be pleased about. We were getting rations of canned meat, cheese, flour, and butter. Some came from the Indian government; the rest was from the Swiss Red Cross. The worst of it was being completely out of touch. There was no news at all. We had no idea what was going on in Tibet. I felt alone, abandoned; and most of the time quite frightened. We all did.'

'So when did things start to improve?' Tenzin asked in a subdued voice. 'How many years did it go on like that?'

Nima Woche smiled. 'Ask anyone . . .', he said, '. . . they'll tell you the same thing. In 1964 the Dalai Lama came down here and talked to us. He said that even though things were difficult, we were going to have to stay. We had to accept that for the foreseeable future Bylakuppe would be our home. It was up to us to make the best of it. When we went back to Tibet, he said, we must be able to return with pride and dignity. Above all we must set an example to the Indians. Not just accept their charity, but show them how things should be done. His Holiness then went out into the fields and encouraged the people individually. He explained that various agricultural experts were on their way to help us and that if we listened to their advice and worked hard then things would be sure to get better.

'Shortly after he had gone back to Dharamsala two bulldozers arrived, which meant we could get out the big tree stumps and prepare the land for ploughing. Then a Swiss man came who taught us how to grow maize. But the real difference was in ourselves. Overnight our attitude to the place had changed completely. We set to work again in an entirely different spirit: with a new confidence. We no longer felt isolated. The Dalai Lama was with us. We were back in touch with the world and with the rest of our people.'

'I suppose . . .', I said, '. . . that it's only when an exile accepts his misfortune, suppresses his longing for home, that things can really improve.'

'That's it,' replied Nima Woche. 'As long as you think of your position as temporary, then you are miserable and achieve nothing. If you want to be happy, then you must build a new life. You don't put up brick houses, and schools, and try to get the best out of the land, if you're thinking "Tomorrow I'll be going home; or maybe the next day". We had to assume we would be here for ever. In a sense, giving up hope was the only way forward.'

'But you still think of Tibet?'

'Of course. Though I remember what it was like when the Chinese came and I am grateful to be here, free from the fear of torture and imprisonment.'

'Why, did you have any particular reason to be afraid?'

'Yes,' said Nima Woche simply. He stared past us for a moment into the middle distance and then began again with renewed equanimity.

'My uncle had a shop in Shigatse. I think he had been supplying the Tibetan guerrillas. He was certainly in touch with them. The Chinese found out, but he managed to get away. So then they came looking for the rest of the family. I was arrested with my father and thrown into gaol. Every day they interrogated us and beat us up. There was actually very little we could tell them, but they didn't know that. Some days they said that if we confessed our crimes, then things would work out all right for us. Then the next day they would beat us and say that we were "Enemies of the People" and were going to be shot. Of course we spent most of the time thinking about how we might try to escape. Fortunately we were being held in an old building in Shigatse, the walls of which were very thick, but made from mud bricks. Mud brick sets very hard, but with some kind of metal tool you can work your way through it. Anyway, there was a famine in China at that time and because they had hardly enough rice for themselves, the Chinese soldiers used to let families send in food for the prisoners. After a while they didn't bother to check the parcels very thoroughly. They would just take what they wanted and give us what was left. In this way our relatives managed to smuggle in an old bayonet and also a note telling us when we should try to escape. So one night we dug our way through the wall and managed to climb down to the street. There, at the back of the building, we found the rest of our family waiting for us with horses. We got clear away: to Sikkim.'

'So when you think about Tibet it's primarily the fear that you remember?'

'Yes. Fear of pain; fear of death. At the beginning I was very unhappy down here in South India, but even then I was better off than I would have been in prison in Shigatse. Nowadays I am much more fortunate then the Tibetans who remained in Tibet. I am an old man and I would like to see my country again before I die, but no one here will return until the Chinese have gone. But on the day the Chinese troops go back to China, everyone in Bylakuppe will pack up and get ready to leave. Even though we have built something here, no one will be tempted to stay.'

'We're going to my cousin's house for lunch,' Tenzin announced unexpectedly, after we had waved goodbye to Nima Woche and watched his slight figure diminish down the dusty road, buffeted by a raucous mêlée of schoolchildren. It seemed inevitable they would knock him over, but somehow he managed to stay on his feet: at least as far as the first bend.

'Really? I thought all your relatives down here were in Sera monastery.'

'No, not all of them. The man we're going to visit lives with his wife. He keeps a shop and grows maize. Actually the whole family has tried to persuade him to make more of himself, but somehow he seems quite happy with what he's got.'

We set off in the direction of the Old Settlement. The sun was vertically overhead, but seemed to be generating more light than heat. The glare was blinding. Most of the maize crop had already been harvested and the fields were golden brown with stubble. Here and there people could be seen stripping off the outer husks and tossing the corn into piles.

After about three-quarters of an hour we came to the outskirts of a small village. There was no one about and the whole place seemed to be cocooned in a noonday hush: a kind of South Indian siesta. In fact, looking around, I decided it was not at all unlike one of the poorer, quieter bits of Andalucia. There was a temple inside a walled compound, its prayer flags motionless in the humid air, and a couple of hundred low, white-washed houses, built close together along narrow lanes of compacted earth. Several, I noticed, had carefully nurtured gardens in which gaudy clumps of livid scarlet and shocking pink fought to outdo one another in exuberant vulgarity. There was also a wide central square with half a dozen dusty trees. Beneath one of them, two Jersey calves were lying on a mat of straw, liquid-eyed and chewing automatically. Everywhere, yellow corn cobs had been laid out on the ground to dry. I picked one up and bit it, but despite a promising appearance, it was hard and tasteless.

'You can't eat it like that,' said Tenzin, with amusement. 'This isn't America, you know. You either grind it to make a kind of flour, or sell it for animal feed.'

When we arrived, Lobsang Drakpa and his wife, Dorje,

were in the kitchen, straining rice. Dressed in a T-shirt and jeans, he seemed a reserved, rather shy man, who was nonetheless determined to be hospitable. She on the other hand, despite her sober dress and apron, gave me the impression of being an energetic woman, whose zest for life was inadequately channelled into domestic competence and pride. They had no children. The kitchen itself was quite large, but at least half of the floor space was taken up with an enormous pile of maize, reaching to within six inches of the roof. 'Three thousand kilos,' our host remarked, intercepting my astonished stare. 'This year's crop. We have two acres. Last year there was no rain and from the same land we got only two hundred kilos. Less than one tenth the amount.' His wife meanwhile had returned to an earthen range. The stove was a simple arrangement with long branches pushed in through a hole at the side, but it clearly worked well enough. The only drawback was the smoke, which hung about among the sooty rafters before eventually leaking out through invisible chinks in the tiles.

Apart from the kitchen, the house had only one main room, though this was big enough to accommodate two tables and four single beds – covered with embroidered quilts of Chinese origin, presumably bought in Nepal – which served as sofas during the day. Along one wall there was also a substantial varnished sideboard, with glass-fronted cupboards, in which were displayed a number of gilded Buddhas and half a dozen books bound in yellow cloth: Tibetan equivalents to the Bible, Shakespeare, and the OED. Next to it were hung several silk *thankas* and a framed portrait photograph of the Dalai Lama. The room's only other decoration was provided by a fading collage of colour prints, showing cheerful family groups against a backdrop of snow-covered mountains.

I sat down on one of the beds, Tenzin and his cousin being locked into a rather intense family conference.

Behind my head, a small window looked out into a yard at the back, where a black Tibetan mastiff lay in the shade panting, his extended and quivering tongue lolling on froth-spattered paws. Sundry rustlings and munchings suggested that at least one other large animal was tethered to the wall of the house. Presently the uncertainty was cleared up, when the black and gleaming muzzle of a cow thrust its way into the room and started snuffling at the back of my neck. While I was evading this attention, a Lhasa Apso puppy jumped into my lap and promptly fell asleep. I began to wonder whether I had accidentally stepped into some sentimental genre painting, depicting blissful rural poverty.

Dorje Drakpa lifted the curtain covering the open door and set out a meat stew with onions and chillis, a pan of rice, a basket of flat bread similar to *naan*, and an earthenware bowl of yoghurt. Her husband leapt up to help. 'My family were nomads,' she said, laughing as she dispensed Goliath portions. 'I was born out of doors and brought up on big meals. Mind you, I'm not sure I'd care to go back to that kind of life: I've come to prefer houses to tents.'

Her good humour and self-confidence prompted the thought that one of the reasons why Westerners and Tibetans generally find it quite easy to socialise is that their everyday domestic customs and taboos are not particularly dissimilar. Tibetan women are well respected and have plenty to say for themselves, and in consequence family life is natural and relaxed.

Buoyed up by the mood of general conviviality, I complimented Lobsang Drakpa on his pleasant house and general good fortune. Fork arrested in mid-air, he stared at me, unconvinced. 'Uh-huh,' he said at last, before resuming his meal. Chastened, I reflected that pastoral idylls were all very well if one volunteered for them. Enforced Rousseauesque simplicity was doubtless a different matter entirely.

Chapter 12

SERA

The battered jeep pulled up on the brow of a low hill and its driver jumped down in the dirt road's loose and rutted surface.

'There's Sera!' he exclaimed, gesturing grandiloquently at the middle distance. One might have been forgiven for thinking that the jumble of utilitarian buildings up ahead was in fact an outlying part of the agricultural cooperative, instead of one of the world's larger monasteries, home to 1200 Tibetan monks. Taking a hard look at the present landscape – the level and distant horizon, the stubbled maize fields and scattered tropical woodland – I tried to relate it to my memories of a sunny spring morning in the Lhasa Valley. And failed.

In Tibet, large monasteries were often built up hillsides, so that even if most of the components were modest in scale, the overall effect was one of magnificence and Cyclopsean invulnerability. Here, spread out over the flat land, Sera seemed sadly diminished: diluted by space.

'Most of the people we'll meet this morning come from around my home town of Kanze,' Tenzin explained, as we jolted along the final mile of potholed road. 'These days

Sera is made up of two separate colleges – Sera Me and Sera Je – each of which has its own abbot and is divided into houses. All the monks who come from Chamdo live together; all those from Lithang live together; and so on. The houses are called *khangtsen*. Kanze; *khangtsen*; it's a bit confusing I'm afraid.'

'Is that the way it used to be in Tibet?'

'Just the same, except that in Lhasa there was another college called Sera Ngag-pa. I was in Sera Je, and I used to live with my uncle in the *khangtsen* of Kanze.'

Driving straight into the middle of the monastery complex, we stopped outside the main assembly hall. Groups of monks were standing around in desultory conversation, almost as if waiting for a bus, while others, generally the younger ones, hurried past with pails of water, baskets of cabbage, or tottering piles of flat Indian bread. A pariah kite, sitting on a fence post, kept watch on all this culinary activity with a glinting and unscrupulous eye. Our arrival seemed to cause very little surprise or interest – even the kite ignored us – so having taken directions we set off unescorted down a narrow lane lined with small, square white-washed houses and populated chiefly by mongrel dogs, all looking by Asian standards remarkably sleek and well pleased with life.

We found Tenzin's monastic relations living in an airy, well-swept, room, with pink hibiscus poking in at the window, rush matting on the floor, and electric lights to read by. The walls were decorated with lurid colour pictures of Tantric deities, while in the corner stood a pile of embroidered quilts. On a sultry October day, it was hard to imagine when they might be needed.

Tenzin was received with (literally) open arms and unfeigned gurgles of joy, before being ushered inside with immense deference and ceremony. Initially this struck me as rather odd, as in most Buddhist societies even the most eminent citizens are expected to show conspicuous humility towards members of the clergy, or *Sangha.* But it soon became apparent that he was being honoured as the head of a family which had long proved itself to be one of the most consistently generous of Sera's many benefactors.

'Roughly how much have you donated over the years?' I enquired as discreetly as I could when the hubbub had finally died down.

'Oh, around 75,000 rupees I suppose,' Tenzin replied after a brief mental calculation.

At its outset, in the fifth century BC, Buddhism was a mendicant religion, one whose practitioners were enjoined to beg for their daily food and to seek shelter only during the annual monsoon. It was a faith which saw the world as a snare and an illusion, a place of suffering from which it alone provided a trustworthy path to liberation. A compromise with the world, however, was soon found to be a practical necessity. To survive and prosper, it needed powerful, wealthy patrons and a permanent establishment. By the eleventh century, when Buddhism finally became secure in Tibet, it had long since been a religion of temples and libraries, one in which ritual and scholasticism had largely succeeded ideals of holy poverty and the austere pursuit of enlightenment. In time, Tibet acquired some of the largest and grandest monasteries in Asia and far from shunning worldly affairs, the clergy set up a form of theocratic government, dominated by the reincarnate lamas: of whom the Dalai Lama was chief. Still, old ideas can be extremely resilient and throughout the Buddhist world – Tibet being no exception – there remained a tension between the forces of hierarchy and those of disestablishment, between the monk in his library and the hermit in his cave, between the seeker after knowledge and the seeker after truth.

Another aspect of this debate, which runs like a warp through the weft of Buddhism's long and complex history, has concerned the respective roles of the monk and the layman: the priest and his patron. Initially it was believed that only a monk could make significant spiritual progress, could sufficiently improve his karma so as to ensure a succession of favourable rebirths, a process leading eventually to escape from the clutches of the world into a mysterious state of beatitude, enlightenment, or nirvana. If a layman lacked the motivation to be a monk, it was only because his karmic condition was inadequately advanced. Such attitudes were of course rather dispiriting to the ordinary member of the Buddhist congregation and over the centuries modifications were introduced to satisfy the religious aspirations of the laity. Before long, the development of compassion for one's fellow man came to be considered an essential concomitant to the pursuit of spiritual wisdom. Virtue now required an object, and religious self-advancement was no longer by itself a sufficient, or indeed entirely laudable ambition. Various forms of ritual observance were introduced, and an enormous pantheon of Buddhist deities constructed to accommodate the people's ancient gods and their incorrigible superstitions.

In Tibet, Buddhism swallowed whole the old popular relgion, Bon, finding new employment for its daemonic personnel and enlisting the powers of the occult in the service of a worthier cause. Meanwhile the monks strengthened their relationship with the laity by practising their skills in medicine, exorcism, and astrology. The boundaries between clergy and laity were further blurred by the increase in the number of monks. Virtually every family would send at least one son to the monastery –

irrespective of his sense of religious vocation – thereby becoming intimately involved in the ecclesiastical world. It was a system which commanded the affection of the people, proved remarkably stable and durable in consequence, and which gave Tibetan society its uniquely religious character.

And it is, of course, precisely this unique relationship between clergy and laity which the economics of the modern world would forbid ever to be re-established. No country, especially not one with ambitions to spend large sums of public money on national reconstruction, could possibly afford to have 20 per cent of its healthy adult population immured in a monastery. However favourable the future may turn out to be, some aspects of the old Tibet are undoubtedly gone for ever.

'You seem very comfortable here,' I observed to Yonten Namgyal, one of the more senior monks, while Tenzin dispensed stout bundles of Choegyal family largesse. He smiled engagingly, a middle-aged man, he had soft, plump features, a matronly figure, and an expression of great benevolence.

'Well, it's certainly better than when we arrived.'

'Why? What was here then?'

'Nothing very much; just trees, tents, a few huts. The land was still being cleared with bulldozers.'

'So who built Sera as it is today?'

'We did. The money came from lay Tibetans like Tenzin here; the skilled craftsmen were mostly Indians; but the labour was provided by the monks. For the first eighteen months we were clearing the ground and then afterwards we began to put up these houses. Even today we have to work, you know. At harvest time all the monks, except the *tulkus* (reincarnate lamas) of whom there are about thirty, go out into the fields. Fortunately, bringing in the maize only takes about a month, so the rest of the time we can devote ourselves to religion.'

'And you pursue your studies much as you would have done in Tibet?'

'Yes. Nowadays we do. The Dalai Lama came here recently and said he was fairly happy with the general standard of learning. Of course there are problems: the heat for example. If you tried to study too much during the middle of the day you would go crazy. We tend to get up very early: before dawn. And also we read at night when it is cooler. I suppose we spend slightly less time studying than we would have in Tibet, but things seem to get done in the end. Next year I hope to pass my *geshe* examinations. To reach this stage has taken me twice as long as it would have in Lhasa, but the delay has mostly been due to the events of the '60s and '70s. And I also have to teach the young monks, which is quite time-consuming.'

'How old are they when they arrive?'

'About sixteen generally.'

'There is still no shortage of candidates then?'

'There certainly is not,' said Tenzin, now being free to give our conversation his full attention. 'There are actually too many. Sera is getting overcrowded. People still manage to escape from Tibet and they come down here, chiefly because they are desperate for an education of some kind.'

Yonten Namgyal nodded in agreement. 'Life in Tibet is very hard and so people think they would like to become monks. That way, they think, they will at least have enough to eat and be free from persecution. Some also hear that people in the outside world are very wealthy and that a few of the exiled Tibetans can now afford their own cars and televisions and even take holidays in foreign countries. Of course, when they come to India they find that most of us still live very simply, and because it is very difficult to get started in business, they cannot make a living and have no alternative but to go to a monastery.'

I remarked that this didn't seem like a very good way to turn out first-class Buddhist scholars, never mind saintly contemplatives, but before Yonten Namgyal could respond a group of about a dozen monks had squeezed its way into the room in order to present white *khatas* to Tenzin. One man had also brought two packets of orange creams and a box of Bourbon biscuits.

'The Dalai Lama has said that he is in favour of quality not quantity: that he is happy to see fewer monks, provided they are better educated ones,' Yonten Namgyel replied defensively, as soon as his visitors had been seated and provided with butter tea. This opinion did not, however, meet with the approval of one of the new arrivals, Jampel Senge, a thin man with a rather incongruous wispy moustache.

'Rubbish,' he said, his mouth full of biscuit. 'The more the better. Out of quantity will come quality. In this degenerate age we need all the monks we can get.'

'Does that mean you disagree with the Dalai Lama?' I enquired innocently.

'I would not dream of disagreeing with His Holiness. He is something holy; something divine.' He paused for a moment and then went on rather belligerently: 'I'll tell you something though. If we're not careful, this Dalai Lama will step into the shoes of the Panchen Lama and give the Chinese everything they want. All this talk of letting the Chinese keep sovereignty in Tibet, provided they allow us autonomy. It's ridiculous: everyone knows the Chinese only understand strength.' He seemed remarkably freethinking for a monk.

'I shouldn't take too much notice of Jampel Senge if I were you,' said Tenzin when the object of his evident disapproval had moved away out of earshot. 'He's a funny guy. A few years ago he used to be a real groover in Kathmandu, with hair halfway down his back. Now he's a monk, but there seems to be some part of him which hasn't changed very much. Even if he has shaved his hair off, he's still got the moustache.'

Such eccentricities notwithstanding, my first impression of Sera was, I reassured him, entirely favourable. The monks seemed intelligent and friendly, while their monastery had a calm, but far from lethargic atmosphere. Tenzin nodded, before resuming an earnest discussion about the cost of a religious service recently held on his family's behalf. 'It was for my brother's little girl,' he explained when the necessary arithmetic had been completed and what looked like a colossal sum of money handed over. 'She had a blood complaint.'

'I thought she went to hospital in Bangkok.'

'She did. But we also took advice from the astrologers in Kathmandu. They said we should get the monks here to help, especially as we have a family connection with Sera.'

'So what precisely did you ask them to do?'

'A hundred thousand mantras to Tara. You know: the Tibetan goddess of compassion. It took eight hundred monks three days to chant them all, which is why it's so expensive. Twelve thousand rupees altogether. Anyway I've sorted out the bill. Why don't we go over to see the library.'

We found Tamdin Gyaltso, a weather-beaten monk with grizzled hair, sitting cross-legged on a pile of faded cushions, once red, now a rather louche shade of magenta. In front of him was a rough-hewn lectern, on which rested a delicately carved printing block about two feet long and four inches wide. By his side was an old tin tray of black ink, a roller, a scrubbing brush, and a pile of paper strips already trimmed to size. Dipping the brush in the ink, he scrubbed at the block to ensure that every curlicue of the Tibetan script would be clearly reproduced, gently placed the paper in position, and finally ran the roller briskly up and down it, twice. The whole procedure took about thirty seconds.

'We're printing the collected works of Tsongkhapa,' he said without looking up or pausing in his work. 'He was the founder of the Gelugpa Buddhist order and we need a large number of copies. Each one has about seven hundred and fifty pages.'

It occurred to me that since the Chinese had dismantled Tibetan libraries with artillery, a speedier method of reassembling them might well be called for.

'Isn't block printing rather a slow process?'

'We've been printing books like this for a thousand years. Actually, we learned the technique from the Chinese. And anyway we couldn't possibly afford modern printing machinery.'

'It must be very boring for you.'

'It is quite,' he replied cheerfully. 'I've been doing this for about three years now. I'm a *geshe*: back in Tibet the actual printing of books was done by the lay people. Only the craftsman who carved the block was a monk.'

'Who makes the blocks now?'

'There's a man from Derge in Kham. Before the Chinese came, the monastery in Derge was famous for its woodblocks throughout the whole of Tibet. He began work as soon as he left Buxa, but unfortunately each block takes him over a week.'

As the Tibetan primary scriptures are made up of the *Kanjur*: 108 volumes containing, among other things, the discourses attributed to the Buddha himself; and the *Tanjur*: 225 volumes of commentaries; it seemed that the individual concerned was in little immediate danger of unemployment.

'Did you manage to bring many books with you from Tibet?'

'Very few. I'll show you the ones we've got if you like.'

So saying Tamdin Gyaltso got up stiffly, clasped the small of his back, and taking a large rusty key off a nearby shelf, led the way out into the ferocious sunshine. The library was really a combination of storeroom and workshop, a dour concrete building with no facilities at all for readers. Opening the door of a small annex, he ushered us inside. Piled on the shelves of a metal cabinet, also locked, there were just two or three dozen books, bound up in cloth.

'These are the rare ones that we managed to save. Take this for example.' He reached down a bundle and gingerly unwrapped it. Inside was the usual neat pile of loose-leaved sheets, but on this occasion made from a fine black paper. The script was printed alternately in silver and gold. 'This is three hundred years old. The ink contains real gold and silver. In Lhasa we had an entire *Kanjur* in this style: a hundred and eight volumes. Now we have just one book. I imagine that it's the only one left. The Chinese burned nearly everything.'

After a lunch of *momos* – meat pastries, cooked by the monks on a kerosene stove in the courtyard outside their room; food from the monastery's own kitchen being deemed much too modest for a distinguished visitor like Tenzin – we were taken over to Sera's main hall, the *Tsog-chen*, where an afternoon service was already in progress. The monastery disciplinarian, a genuinely intimidating individual, kitted out with enormous boots, pointed firmly to a vacant patch of sunlit floor next to the main entrance and Tenzin and I obediently slumped down where indicated.

His boots looked even bigger from ground level, and I was reminded of one of the more controversial aspects of Sera's recent history. Before the Chinese invasion, the great Lhasa monasteries of Sera, Drepung, and Ganden were so populous that they required their own monastic policemen to maintain some semblance of order. Those at Sera, known as *dob-dobs*, came to have an unenviable reputation for being a law unto themselves, their habitually loutish behaviour at the New Year festival of Monlam attracting a surprising amount of popular odium. In effect, Sera possessed a small private army, a fact illustrated by the monastery's participation in the civil war of 1947, during which the monks of Sera Je tried to restore to power the deposed Regent, Reting Rinpoche. In nearly two weeks of fighting, Sera was intermittently shelled by the artillery of the Tibetan army and around two hundred monks were killed. Reting Rinpoche himself later died in mysterious circumstances in one of the dungeons of the Potala.

'I suppose this must remind you of your boyhood?' I whispered to Tenzin surreptitiously as soon as the disciplinarian was occupied elsewhere, extirpating indecorous frivolity among some of the younger monks. The hall was full to overflowing: row upon row of red-robed figures, swaying gently from side to side, chanting in a harmonious swelling chorus. The two lines either side of the central aisle were composed exclusively of *geshes*, the monastery's most able and highly qualified scholars, while up near the abbot's dais was a group of young *tulkus*: children identified as the reincarnations of specific spiritual masters.

'Not particularly. Sometimes I find it difficult to believe that I was ever a monk. Take all these statues, for example: nowadays, I'm hopeless at remembering which is which.'

'Well, if it's any consolation most Christians know

almost nothing about the iconography of their cathedrals.'

'Of course, I still recognise the most important ones,' Tenzin continued, somewhat defensively. 'You see the statue up there? That's Tsongkhapa. It was donated by one of my brothers.'

Looking round, it seemed to me that the hall was quite well supplied with religious images – most of obviously recent manufacture – while from the scarlet pillars hung long *thankhas* mounted on golden cloth: some freshly painted, some of self-evident antiquity. With the prayer hall of the original Sera, however, there seemed to be little obvious similarity. Here were no great frescoes, writhing with life on the edge of the musty, sacerdotal gloom; no intimidating shadows crowded with jostling ghosts; no sticky sweet smell: the compound of butter lamps, incense, and centuries of unwashed feet. The new Sera was sanitised and safe, its atmosphere sterile as a laundrette.

Light surged in through open windows, while outside in the South Indian glare, some crows squawked disrespectfully and squabbled over scraps in the dust.

The service concluded, and its five or six hundred participants once more evenly dispersed throughout the monastery, Tenzin and I were escorted to our appointment with Lobsang Tsering, the abbot of Sera Je. After a brief stroll through a tangle of alleys, we were shown into a room with a long narrow conference table, on either side of which was a line of red plastic chairs, upholstered with squares of canary yellow carpet. The walls were painted a virulent turquoise and decorated, rather like a sports pavilion, with team photos of Sera's distinguished alumni. This apparently was where the monastery conducted its official business with the outside world.

Some of the monks who had come with us drifted back to their studies, while those who remained showed little of their former ebullience and wore subdued expressions, tinged apparently with slight trepidation. As a displacement activity, six or seven people set about polishing cups and saucers, pouring out butter tea, and then agitatedly discussing whether, after all, it mightn't have been better to have waited for the abbot's arrival, before having done anything remotely so presumptuous.

After about twenty minutes of such uncomfortable indecision, Lobsang Tsering swept into the room, sucking along in his slipstream a small, flustered, and breathless entourage. His powerful physique, close-cropped hair, and confident, almost aggressive manner suggested a victorious Spartan general more than a self-effacing man of religion. Clearly accustomed to prompt obedience, he seemed to have very little time for the prevarications of Athenian smoothies. Nodding to me, he greeted Tenzin with brisk cordiality, before issuing a volley of orders, dispatching a bevy of messengers, and then seating himself with awe-inspiring gravitas.

I was still absorbing the impact of this entrance, when I noticed a tall, frail individual, wearing heavy spectacles – several sizes too big for him and held together with Sellotape – vainly struggling to get behind the abbot's chair, the back of which was now jammed up against the wall. After a couple of minutes' futile wriggling, Lobsang Tsering became aware of the poor man's plight and with a magisterial gesture graciously allowed him to pass. The newcomer thereupon lowered himself into a vacant seat – deftly catching his glasses which fell off in the process – clasped his hands together in his lap, put his head slightly to one side, blinked a couple of times, and then sat staring fixedly at the table, rather like a rare and endangered species of stork.

'Who on earth's that?' I asked, leaning across to Tenzin.

'He's the abbot of Sera Me. You know the other *dratsang*: the other college.'

'You mean he's just as important as Lobsang Tsering?'

'Oh yes, certainly. They run Sera between them.'

'But they're so completely different.'

'Well . . .' said Tenzin, unanswerably, '. . . why not?'

Before I could continue with this conversation, Lobsang Tsering began to speak, loudly and fluently, with fire and indignation, sawing the air with his right arm for additional emphasis. He had plainly had enough of preliminaries and was determined to get our interview started – and hence over and done with – just as soon as was practically possible. Asking questions being impossible, I settled back to wait for the end of his oration. Tenzin meanwhile gave a very good impression of a man being forcibly held down and pummelled with rhetoric. The abbot of Sera Me, perhaps having heard it all before, appeared to fall into a deep doze. On subsequent reflection, I decided that he might well have been meditating. Suddenly there was silence.

'What did he say?'

Tenzin, whose expression suggested that he had trodden on an electric eel, flapped a hand limply in my direction and opened his mouth a couple of times without emitting any organised sound whatever. Eventually he mustered sufficient resilience to recover his powers of speech.

'Er . . . er . . . quite a lot really. I suppose I could . . . er . . . give you the gist of it if you like.'

Lobsang Tsering, although not understanding a word of English, plainly didn't care for the sound of this feeble exchange and began drumming his fingers on the table with impatience.

'He wants you to know what happened to him in Tibet and what he thinks of the Chinese in consequence.'

'But I thought he was going to tell us about Sera?'

'Maybe he will, but first he prefers to talk about his experiences. He says that as you're a journalist, you ought to know about them.'

At this point the abbot lost patience and began again, Tenzin doing his heroic best to provide a simultaneous translation.

'In 1959, at the time of the Uprising, I was in Ngari, western Tibet, near the Ladakh border. I could have escaped very easily. But I returned to Lhasa of my own free will. Of my own free will, you understand. And what happens? The Chinese immediately throw me in gaol. What have I done to deserve this? Nothing. I was put in a prison near Shigatse. They bound my hands to my ankles, so that when they finally untied me I couldn't stand up properly for weeks afterwards. I still have trouble with my back. To eat they gave us a few ounces of *tsampa* a day, and two or three spoonfuls of boiled cabbage. The rations got less and less until after a while all the prisoners were starving. People became so desperate that they would fight each other for a half a mugful of cabbage water. I myself was reduced to digging for earthworms.'

Lobsang Tsering paused, temporarily speechless, his mind flooded with the horror and humiliation of it all. It occurred to me that this might be the source of his astonishing energy. His vigour, his impatience, his will to power, were all manifestations of sublimated rage.

'And we were the lucky ones. Those of my friends who were sent to China never came back. Many of the monks in the Shigatse prison committed suicide. Others died of malnutrition. I would say that only about 20 per cent of us – the youngest, the strongest, *the most determined* – were able to survive.'

Suddenly his manner changed and he looked at me almost, it seemed, in supplication. The mask of power fell away and instead I saw a man haunted by his own impotence in the face of a continuing calamity.

'You should know these things so that you can write about them. The world must know what happened in Tibet and you are in a position to tell them. I am not. Not here. Down here in South India. And today in Lhasa such things still go on. Just the same. Monks imprisoned, beaten, tortured, killed. . . .' He paused while authority and composure ebbed slowly back.

'As I say, I was relatively fortunate. After three or four years, they sent me to another gaol in Shigatse where the lay people were allowed to bring the prisoners food. I tell you, they gained more spiritual merit by feeding the starving than from all their prayers in Tashilhunpo. Then in 1966 I was released: on the condition that I would not try to teach religion. If I did, the Chinese said, I would not be given another chance.'

'It seems a strange time for them to have let you go – right at the beginning of the Cultural Revolution.'

'Maybe, but in a way it made things easier. I was determined to get out of Tibet and very soon there was so much turmoil with fighting between the Chinese authorities and Mao's Red Guards, as well as between the Chinese and the Tibetans, that I was able to slip away unnoticed. It took me twenty days to walk to Sikkim. There the authorities locked me up for a month while they decided what to do with me, but eventually they allowed me to carry on to India. I was sent down here almost immediately. In the '70s I was the monastery disciplinarian and then, two years ago, I became the abbot of Sera Je.'

'So after a quarter of a century, can the Bylakuppe Sera be compared with the original institution? Has Tibetan monastic culture really been preserved here? Or is this just an imitation? A good pretence?'

'No, it's not a pretence.' Lobsang Tsering condescended to be more amused than annoyed. 'I'd say that we've been quite successful. The monks work just as hard as before and follow the same course. There are distractions and the climate is not favourable, but overall I am quite optimistic.'

'But suppose the Chinese don't leave. Could you go on like this indefinitely?'

'Perhaps. I should think so. Why not? The big problem of course is money. We have so many people arriving from Tibet that we have nowhere to put them. Some monks sleep ten to a room. This is highly unsatisfactory and makes it extremely difficult for them to study. Fortunately, these days we receive some foreign donations. As you know, there are now many Tibetan lamas living abroad: in Europe, Canada, the United States. . . . Thanks to them and to their followers we manage. Problems arise, but solutions are found. If the Chinese remain in Tibet for a hundred years, Sera monastery will survive.'

As if to reassure himself, Lobsang Tsering glanced along the table to his silent and enigmatic colleague, but the abbot of Sera Me merely smiled seraphically and said nothing.

'Just as long as the Indians let us stay here. They are so anxious to be friends with the Chinese, you can never be sure. If Nehru hadn't been so foolish in the first place, perhaps we wouldn't be in this mess. And of course the Indians wouldn't find themselves with a hostile army all the way along their northern frontier. They've only got themselves to blame.'

Did he not, I wondered, find that worldly considerations – money, for example – interfered with a religious life?

'No,' said Lobsang Tsering shortly. 'Anyway, what do you mean by a "religious life"? One thing you should not forget is that Sera is a Gelugpa monastery. We believe in the importance of study; in the importance of logic and philosophy. In the hills above Dharamsala, there are today around fifty hermits, yogis, meditating in caves. But they have all studied at somewhere like Sera beforehand. Unless you have such a solid grounding the pursuit of enlightenment is futile: a complete waste of time.'

After tea, on our way back to the Bylakuppe guesthouse, Tenzin and I called in at Tashilhunpo, the small monastery established by exiled followers of the Panchen Lama. On a patch of scruffy ground directly in front of the *gompa*, about a dozen monks, all wearing their distinctive, shaggy, yellow, crested hats, were listlessly watching one of their more vigorous and muscular brethren, stripped to the waist, swinging a great, rusty axe at a rapidly splintering tree trunk. Jagged chips of wood flew in all directions, imperilling the eyesight of anyone within twenty feet, while rivulets of sweat ran down the monk's forearms, marooning islands of white dust on his dark and hairless skin. Every few moments he put down the axe to dry his palms on a scrap of ragged and filthy towelling.

'Fuel for the kitchen,' one of the spectators explained presently. He seemed shy, almost apologetic, his manner an immediate contrast to the ebullience of his compatriots at Sera.

'Quite a change from Tashilhunpo in Shigatse,' I remarked crassly, looking round at the modest buildings, the rough pathways overgrown with weeds, and sensing an atmosphere suggestive of poverty and grim resignation. My new acquaintance shrugged and his face took on an expression of profound gloom. 'Wouldn't know,' he replied shortly. 'Haven't been there.'

Today, the original Tashilhunpo is Tibet's largest surviving monastery with around six hundred monks; a mere 18 per cent of its full complement on the eve of the Chinese invasion. However, its buildings had been left relatively unscathed by the mayhem of the past thirty years, a state of preservation particularly startling when compared with the dereliction of the shattered Lhasa monasteries. Precisely why Tashilhunpo should have been so specially favoured is, among Tibetans, a matter of some controversy.

The title of Panchen Lama was created in the seventeenth century by the 'Great Fifth' Dalai Lama, the inventor of the unified, theocratic, Tibetan state. Having carved out for himself and his successors a position of unprecedented power (and prior to work beginning on his immense new palace, the Potala), he seemed to have felt that a gesture of humility might not, in the circumstances, come amiss. His venerable tutor and abbot of Tashilhunpo, Lobsang Chokyi Gyaltsen was duly pronounced to be an incarnation of the Buddha Amitabha – a spiritual rank actually superior to that of the Dalai Lama himself – in a lineage henceforth to be known as that of the Panchen ('Great Scholar') Lama.

Doubtless the Dalai Lama felt genuine respect and affection for his elderly mentor, but given his consummate skill as a politician it is astonishing that he did not realise what problems he was storing up for the future by creating a rival powerbase within the ruling Gelugpa Buddhist hierarchy. Over the centuries the Chinese – a people seldom guilty of political naivity – have accepted his gift with enthusiasm, constantly playing one lama off against the other on the reliable principle of divide and rule. In 1728, the Manchu Chinese Empire even went so far as to declare the Panchen Lama to be the autonomous ruler of the western province of Tsang, an assertion which the Tibetans sensibly chose to ignore.

In more recent times, however, Chinese efforts to sow division have fallen on more fertile soil and the relationship between Lhasa and Shigatse has been anything but harmonious. In 1922, while trying to reimpose his authority on Tashilhunpo by insisting that it make a contribution to the cost of maintaining a Tibetan national army, the Thirteenth Dalai Lama caused the Ninth Panchen Lama to flee to China, presumably in fear of his liberty, or continued personal wellbeing, or both. There he lived out the remainder of his days, his exile a focus for endless speculation and damaging intrigue.

His successor, born in 1938 on the border of China and the Tibetan province of Amdo, was effectively the candidate of the Chinese (Nationalist) government, and only after the (Communist) Chinese invasion did the religious authorities in Lhasa finally agree to endorse him as the true reincarnation: in which decision, by then, they doubtless had very little choice. Educated in China and groomed by the Chinese as their protégé and, if necessary, heir apparent, the Panchen Lama finally arrived in Shigatse in 1952 escorted by troops of the People's Liberation Army. It was not, however, until the flight of the Dalai Lama to India seven years later that he could be fully utilised, applying a veneer of spurious respectability to armed aggression, ideological persecution, and the murderous suppression of dissent.

'In short, a wonderful situation prevails in Tibet today,' he famously declared in December 1960. 'Prosperous scenes of labour and production are found in every corner of the vast countryside. . . .'

However, history has proved the Panchen Lama's character to be nothing if not contradictory. Despite being for years an apparently willing Chinese pawn, his relationship with his sponsors seems to have crossed a fateful Rubicon when, taking advantage of his temporary absence in Peking, they began to round up the monks at Tashilhunpo, persuading the obstreperous ones to be silent by the simple expedient of a bullet. His dissatisfaction with this new and unwelcome state of affairs finally came to a crisis in March 1964, when, having been required to address a mass rally in Lhasa and to spout the usual mixture of slogans, platitudes, and lies, he took the opportunity to speak warmly in favour of Tibetan independence and to pledge his undying loyalty to the exiled Dalai Lama in just about the most ostentatious and public manner possible. Whether this outburst may best be described as brave or foolhardy remains open to question.

The Chinese, aghast, roughly seized their erstwhile puppet and, having gone to considerable lengths to persuade him of the error of his ways, threw him into gaol and left him there to rot. The Cultural Revolution then intervened and it was not until 1978 that the Panchen Lama was heard from again.

After fourteen years of imprisonment and torture, his next public utterance was, understandably, rather more cautious. Having apologised for his 'mistakes', he went on: '. . . For a period of time I discarded the banner of patriotism and committed crimes. Guided by Chairman Mao's revolutionary line I have corrected my errors.'

Fortunately for the Panchen Lama, the Chairman's revolutionary line was becoming of less consequence by the minute. Following Mao's death in 1976 and the thwarting of the ultra-leftist Gang of Four, a more pragmatic regime had come to power, one which was dimly aware that the Panchen Lama might still, conceivably, be of use.

For more than a decade, up until his death in January 1989, the Panchen Lama prospered. He married (a Chinese woman) and had at least one child, indulged his legendary appetite at the more expensive Peking restaurants, and invested in a number of business ventures in Lhasa and Shigatse, the probity of which was never established to everyone's entire satisfaction.

On the other hand, his advocates insist, he encouraged the Chinese to patch up some of the remaining monasteries and in general acted as a buffer between the authorities and their unfortunate colonial subjects, moderating Peking's instinctive vengefulness and restraining the Tibetan hotheads intent on expelling the PLA armed only with a penknife and their righteous indignation. To the end he remained an enigma: revered by some, reviled by others; a Tibetan Quisling; a pragmatist who pursued the art of the possible; a courageous man who concealed his true affections; a wily old rogue who looked out for the main chance and whose gluttony finally killed him. What is not in dispute is that he died in Shigatse of a heart attack. Of course, some people muttered that he must have been murdered while others maintained, without any obvious signs of grief, that the Chinese had just lost their most important and irreplaceable ally.

Having been invited inside, Tenzin and I strolled around the *gompa*, pausing eventually before two large black-and-white photographs of the Panchen Lama hanging in pride of place on a pillar beside the abbot's throne. Our guide, one of the younger monks, explained their origin, more, it seemed to me, from a sense of duty than any particular enthusiasm.

'When the Panchen Lama visited Tibet in 1985, we were able to send a representative to meet him in Shigatse. He gave us these.'

'Was he interested to hear about his monastery in South India?'

'Oh yes. Of course. He said that he wished he could come down to see us.'

'So do you have much contact with Tashilhunpo nowadays?'

'No. None at all really.'

We wandered slowly back across the scrubby and uneven ground to an anonymous building, apparently used as a kind of common room. Three elderly monks seated on rickety wooden chairs stared up at Tenzin and me as if utterly bemused by our appearance there. They were clearly astonished to find themselves the object of anyone's attention or concern. Tea was brought and we sat for a few moments in silence, listening only to the sound of the flies which swarmed everywhere like the advance guard of a Biblical plague, landing on the monks' bald pates, and striding about with the assurance of a duke on his grousemoor. One bluebottle of specimen size dived into my tea, where it proceeded to practise a vigorous, if splashy backstroke. In deference to my hosts' Buddhist sensibilities, I hoicked him out and let him run around the table to dry off.

'No one has come from Tibet since 1982,' said the younger monk at last, bravely attempting conversation. 'There are only fifteen monks here now who came from Shigatse.'

'But there seem to be quite a lot of young novices. Where are they all from?'

'We have a school. The students start when they are eight, and we have paid teachers for English and Hindi. They are mostly the children of Ladakhis and exiled Tibetans living in Kulu. Also the people from Lahaul and Spiti – the regions to the north and east of Manali – send their boys here. It's a tradition that still continues. They always educated their sons at Tashilhunpo before the Chinese invasion. And actually the same applies to the Ladakhis. For them, and all of western Tibet, it was primarily Shigatse they looked to; not Lhasa.'

'So the monastery here is thriving?'

'Well. . . . The problem is money really. You see, we were only given land for eighteen people. Also in the beginning we did not receive any money from the aid agencies.'

'Why was that?'

'I don't know I'm afraid. And then for the last few years there has been a drought in South India, which had made things a great deal worse. We have some sponsors of course – in a small way – and we can get any schoolbooks we need from Delhi, but still money has been very difficult. Also . . .', the monk hesitated, '. . . we have not really been accepted here at Bylakuppe.'

'Accepted by whom?'

Withdrawing behind a haggard protective mask, the monk shrugged, resolutely declining to commit himself further.

Chapter 13

HUNSUR

The following morning, the welfare officer from Bylakuppe New Settlement (who until now had been away on official business in Mysore) came over to the guesthouse for breakfast. As all that was on offer was a greasy fried egg, it did not seem likely that the motive for his visit was solely gastronomic. And indeed so it proved. Perhaps, he suggested after a while, looking studiedly unconcerned, we had by now seen all that we wanted to and hence might feel inclined to move on to Hunsur, which we would be sure to find equally interesting; if not more so. Not, of course, that there was any problem with the Indian authorities – far from it – or that he himself wished to be anything less than entirely hospitable; it was just that perhaps, well, perhaps we had finished anyhow. And there would be no problem about transport as a local Indian of his acquaintance was the owner of a car. Admittedly it was a rather old and potentially unreliable one, but then Hunsur was only a couple of hours away and the road was in good condition for the most part, only the last few miles being unsurfaced and in consequence a little bumpy and uncomfortable.

*

As it seemed that our welcome might easily be overstayed, by eleven-thirty we were off, trundling through the hot South Indian countryside, our progress shadowed by a line of distant, beckoning hills and punctuated by dusty villages, where white, skinny cows cropped the grassless soil around ponds of slimy, scum-flecked water. Eventually, having learned to disregard the confident directions provided by local people (who from excessive sympathy merely told us what they thought we wanted to hear, as opposed to the bald and unpalatable truth that we were hopelessly lost), we located a track that led to the Tibetan settlement, and quite by accident drove up the front drive of Hunsur's Lower Tantric College. Tenzin relaxed visibly and smiled.

His pleasure proved to be surprisingly short-lived, however, as our arrival seemed to cause immediate consternation among the senior monks who came out to investigate the source of all the commotion. Irritated by this unexpected response, Tenzin paid off the driver and then departed in search of an explanation. He returned shortly looking puzzled.

'It seems Dharamsala has blessed the settlement with a new representative who's completely neurotic about foreigners. They're all in a terrific state about it. Even the abbot appears to wish that we hadn't come. I can't think what all the fuss is about.'

It was at this point that an extremely smart Ambassador car – its paintwork immaculate, windscreen spotless, and wheel hubs burnished like Achilles' shield – drew up with a scrunch beside us. A dapper little man jumped out, wearing a starched white shirt, grey slacks, and with his black hair so neatly trimmed, severely parted, and gleamingly oiled, that he might just have returned from the barber's, via perhaps the car wash and the laundry, had this bit of Karnataka possessed any of these services; which of course it didn't. Dashing over to where Tenzin and I were standing, he seized me by the arm and propelled me firmly towards the rear door of the car.

'Get in, get in, get in,' he hissed, his manner a curious mixture of coercion and entreaty. Being completely nonplussed, I complied without a struggle, while Tenzin, equally bemused, climbed into the front seat. Meanwhile, the representative – for this was he – flung our bags into the boot, ran round to the driver's side, threw himself in through the door, started the engine, and drove off.

We had been going for at least a mile, during which time Tenzin and I exchanged looks of mingled amusement and incredulity, before our self-appointed chauffeur had composed himself sufficiently in order to be able to speak.

'You shouldn't have come you know. You shouldn't have come. You'll have to leave first thing tomorrow. I'd take you to Mysore myself now, but I can't. Of course I shan't inform the authorities, but if they find out, what then? Tell me that. What then?'

'What authorities? Where?' Tenzin very sensibly enquired, staring out at the passing fields that stretched away to a distant horizon, uncluttered by so much as a house, still less a village, or any other likely source of cantankerous, uniformed officialdom. In the imagination of the representative the landscape was clearly swarming with agents and informers, eagerly awaiting just such an opportunity to contrive his arrest, imprisonment, humiliation, and disgrace.

'You'll have to stay inside until it's dark,' he went on, ignoring the question completely.

It occurred to me that one simple way of getting the conversation onto a more constructive footing might be to introduce ourselves, but even this innocuous tactic misfired badly. On being asked for his name, the representative panicked so much that he nearly drove off the road with fright. 'Later, later, later,' he said, looking round desperately for any way out of his ghastly predicament. After a few moments, however, a crafty and rather pleased expression stole over his face, as though he were silently congratulating himself for having thwarted such a nefarious attempt to trap him.

The representative was himself living in the official guesthouse, having, it seemed, taken up his post at Hunsur only a few months previously. It was a pleasant, substantial buiding, much grander than the one at Bylakuppe, with freshly painted green walls, large red arm chairs, mosquito screens at the windows, and a bathroom of positively Caracallan splendour (at least compared with most of those to be found in rural Karnataka). Tenzin and I were shooed inside, our reluctant host hurrying over to bolt the back door, which, as far as I could see, led out into an empty field.

It was while he was busy drawing the curtains to keep out the prying eyes of the incorrigibly inquisitive populace, that it occurred to me to dig out the letter of introduction from the Information Office in Dharamsala, which firmly enjoined all Tibetan officials to be as hospitable and cooperative as their individual circumstances permitted. Presenting it to the representative, I stood back to see what reaction, if any, it would provoke. Seeing the red official crest, he seemed to stiffen slightly before beginning to read, his eyes widening in horror as he began to comprehend the full enormity of his terrible mistake. By the time he got to the end of the letter (it was very short) he was a broken man, his career in ruins, all hope of advancement shattered by twenty minutes of excessive zeal.

'Everything I have is yours,' he said, flinging his arms wide, his voice breaking with repentance and grief.

'Uh?' said Tenzin, startled. 'What did you say?'

'Everything . . .' the representative went on, looking round for some precious object to bestow on us. Finding nothing suitable, he dashed into the nearby kitchen. 'Lunch,' he shouted. 'You must share my food.' This sounded more promising, so Tenzin and I trooped after him, only to find that calamity had once again struck.

'All I have is here,' the representative wailed, indicating the bottom shelf of a very large cupboard, on which stood half a loaf of stiff and elderly bread, a pot of apricot jam sustaining an entire moss garden of colourful growth, and, propped up in one corner, an egg.

'I've never met a Tibetan like him,' I confided to Tenzin in mid-afternoon, while our host was out, attending to his duties in the nearby settlement. 'He even looks vaguely Chinese to me.'

'Well . . . ,' Tenzin replied helplessly, '. . . he's certainly conscientious. I suppose he's so new to the job, that he feels very insecure. As to his being Chinese, you're actually not far wrong. His family came from the easternmost part of Kham: right on the Chinese border. Not . . . ,' he added doubtfully, '. . . that that explains anything.'

It was dark when the representative returned, but despite the gloom being only slightly diluted by a flickering forty-watt bulb, there was no mistaking the look of triumph that now glowed on his previously despairing face.

'You've been invited to a banquet,' he announced grandly. Both Tenzin and I responded to this abrupt transition from the ridiculous to the sublime with instinctive caution and said nothing. The representative, however, was quite irrepressible. 'Come along, come along,' he said, 'we're going out.'

'Out? But what about the Indian authorities? Aren't you worried about them?'

'Oh no. No one will see you. It's quite dark now.' Evidently fearing that we hadn't noticed, he walked to the door and pointed up at the sky. 'You see,' he said. 'You will be invisible. Anyway come along, we are expected.'

We drove in stoical silence back across the blackened fields – the representative peering earnestly forward along the beams of his faltering and jaundiced headlamps – turning at last into the familiar driveway of the Tantric College. There, a group of Tibetan monks could be seen ushering two slight, white-robed figures through a brightly lit and welcoming doorway.

'Christians!' said the representative, in the breathless and awestruck voice of someone glimpsing a fabulous animal, which he had previously supposed to exist only in the pages of legend. 'English Christians,' he continued; adding as an afterthought, 'From England: your country,' just in case I had been left in any doubt.

'I thought you said that foreigners weren't allowed here.' I objected.

'Ah yes . . .' replied the representative, '. . . but they have permission. *Official* permission from the Indian authorities!'

Father Peter and Brother James turned out to be Benedictines from Gloucester, spry and smiling in immaculate cream cassocks. They were on an exchange visit and the refectory of the Tantric College had been lavishly decorated in their honour with coloured paper streamers and festoons of silver tinsel. Both seemed slightly relieved to see a fellow countryman and darted across the room to seize me warmly by the hand. Father Peter, a thin man with silver hair, was particularly affable. He talked extremely fast, his super-abundant energy otherwise expending itself in a series of small hops from one foot to the other. This resulted in a large wooden crucifix swinging across his chest as if we'd been caught in a sudden earth tremor, during which habitually immobile objects had acquired an alarming and unpredictable life of their own.

In comparison, his hosts all seemed to be the sturdy sons of good Tibetan farming stock: their coarse red robes, grizzled heads, weathered skin, and ham-like biceps a reminder that Tibetan monasteries contain men who in another culture might well have opted for a vigorous existence in the workaday world, rather than for one of spirituality and sequestered contemplation.

We sat down, around twenty of us in all, at a long trestle table which sagged slightly under the weight of a dozen great trenchers of food. A bear-like man on my left – well over six feet tall and weighing in excess of fifteen stone – briefly introduced himself as the college choirmaster, before piling his plate with noddles and stir-fried meat and tucking in as though it were his first substantial meal for a month.

Father Peter coughed: at first diffidently, then with rather more insistence. The choirmaster looked up, his kindly face full of sympathy, but without the least understanding as to the cause of this sudden affliction. However, having no medical advice to offer, he presently resumed his dinner. Like a man on the edge of a very cold pond, Father Peter stared round at the happily munching Tibetans, took a deep breath, and then began to say grace loudly and firmly. The clatter of plates and the rumble of conversation abruptly ceased. After the prayer had ended, an awkward silence continued for some seconds, while the abbot of the Tantric College and three or four of his more senior monks went into a huddle to work out a suitable Tibetan response. This they then intoned solemnly. When they had finished, the choirmaster turned to me, shrugged his shoulders with obvious bafflement, and then, as if to make up for lost time helped himself to a dozen *momos*, some more noodles, and a bowl of carrot salad.

'It's really very impressive,' Father Peter observed when dinner was finally over. He held a cup of instant coffee out in front of him and stirred it thoughtfully. 'The natural religiosity of the Tibetans is unique in my experience. It's very difficult not to be envious coming from Europe where religion is so . . . well . . . ah . . . peripheral nowadays. I suppose one might compare the Tibetans to the inhabitants of Sicily, say, or parts of southern Ireland: places where the old Catholic culture is still substantially intact; where people follow a genuinely religious way of life and where belief is all but unquestioned.' He sighed.

'But do you suppose that Tibetan religiosity can survive exposure to the modern world? Or will it prove just as susceptible to materialism as the religious faith of the West?'

'Ah well . . .', said Father Peter, stirring his coffee slightly faster and generating a small vortex in the unattractive grey liquid, '. . . that, of course, is the question. At the moment religion and nationalism can be equated to some extent. But over time I imagine that the Tibetans will prove little different from the rest of humanity. The pattern we have seen in the West is, it seems to me, highly likely to repeat itself out here.'

Initially this gloomy prognosis seemed to cheer him slightly, but catching himself in possession of such an unworthy emotion, he quickly assumed an expression of extreme seriousness.

'The attractions of materialism seem to be irresistible to the majority of people, irrespective of their cultural background.' He hesitated. 'And of course . . .', he went on, '. . . one can quite understand why,' giving me the clear impression that he personally could understand no such thing.

What, I wondered, did he hope to achieve by his visit to a remote Tibetan monastery. Over dinner, I explained, I had been trying to find out what the Tibetan monks knew about Christianity and so far as I had been able to tell, only the threadbare phrase the 'promotion of world peace' was unspecific enough to bridge the gulf of mutual incomprehension. Father Peter stared at me as though this was the kind of unhelpful remark only to be expected from a journalist. Did he, I persisted, as a Catholic monk, feel any great sympathy for Buddhism; particularly the Tibetan variety?

'There are obviously very great differences between our two religions; though the morality is not altogether dissimilar. But I am convinced that Buddhism is a Way of Truth. You have only to look at the faces of the Tibetan people. There you see real spiritual serenity. As to the "Tibetan variety" I am not at all sure what you mean.'

'Well, Tibetan Buddhism is a far cry from the earlier forms of the religion: with its pantheons of Buddhas, bodhisattvas, protective deities, oracular spirits, reincarnate lamas, and so on and so forth. Thanks to the indigenous shamanism and Indian Tantra, it includes quite a lot the historical Buddha might have found fairly puzzling. Early Buddhism was about the individual's search for salvation – the pilgrim's progress – not all this esoteric, mystical stuff.'

'You sound, if I may say so,' said Father Peter, '. . . like a particularly censorious protestant, outlining his multifarious objections to Catholicism. In view of which, you can hardly expect me to be sympathetic. It would appear that temperamentally you incline towards fundamentalism – or at least Puritanism. I suggest that you talk to the abbot here tomorrow. I wouldn't presume to make out a case for the defence. However, Brother James and I come from a contemplative order and in consequence I think there is much that we can learn from Tibetan practice. In my opinion the similiarities between Christian prayer and Buddhist meditation are a good deal more interesting than the differences. And now . . .', (the abbot of the Tantric College was waving at him vigorously from the other side of the room), '. . . I believe our presence is required at the screening of a film.'

We trooped outside. A light shower had fallen during dinner and the still night air was as fragrant as an incense factory, saturated with an intoxicating perfume for which no particular flower could be held directly responsible, but which seemed to be exhaled by the ground itself, the smell of universal fertility, a volatile elixir of life. We crossed a patch of damp, rust-coloured soil to the main chanting hall. The local frogs, partying vociferously, rendered any attempt at conversation futile.

Inside, three or four hundred monks, mostly in their twenties or thirties, had packed themselves in untidy rows behind a small projector. Brother James and Father Peter were immediately ushered into the midst of this heaving throng; two visiting supporters in a football crowd; inconsequential flecks of white in a billowing ocean of maroon and yellow. The lights were dimmed and the film began. It seemed that the three days of their stay at Hunsur had been chronicled by someone with a video camera and edited highlights, dwelling particularly on the guttural chanting for which the college is famous, were now being shown for the general edification of the monastery. The audience, however, was in no mood to sit in decorous silence. Whoops of delight broke out whenever someone in the hall recognised himself on the screen, his friends joining in with a chorus of full-throated cheering. One or two of the senior monks at the front of the hall began to turn round in their seats and to direct long, disapproving stares at the instigators of this vulgar commotion. Eventually, when silent admonition had proved to be of no effect whatever, the projectionist was instructed to hurry up proceedings and to bring them to a premature conclusion. This meant, however, that each time the video tape was run on fast-forward, venerable figures (including the abbot), could be seen hurtling about the screen at preposterous and unnatural speed. The massed ranks of the assembly rocked with gleeful and cacophonous laughter.

What brings them here? I found myself wondering when the pandemonium was at its height. All these young men forsaking the life of the world to learn fiendishly complex Tantric ritual, afterwards immuring themselves on meditation retreat for three years or more. Why should so many of them opt to live like this? After all it *is* celibacy. And unless one is blessed with an intensely spiritual or philosophical cast of mind – which not all that many people are – the substitutes of work and companionship cannot be particularly adequate. Of course a monastic life is free from want. You accept the moderate comfort of relative poverty and in return are freed from the terror and suffering of absolute destitution. But here in South India such considerations are nowadays irrelevant. Life in the Tibetan settlements is secure enough; everyone is housed and nobody starves; even leisure is not a complete impossibility.

In the old Tibet, for the mass of the people the monasteries were the only source of education and therefore the only escape from the grim routine of manual labour. As monks ran the civil administration – they were the country's white-collar workers – the pleasures of the flesh might reasonably be exchanged for social advancement. But nowadays secular schools provide a far less penitential route to the comforts and civilities of middle-class life.

So could it be karma, the Buddhist version of brimstone and hellfire, the fear of being reborn an animal (or worse), which fills the cloisters with each succeeding generation? Looking round, it seemed distinctly unlikely. I had seldom seen a less angst-stricken bunch. No, the majority of these young men had taken orders simply out of obedience to cultural tradition; they had no religious vocation, no ulterior motive; they were doing merely what their society expected of them.

On our way home the representative was in almost euphoric good humour. The malign phantoms which had haunted his daytime world – notably Indian policemen – were by now all safely tucked up in bed. Everything had gone extremely well, he said. The banquet, he was sure we would agree, had been a tremendous success. Furthermore, he had good news for us. Although in the morning he had to drive Father Peter and Brother James to the station in Mysore – they were apprently going to visit an ashram near Madras, before returning to Dharamsala – he had arranged for us to spend the day at the Tantric College and would drive us over there for breakfast with the abbot at nine. He beamed at us, his face glowing with renewed confidence and self-esteem.

Even the realisation that a window had been left open with a light on – in consequence of which the guesthouse had been occupied in our absence by a rag-tag army of South Indian fauna – failed to depress him greatly. A colossal toad, which looked as though it might well dine out on squirrels or stray cats, glared sullenly at us from the doorway, resolutely declining to move. The representative poked it tentatively in the ribs with a broom. 'Surprising,' he said, stepping backward slightly. 'Most surprising. It seems a very determined creature.' Moths the size of saucers blundered about the rooms through a haze of mosquitos, whacking into light bulbs and leaving them swinging wildly; while on every available flat surface, including the ceiling, bulging lizards smacked their lips with whip-lash tongues, beady-eyed with insectivorous gluttony.

As order would clearly have to be restored in daylight, I retired to bed, only to discover that a column of soldier ants had got there before me: in battalion strength at least.

The original Lower Tantric College (Gyu-me in Tibetan) still stands in the centre of Lhasa, though not a great deal happens there nowadays. A focus of particular hostility in the Cultural Revolution, it was ruthlessly desecrated, and its 500 monks murdered, imprisoned, or otherwise dispersed. Thirty or forty have subsequently drifted back to eke out an uncertain and uncomfortable existence.

The institution was founded in 1433 by Je Sherab Senge, a follower of the great religious reformer Tsongkhapa, who had been charged by his famous mentor with the preservation and dissemination of his specifically Tantric teachings.

The principal characteristic of the Tibetan form of Buddhism is the faith it places in Tantric techniques for achieving enlightenment. Traditionally, Buddhists had assumed that only the gradual improvement of karma (the slow accretion of meritorious actions), by effort sustained over a long succession of lives, could bring about the conditions in which final spiritual salvation might be attained. But Tantra claimed to be able to truncate this process into the single lifetime of a determined and disciplined individual. Impatient of a philosophy which had degenerated into arthritic scholasticism,

Tantra promised results (as, incidentally, did Zen, which developed in China at much the same time, for some of the same reasons). Tibetan Buddhism does not deny the validity of earlier practices and beliefs, it merely adds this extra, highly significant component.

The precise origins of Tantra still remain obscure, but generally it is accepted that Tantric ideas and practices began to be of importance in India around the fourth century AD. Tantric Buddhist texts survive from the sixth century, about a hundred years before the first introduction of the religion to Tibet. Tantra was not, however, a specifically Buddhist development: it was rather an Indian cultural phenomenon, of comparable importance in the history of Hinduism.

The guiding principle of Indian civilisation throughout the centuries has been an insistence on the primacy of the spirit. Indian religions have always distrusted, or dismissed, the evidence of the senses and have instead placed value on the perceptions of the mind, particularly the mind when stilled and focused through meditation. The world is generally seen as an illusion, a place which is inherently incapable of satisfying the higher aspirations of man, and from which we should make every effort to escape.

There have, however, been one or two modifications to this habitual point of view. Both Buddhist and Hindu Tantra support the orthodox position that sense perception is profoundly misleading, but nonetheless maintain that life contains experiences which may be put to practical use. Controversially, they insist that the sexual impulse may be redirected and controlled for spiritual purposes. Hindu Tantra considers the human libido to be identifiable with the creative, energy-essence of the universe, as a result of which various yogic practices were devised, in which coition between male and female initiates was permitted in the quest for states of higher consciousness. (Needless to say, Europeans in India during the colonial period were aghast at the very idea of such behaviour, regarding sexually explicit Tantric sculpture and painting as so much pornography. Even though we are nowadays pleased to think ourselves more sophisticated, Westerners are still happier with the idea that civilisation is the result of repression. Mankind, we prefer to think, has progressed by taming the rampant Eros and putting him to useful and productive labour.)

Unlike Hinduism, Buddhism does not believe in the existence of any cosmic positive principle, insisting that all things are ultimately empty of inherent meaning. Nonetheless, Buddhist Tantra likewise sees virtue in manipulating the energy of sexual desire. Generally this has been through imagination rather than actual intercourse, Tibetan Tantric Buddhism having retained a fundamentally ascetic character. (In Tibetan art and sculpture the sexually united male and female also became a crucial symbol for the marriage of wisdom (female) and yogic technique (male) required for the attainment of enlightenment.) Most importantly, Tantra insists that the physical basis of psychic life is a 'subtle body' of energy, which if properly understood and controlled can be the means by which the mind is brought to the mystical experience of 'clear light'. In Tantra, therefore, enlightenment is not simply the result of progressive refinement of the mind, but is a psycho-physical transformation.

Tibetan practitioners of Buddhist Tantra tended to be either hermits (yogis) independent of any particular religious institution and often living in isolated Himalayan caves, or monks who had studied the traditional texts (sutras) for many years and then opted to commit themselves to a teacher (guru) in the hope of reaching a higher level of religious development.

The esoteric Tantric scriptures are quite incomprehensible without the help of such a spiritual cicerone. As a consequence of the Tibetans' exile, some of them have recently been elucidated for the benefit of Western curiosity, but the vast majority remain untranslated and obscure to all but a handful of Tantric masters.

Gosok Rinpoche, the abbot of the Tantric College, was a corpulent, uninspiring man to look at. His complexion seemed in immediate need of fresh air and he wore thick pebble glasses, through which he peered in an unfocused, perplexed kind of way. He was, I decided, the precise physical opposite of the emaciated Himalayan yogi, cross-legged on a glacier in his loincloth. Next to him sat the burly, jovial figure of Geshe Tashi, the College's Chanting Master, who had evidently agreed to keep him company and lend him moral support. Tenzin and I had joined the two monks for tea and biscuits in the refectory. The room was still decorated with paper streamers from the night before, which fluttered and rustled in a feeble and listless breeze. Outside the day was building up into a sullen, tropical torpor. From the nearby *gompa* came the sound of lethargic chanting.

'Me?' said Gosok Rinpoche in surprise. 'You want to know about me?' He looked helplessly at Geshe Tashi, who looked equally bemused and said nothing. I explained that I was very interested in the lives of individual Tibetans: particularly those occupying such important positions in society.

'Whereabouts in Kham do you come from?' enquired Tenzin in his most unthreatening, psychoanalyst-in-search-of-a-confidence voice.

'From Lithang.'

'And when did you leave?'

'In '59. To get away from the troubles in Lhasa. I was only twelve at the time. The Dalai Lama had already gone and in Tibet there was nothing but violence. Actually I soon began to wonder if I'd made a mistake: I had a very hard time walking through Arunachal – which is a remote and wild part of India – and ended up in first Misamari, then Buxa, both of which were extremely unpleasant. There were very few books and nearly everyone was sick. Fortunately I survived and after a while was able to come down to Sera. I eventually sat my *geshe* exam there at the age of thirty-two.'

'So how long have you been abbot here?'

'Since last year. His Holiness appointed me about twelve months ago. The abbot of this college serves only a three-year term and then the position passes to someone else. Nominations for the post are sent by the monastery to the Dalai Lama and he then makes the final decision. I joined the Tantric College in 1979 and became abbot ten years later. You see, the basic study of Tantra takes nine years; though of course the subject is vast and there is no limit to the time one may spend on it. Nowadays I continue to study texts and to teach the younger monks at the same time.'

'And the course is the same as it was in Tibet?'

Gosok Rinpoche paused to consider the matter. 'If anything, there is more emphasis on intellectual rigour than there was in Lhasa. And of course no one may *begin* to study Tantra here until he has a thorough knowledge of Sutra, which will take him at least fifteen years, if not longer. When monks arrive here, they are the particular responsibility of the abbot. After one year they have to give an oral exam to me, based on a hundred and sixty pages of memorised text. Then they have to participate in three days of formal debate on various Tantric subjects. During their first year they are also under the instruction of the Chanting Master; they learn how to construct various sand mandalas; and they practise two types of meditation.'

'So would you say that your years in exile have at last brought a kind of normality?'

'Normality? Of a kind, I suppose. I am personally content, but the monastery has many problems, and these naturally cause me some anxiety. These are to do with money mostly. We were allocated land, just like the lay settlers, and this is really our only source of revenue. For example, the *gompa* here had to be built by the monks themselves. We must all work to survive and even then it sometimes seems that there will not be enough to go round. We were able to bring almost nothing with us from Tibet: just a few *thankas.*'

'Do you have any contact with Gyu-me in Lhasa?'

'No. None. But I know that about forty monks have returned there and that the assembly hall is still standing.'

'And how many monks are there here in Hunsur nowadays?'

'Five hundred. The college is completely full. You see, all those monks who pass the exam of Geshe Lharampa, the highest grade, are obliged to go to one or other of the Tantric Colleges: either here, or to the Upper Tantric Colleges at Bomdila in Arunachal.'

'The two colleges teach the same thing?'

'Yes. There may be some slight difference in the chanting – I am not sure – but that is all. Anyway, despite the fact that these outstanding scholars are *required* to attend a Tantric College, they still have to write to us, often two or three times, for permission to enrol here. We have to find room for them somehow, but it is not always easy.'

'Still, it must be encouraging to be oversubscribed. At least it shows that your cultural tradition remains healthy, despite all the traumas it has suffered.'

'Oh, I am not in the least concerned about that. I am

sure that the Tibetan Tantric tradition can survive indefinitely, whatever the financial hardships. Such problems may be a nuisance, but they will be overcome somehow.'

'So when the students come here, what exactly do they learn?'

Gosok Rinpoche paused and glanced across to Geshe Tashi. 'To those capable of taking desire into the path . . . ,' he began, '. . . the Buddha taught the vehicle of the Vajrayana.' He stopped, as if aware that this formulaic reply was not really going to meet the needs of the occasion, and turned to Geshe Tashi for assistance.

'Well . . . ,' said Geshe Tashi slowly, '. . . it's a bit hard to summarise really.' He looked at me carefully and appeared moderately reassured by what he saw. 'To be honest, Western people have often misunderstood Tantra very badly. Of course, this was partly because the texts were secret and they tried to imagine what must be in them. Fortunately, things are better nowadays. One or two scholars have recently written quite good books in English. You've probably read them? There's a man called Jeffrey Hopkins: an American. And then His Holiness has tried to bring some aspects of Tantric ritual more into the open – the Kalachakra initiation at Bodh Gaya, for example – which has helped to give Western people a different impression. All this is very positive. But to be honest, it's not possible to explain simply what we do here. To understand our meditations and our rituals, you have to have reached an advanced level in the study of Buddhist philosophy. And quite a lot is still kept deliberately obscure. Our famous chanting, for example, was developed partly to prevent the uninitiated from knowing what was going on.'

'In the Tibetan Buddhist tradition, it is claimed that Tantra provides a short-cut to enlightenment, which may be achieved in the course of a single lifetime.'

'Yes, that's true. Tantra is not suitable for everyone, but for some it can provide such a path.'

'So how many people here are seriously attempting to become enlightened: as opposed to simply pursuing a scholarly discipline and an ascetic way of life?'

Geshe Tashi looked taken aback. '*Everyone* here is working for enlightenment. We have a queue of people waiting to do three-year meditation retreats; so many in fact that it is hard for us to ensure that they all get a chance. But generally the necessary teaching and facilities are there. I must tell you . . . ,' he said with sudden and compelling earnestness, '. . . that enlightenment is definitely possible. We have many monks here – one cannot say precisely how many, but a significant number – who have advanced very far along the path.' He glanced at the abbot for confirmation and Gosok Rinpoche sagely nodded his assent.

'Westerners say: "What is enlightenment? How can we be sure that it exists?" But for us such questions have no meaning. If you follow the path, then such doubts disappear. Hundreds of Tibetans over the centuries, who have practised with great devotion and intensity, have had similar experiences. But of course I am not suggesting that it is easy to become enlightened.' His voice faltered and his eyes dropped to the tablecloth.

'My own guru was the highest Geshe Lharampa and he studied Tantra for twenty-seven years. He lived until he was seventy-nine years old, and just before he died – here at Hunsur – he told me that for him, one life was not enough. And he was a very great man.'

To my amazement, when he looked up his face was shining with tears. The genial, rubicund, Geshe Tashi had collapsed into utter misery. Gosok Rinpoche reached across and grasped his wrist.

'In our tradition . . . ,' he said, clearing his throat, '. . . in the Tibetan Tantric tradition, such devotion by the disciple for his guru is necessary for there to be any hope of success. Without such trust, such spiritual love, it is not possible to succeed.'

The two men sat side by side in silence for at least half a minute. I looked at Tenzin who was evidently moved. Here, I thought, is true religious feeling. This is not scholasticism; these men did not become monks for the sake of an easy life. Here I am standing at the border of another country, of whose geography and inhabitants I know little. I felt a sudden and unexpected wave of humility.

Chapter 14

DHARAMSALA (II)

'Oh, so you've come back at last,' the Dalai Lama's Private Secretary exclaimed with cheerful incredulity, as Tenzin and I accosted him on the outskirts of McCleod Ganj. 'How was it? Did you get down to South India? Oh really. I'm not surprised. We've had problems before with the authorities there. You'd better tell His Holiness: he likes to know these things. Give me a ring after lunch and I'll see when he can fit you in. Friday afternoon might be a good time.' Waving affably he continued on his way, an austere, black-robed figure, down the treacherous, stony footpath to the Tibetan government offices at Gangchen Kyishong.

A three-hour flight from Bangalore, overnight on the Jammu Mail from Delhi, and we were back in the Himalayan foothills. During our five-month absence little seemed to have changed: the Kangra Valley was a bit greener thanks to the residual effect of the summer monsoon; the streets were empty of Indian tourists – who were now all back hard at work in Chandigarh – but otherwise we might have been away for no more than a week. Out in the Great World dynasties might fall, but in

Little Tibet life in exile carried on with every appearance of serene normality.

It was while we were sitting on the roof of Wangchen's hotel – having stuffed ourselves with *thukpa* and been regaled with the tastier morsels of Dharamsala's political and amatory gossip – that Tenzin announced he had already finalised the afternoon's itinerary. He had, he said, been pushing Dharamsala's telephone system to the limits, and as a result everything was now settled.

'I've spoken to the Religious and Cultural Affairs people about going to see the hermits behind the Children's Village in Forsyth Ganj. They said I should talk to Mrs Pema Gyalpo's gardener. He knows where they all live and has agreed to come with us. They seem to think it's all right to go up there. I mean, we won't be disturbing anyone. At least that's what they say.'

Although Wangchen clearly approved of Tantric yogis in principle – as an indispensible part of the Tibetan cultural scenery – he seemed to find it hard to understand why anyone should want to spend their time actually talking to one. Lunch over, he therefore gave the excursion his unqualified blessing, before shuffling off for a strenuous session of mah-jong.

Driving through the quiet woods round a spur of the Dhauladar, we clattered up the hill into Forsyth Ganj, past a small muddy lake where children from the TCV were feeding bread to the swirling fish, and stopped next to the school's basketball court. There our guide was waiting for us as arranged.

We set off up the slope on foot. As the ground was very uneven and covered by dead leaves – so many in fact that they appeared to have lain there undisturbed since the beginning of time – I found it extremely difficult to keep my footing. The playground shrieks of triumph and disaster were rapidly dulled by the surrounding forest and very soon a primeval silence closed around us like a wall.

We had only been stumbling along for about twenty minutes, when we came across Drakpa Thupten sitting on a pile of logs at the door of a rough wooden lean-to. A middle-aged man, he was dressed in the woollen robes of an ordinary monk and didn't seem especially surprised to see us. Initially it was hard to tell whether he regarded our arrival as a gross intrusion, or an agreeable diversion, but Tenzin having explained what we were doing there, he politely indicated a couple of moss-covered stones for us to sit on: arm chairs in his open-air living room. On closer inspection, it appeared that his home was propped up against a rocky outcrop and consisted of one windowless room, the gaps in the planking being sealed with ragged scraps of old plastic sack.

'Oh, there are hermits all round here,' he said in response to my initial enquiry, flapping an arm in the direction of the encircling trees. 'About thirty I suppose. Then there are some more higher up. I believe there are fifty or sixty altogether. Some of us live in huts like this; others in caves.'

Wasn't he, I wondered, a bit too close to civilisation at this relatively low altitude? Drakpa Thupten considered his objection for a moment.

'Well, I *prefer* it up higher,' he said. 'And sometimes I go and stay there for a while. It is certainly much more tranquil. But if you go up close to the snowline, it is very cold for much of the year. Also you have a problem about food. Some yogis have trained themselves not to mind the cold, and some can live with hardly anything to eat, but I have not reached that level of attainment. Here, I may not have isolation, but at least I do have solitude.'

'What do you do about food?'

'The hermits are helped by the office of His Holiness the

Dalai Lama; also the villagers sometimes bring *tsampa* or bread.'

'So what made you choose this existence, as opposed to say, life in one of the famous monasteries?'

'In Tibet, before the Uprising, I *was* in a big monastery: Drepung, near Lhasa. There were hermits who lived in the hills there, and I suppose even then I found them interesting, and wondered whether I might join them one day. But in 1959 Chinese artillery shelled Drepung and I decided to follow His Holiness to India. It was the only thing to do, but even so, life soon became extremely difficult. Because I was a junior monk, I could not get a place in one of the lama camps like Buxa, and for three years I had to labour on the roads in Assam. The work was very hard and there was only time to study for one hour in the morning and one hour in the evening. It was most unsatisfactory, so in order to have a better life, I decided to join the Indian Border Police. I was young and fit and I thought that at least I would be physically close to Tibet. At that time, we all thought we'd soon be going home.'

'It must be more than quarter of a century ago now.'

'I suppose it must. Anyway I stayed in the Border Police for about five years. It wasn't such a bad life – certainly a lot better than road work – but again opportunities for study were very limited. You see I'd already taken vows in Tibet. I'd mentally committed myself to a religious path and couldn't help feeling that I was wasting my time. The turning point came when I realised that we were not going back; at any rate not in the foreseeable future. By then the Tibetan government had been set up in Dharamsala, and the religious institutions were beginning to get themselves organised once more, so I handed in my resignation. That was eighteen years ago.

'I came to McCleod Ganj and talked to the lamas here and asked them what opportunities might now be open to me. But almost immediately I realised that what I really wanted was to become a hermit.'

'Why exactly? It must be such a demanding and uncomfortable life.'

'There was no particular reason for my decision. It was more a feeling: a feeling that wouldn't go away. A constant awareness that a simple, solitary life would suit me best. A life in which I could concentrate on training my mind, without all the distractions of a monastery. I somehow knew that this was the way for me personally to achieve the greatest happiness.'

'Had you been very unhappy since you were forced to leave Tibet? I mean had you despaired of your fate and that of your fellow countrymen?'

'No. I could not say that I had suffered greatly compared with many others. Some who now live here were tortured. Some were in the Chushi Gangdruk and killed Chinese soldiers. Perhaps their experiences drove them to a life alone in the forest. Maybe they are trying to relieve their feelings of guilt: trying to come to terms with the karmic consequences of their actions. There was a man who used to live in a cave just up the hill who was rather like that. He was called Lobsang Tenzin and he came from Phenpo in Central Tibet. He was regarded as one of the most accomplished Tantric yogis. Obviously I don't really know what he felt inside, but certainly he had been in the resistance, captured, and beaten so badly that he was partially blind. I believe he had been betrayed by his own brother, which was a great sorrow to him. His wife and three children had also died. Eventually, by pure chance, he managed to escape from gaol. He then crossed the mountains and joined the Tibetan battalion of the Indian army. But in 1971 India went to war with Pakistan over Bangladesh, and the Tibetan soldiers who had volunteered because they thought they might be able to fight the Chinese, suddenly found themselves in the middle of another battle, the reasons for which they barely understood. I think it was as a result of his experiences there that he finally decided to become a hermit. Even though he was not a well-educated man – indeed at first he could not even read – he came to Dharamsala to receive instruction.'

'You seem to know a lot about him.'

'Well, as I say, he was highly respected for his attainments. On one occasion he was even taken to America by some scientists.'

'Why was that?'

'They wanted to test his ability to generate internal heat. You've probably heard of Milarepa, the famous Tibetan poet.'

'Of course.'

'Then you'll know that he lived about a thousand years ago and that even in the middle of winter he would meditate high in the mountains, dressed only in light cotton clothes. He was a practitioner of *tum-mo*: the form of meditation which generates internal heat. In the Tibetan Tantric tradition we believe that as well as the gross physical body, there is a subtle body of energy flowing through a network of psychic channels. Well, a skilled yogi can concentrate this energy at certain points through meditation. Of course, the main purpose of controlling this energy is to help generate the mind of enlightenment – the so-called experience of clear light – but the technique also has practical uses. Anyway, these American scientists wanted to carry out various tests in their laboratory.'

'Do you yourself practise *tum-mo* meditation?'

Drakpa Thupten smiled shyly in self-deprecation. 'No, I am not a very advanced practitioner. I am still at the stage of generating *bodhi-citta*: the mind of compassion,'

'But you do spend much of your time in meditation?'

'Oh yes. I do four sessions of meditation a day – two in

the morning, two in the afternoon – each of about three hours in length.'

'And you still receive instruction?'

'Yes, of course. I walk down to Dharamsala to see my lama quite regularly. He teaches me the various techniques of meditation – like visualisation, for example – and gives me philosophical texts to read. These we discuss on future occasions, so he can assess my understanding and correct any errors of interpretation. You see the lamas are very concerned for the welfare of the hermits here. Accomplished yogis like Lobsang Tenzin even have audiences with His Holiness the Dalai Lama to discuss their spiritual progress.'

'So where is Lobsang Tenzin now?'

'Unfortunately he died in the autumn of 1988. He went to hear a teaching given by His Holiness in Manali, but for some reason fell ill. He returned here, to his cave on this hillside, but only survived for a few more days. However, as he was spiritually very advanced, he was able to remain in meditation for several days after his death.'

Something in my expression clearly alerted Drakpa Thupten to the presence of an unregenerate sceptic. Had I, he enquired, ever studied the Tibetan teachings on the subject of rebirth? I replied that to some extent I had, but my knowledge, such as it was, was undoubtedly very superficial.

'Tibetans believe that skilled practitioners are able to control the departure of consciousness from the body. After physical death has occurred, a subtle form of consciousness may remain for a while, before proceeding to the *Bardo* – or intermediate state – and ultimately taking rebirth.'

'Even some Westerners now believe in the reality of what they call "after-death experiences",' Tenzin interjected to Drakpa Thupten's evident approval.

'You must go up to the home – the *labrang* – of Ling Rinpoche, the Dalai Lama's senior tutor,' he went on. 'Ling Rinpoche died in 1983. After his heart had stopped beating, he remained in meditation for thirteen days, during which time his colour did not change and his body did not deteriorate. When his consciousness finally departed, his remains were embalmed in the traditional Tibetan manner and made into a statue. You can see it in the shrine-room there. His twenty-second reincarnation, a four-year-old-boy, now lives at the *labrang*. It may be possible for you to obtain an audience.'

Thanking Drakpa Thupten for his advice, I said that we would be sure to pay the young rinpoche a visit. From his own experience, I wondered, had he found Dharamsala a good place in which to meditate? It was, after all, very different from Tibet. The landscape there was so vast and awe-inspiring and the light so clear and penetrating, that even the most mundane objects could appear to be endowed with numinous significance. In such an atmosphere, a random arrangement of stones by the roadside could strike one as having the force of an ancient symbol: a cryptogram to be deciphered in a dramatic access of vision. Tibet, I said, had struck me as a kind of immense laboratory of the spirit, a place which might have been provided by a thoughtful Creator for metaphysical experience and speculation. Whereas in Dharamsala, nature might be tranquil and aesthetically delightful, but it offered few intimations of a transcendent reality. His forest hermitage was quiet and unsullied, but it was also damp, dark, and perhaps at times claustrophobic. Wasn't such an environment rather inhibiting?

Drakpa Thupten smiled uncomprehendingly. 'The precise location is quite unimportant. Such experience is only in the mind. Surely you know that Buddhism dismisses the validity of gross physical phenomena. The doctrine of universal impermanence makes it impossible for us to attach such values to the appearance of the material world. From this point of view, one place is much like another.'

'In that case, if Tibet were liberated, would you go back?'

'Of course.'

'And you would continue to be a hermit?'

'Certainly. I would live in a cave somewhere near Lhasa – ideally in the hillside behind Drepung – so that I would be near His Holiness and could still receive teachings from the lamas. But then I have already explained that my decision to become a hermit was not influenced by the difficult circumstances of our exile. It was a purely personal decision.'

We left Drakpa Thupten bending over a small fire to tend a battered and blackened kettle. Blue woodsmoke filled the empty spaces of the forest, illuminated by shafts of intrepid autumn sunshine. When finally we came out onto the open ground, a surprisingly chilly breeze caused me to glance up at the distant crags of the Dhauladar. There, a faint dusting of white clung to its sheer rock walls, a presentiment of winter nights, of finger-numbing frost and silent snowfall.

The road from McCleod Ganj bazaar to Ling Rinpoche's *labrang* was narrow, steep, and circuitous. The first hundred yards up to the Mountaineering Institute were surfaced after a fashion, but from then on it was only a dirt track and a particularly ill-maintained one at that. After a brief altercation with the Indian army, some of whose vehicles were coming in the opposite direction – assuming for some reason that they were in possession of an inalienable right of way – we surmounted a final hummock and came out onto a level patch of ground. On it had been built, a hundred or so years before, a colonial bungalow of unusual size, its broad verandah overlooking the hazy splendour of the Kangra Valley, whose smoky corrugations rolled in a rhythmic sea-swell to the distant plains of the Punjab.

I was on the point of confiding to Tenzin that I had discovered my dream home at last, when a small Tibetan boy came hurtling round a corner in pursuit of a large Alsatian guard dog. To discourage him from sinking his teeth into the tyres of the jeep, the young rinpoche – who was chewing pink bubblegum – picked up a small rock and threw it at the dog's head. Being a tolerant and well-intentioned animal, the Alsatian declined to take exception to this peremptory treatment and merely shuffled off, looking aggrieved.

Just then, an elderly monk and a middle-aged woman (who subsequently turned out to be French), emerged briskly from the house to investigate the causes of such an unseemly uproar. The monk, who had been expecting our arrival, but who still looked less than overjoyed that it had actually occurred, led us onto the verandah where he slumped into the kind of rattan-backed easy chair once favoured by pukka sahibs for the consumption of their evening chota peg. A playpen had been constructed nearby, which now contained, among other things, a plastic motorbike and sidecar, a large red fire engine, and a striped inflatable dolphin which, owing to a lack of air pressure, seemed to be extremely poorly. This the young rinpoche handed to Tenzin.

'He wants you to blow it up,' the French woman explained superfluously.

I asked the monk, whose name was Lobsang Lungrig, how he had been chosen to occupy such an important and unusual position.

'I was the personal attendant of the former Ling Rinpoche for nearly half a century. Originally I had been sent by my family to the Medical College in Lhasa, but after four years there, my grandmother decided I should enter Ling Rinpoche's service. I was nineteen years old. In 1959 we left Tibet in the company of His Holiness the Dalai Lama. Since then I have lived chiefly here in Dharamsala and also in Bodh Gaya. For eight years Rinpoche was the abbot of the monastery there. Now I am seventy-four.'

'How old was the Rinpoche when he died?'

'Eighty-one.'

'And what did he die of?'

'Blocked arteries, so the doctors said.'

'By all accounts Ling Rinpoche was a very learned and saintly man.' Lobsang Lungrig nodded. 'And as you had been with him for so many years you must have felt great sorrow when he died.'

'Yes.'

'But was the pain of bereavement in any way moderated by the certainty of his being reborn?'

'No, it makes no difference. The grief is just the same. After all, one may not live to see the new reincarnation. When Ling Rinpoche died I was already quite an old man. Fortunately for me, in this case the search began almost immediately.'

'How was this conducted? One of the problems of exile must be that the Tibetans are nowadays scattered all over the subcontinent. The procedure for finding and identifying reincarnate lamas must be very different from the old days in Tibet.'

'Not really. A reincarnation like Ling Rinpoche has control over the process of his own death: both when it occurs and where he will subsequently be reborn. Anyway, not long after he had passed away, astrologers were called and they said that the reincarnation would be discovered after an interval of so many months. Furthermore, they said, the child had recently been born and his mother was at that moment extremely sick. The Dalai Lama was asked to throw dice to see if he could suggest a likely place, but no clear answer was forthcoming, so eventually people were sent off all over India to search for suitable children.'

'There was no possibility of his being reborn in Tibet?'

Lobsang Lungrig looked at me with unexpected severity. 'Certainly not. Why on earth would Ling Rinpoche want to do that? Anyway, a list of six hundred names was drawn up and these were arranged in alphabetical order. The Dalai Lama was consulted once more and he said that the fifth letter of the Tibetan alphabet would in this case prove significant. With this advice in mind, lamas were sent out to look at the short-listed candidates. Mostly they were in Delhi, or around the Kangra Valley. Of course they didn't know at this point, that Rinpoche had actually been born in Bir, not all that far from Dharamsala. His mother having died in childbirth, he had been taken to the Tibetan Children's Village and placed in the orphanage.'

'Where was his father?'

'His father was a poor man and already had seven other children to provide for.'

'So how was a positive identification eventually made?'

'The lamas who had gone off to search for the reincarnation came back to the Dalai Lama and told him that so far they had not had any luck. The children they had talked to, they said, seemed shy of strangers and showed no obvious wish to communicate anything to them. Although they had interviewed dozens, if not hundreds, of young boys, none had seemed in any way unusual and none had been able to answer any of the questions they had asked about Ling Rinpoche's previous lives. His Holiness then said that they must persevere, that sooner or later they would be successful. Someone had been telling him, he said, about a remarkable child at the TCV. The boy was apparently still very young, but maybe they should go to see him just in case. So the lamas went along to the Children's Village and asked to speak to Thupten Thinlay. For some reason the boy seemed very friendly, very pleased to see them. They asked him if he knew who they were and why they had come and without the slightest hesitation he said that yes he did. So the lamas then gave him a selection of objects, some of which had belonged to Ling Rinpoche, and asked him to choose one or two. The first thing he picked out was Ling Rinpoche's old rosary: even though there were a number of others, all of which were newer and more likely to catch the attention of a small boy. The lamas then asked him why he had made this choice and Thupten Thinlay replied that it had once belonged to him, that it had been lost, and that he had since been looking for it everywhere. He then proceeded to play with it using his left hand, even though he himself is right-handed. I was later able to confirm to the lamas that the previous incarnation of Ling Rinpoche had indeed been left-handed. This unusual behaviour did not of course provide conclusive proof, but the lamas were sufficiently impressed to return to the Dalai Lama and to explain to him precisely what had happened. His Holiness then sent for the child and conducted many further tests. . . .'

'What precisely?'

'I don't know; I wasn't there. But further tests were carried out, the results of which were positive as before. After having consulted with his advisers, the Dalai Lama said that they were in no doubt whatever, that the correct reincarnation had been identified, and that Ling Rinpoche should be brought to live in his *labrang*.'

'You say that you were in Ling Rinpoche's service for nearly half a century. . . .'

'Forty-eight years.'

'Have you ever had any doubts about the correctness of the decision? Do you recognise in this child the man that you knew for all those years?'

'I am quite certain. There is no doubt in my mind whatever.'

On the lawn below the verandah the subject of our conversation was playing football with the French woman and another, older boy, aged about eight or nine. Tenzin, who had by now recovered his breath, having dutifully reinflated the dolphin (he had been translating my conversation with Lobsang Lungrig in between giant gulps of air), looked approvingly at the game and remarked:

'Westerners often claim that reincarnations do not have enough contact with other children; that they are not brought up properly. For example, they say that from a very early age they are treated with an incredible amount of respect and that this must be very bad for them. They think they should be brought up like ordinary boys and allowed to choose their own lives when they are old enough to make an independent decision.'

Lobsang Lungrig's expression darkened. 'But reincarnations are *not* ordinary children . . .', he replied testily, '. . . so it would be quite inappropriate for them to be brought up as if they were.'

'So when will he go to school?' I asked in what I hoped might sound a conciliatory voice.

'He will go to Drepung monastery in South India when he is seven or eight. Later he will receive instruction from the Dalai Lama. Ling Rinpoche became tutor to His Holiness when he was thirty-seven and the Dalai Lama was only four years old. Now His Holiness will be able to return the teachings that he himself received.'

'I've heard . . . ,' I said, '. . . that there is a statue of the former Ling Rinpoche in a small chapel here. Would it be possible for us to see it?'

Without replying, Lobsang Lungrig stood up and led the way round to the back of the house. There he unlocked an ordinary-looking door and, reaching inside, flicked on the light. Ling Rinpoche, or rather the former earthly manifestation of that revered spiritual lineage, was sitting inside a glass case staring out at the world with an expression of the greatest serenity and benevolence. He appeared to be thinking, perhaps resting, before strolling down to the *gompa* in McCleod Ganj, to supervise the evening prayers.

The Tibetan method of preserving such remains is a sophisticated form of taxidermy – the statues both are and are not the physical remains of the deceased – but the person responsible for plastering and then painting the face had undoubtedly been an extremely accomplished artist. Even from a distance of three or four feet, Ling Rinpoche's complexion and expression remained astonishingly lifelike. Indeed, the longer I looked, and the more scope my imagination was given to make mischief, the more lifelike they appeared to become. I felt the hairs on the back of my neck beginning to rise.

'Incredible,' said Tenzin, standing next to me, a tremor in his voice betraying the advent of deep religious emotion. 'Incredible.'

And indeed it was. Despite the fact that Ling Rinpoche had – according to Tibetan tradition – undergone a kind of subtle metempsychosis into the the body of a four-year-old child (currently playing at football no more than fifty yards away), some residue of a powerful personality, of great holiness, or of prolonged spiritual endeavour seemed to have remained in an atmosphere so potent as to be inescapable.

I was, however, released from this temporary state of duress by the sound of Lobsang Lungrig shuffling in the doorway and jangling the keys in his pocket. On the way out I noticed that next to the white *khatas*, laid on the ground by pilgrims, was a selection of soft toys – several teddy bears of varying sizes and an extremely plausible badger – evidently brought for the amusement of the young Rinpoche and now perhaps discarded in favour of more grown-up entertainment.

In our absence, Ling Rinpoche had in fact abandoned football in favour of gardening and was carefully watering the flower pots arranged along the verandah. Having a strong distrust of small boys with hosepipes, particularly in the vicinity of expensive camera equipment, I maintained a safe distance, but Lobsang Lungrig insistently waved me forward.

'Now we get Rinpoche's blessing,' said Tenzin.

This came as a surprise. 'We do? You go first then, just to show me the protocol.'

Detaching Ling Rinpoche from the hosepipe, Lobsang Lungrig led him firmly by the hand to an armchair on the verandah, over which had been thrown a sheet of crumpled yellow linen. Clearly he had done this many times before, as he scrambled up onto his makeshift throne without protest or the need for inducement of any kind. Tenzin stepped forward with a *khata*, knelt down, and offered it to him ceremoniously. It was received with practised nonchalance. Tenzin then bowed his head and, reaching forward, the Rinpoche patted it firmly.

Feeling extremely awkward, I did my best to copy the procedure. While kneeling down, it occurred to me that I had done nothing like it in my life before. I had knelt in church on a fair number of occasions, but never, so far as I could recall, to a fellow human being. Still, I had no wish to offend anyone. As I handed him the *khata*, I glanced up briefly into Ling Rinpoche's face. He looked bored, or at least absent-minded, but there was no denying he was a very striking child. His features were regular, his skin had a mother-of-pearl sheen, and there was an aristocracy of manner – whether inherited or acquired – which was unavoidably impressive.

I got up to find Lobsang Lungrig beaming at me with immense and quite unexpected friendliness. Apparently this simple act of self-abasement had been sufficient to propel me skywards in his good opinion. I was now regarded, it seemed, as an honest pilgrim rather than as an impertinent sceptic. I had performed the simple ritual as required, and could now be regarded as a sympathetic foreigner and valuable friend of Tibet.

We sat on the verandah drinking tea while Rinpoche played with his dolphin. When finally the time came to leave, Lobsang Lungrig shook me warmly by the hand and personally escorted us to the jeep.

It was only on the way down to McCleod Ganj that I began to appreciate fully just how different the experience had been for Tenzin and myself. I had enjoyed the encounter, but had left no more convinced than before by Tibetan arguments in favour of identifiable reincarnation. On the other hand, for my travelled, affluent, worldly-wise companion, meeting the four-year-old Ling Rinpoche had been a great and memorable event. There were rinpoches aplenty in Kathmandu: some venerable; some by all accounts fairly unscrupulous. But this was different. Ling Rinpoche came from a long lineage – this was the twenty-second incarnation – and was an acknowledged spiritual master. Furthermore, he had occupied, and for that matter still did occupy, a prominent place in the affections of the Dalai Lama himself. I found myself impressed, almost envious, that merely meeting a great Lama, the experience of *darshan*, could produce such self-evident exhilaration.

*

Throughout its history, Buddhism has been afflicted by a central, chronic problem. How does a creed of mystics and contemplatives which requires the constant, arduous search for mental refinement, weld itself onto wider society? make itself useful and interesting to the great unlettered mass of the people? One expedient has been to leave in place popular animism, folk religion, and superstitious magic, and to attempt to build on these ramshackle and precarious foundations a superstructure of noble and classsical proportions. Another remedy has been to expand a pantheon of minor deities and bodhisattvas – all of which might be viewed symbolically by the learned, as a colourful mythology of the mind – and to stimulate religious feeling through popular devotion. Unfortunately, in the case of Indian Buddhism, this merely led to it being absorbed into devotional Hinduism, a religion of legendary hospitality, whose rules of admission have come to be drawn so wide as to be almost indefinable.

In Tibet, Buddhism became established over a prolonged period of time: among the nobility, a steadily expanding clergy, and eventually, in a somewhat attenuated form, among the people. They, however, insisted on remaining stubbornly loyal to the pre-existent spiritual hierarchy, and the occult world it had inhabited since time immemorial. The new Buddhist pantheon vied for popular affection with the demons and deities long in residence and, generally speaking, found the going fairly rough.

It was towards the end of the twelfth century, that a system of succession by reincarnation was adopted by prominent abbots within the Kargyupa Buddhist order. No one is entirely sure where the idea originated, but it too probably came from India. Nowhere else in Buddhist Asia has ever entertained the idea that reincarnation might be a process susceptible to comprehension and control. From now on, young children increasingly came to be identified as successors to prominent religious leaders. This innovation might be described, without too much risk of hyperbole, as the most significant development in the whole cultural history of Tibet.

The slight problem with his notion of reincarnation from an orthodox point of view is that the third of Buddhism's three irreducible articles of faith insists that there is no such thing as a soul, or enduring spiritual entity with some self-containing principle of coherence. The self in Buddhism is considered to be a collection of psycho-physical elements which are borne along the stream of karma, disperse at the point of death, and reform in another, subsequent existence. These elements do not, however, in any sense constitute an individual personality proceeding from life to life, unimpeded by the habitual recurrence of death.

This orthodoxy, it must be said, has not been entirely unchallenged. As early as the third century BC a sect known as the Personalists (Pudgalavadins), caused a minor schism by claiming that the impersonal psycho-physical elements did indeed have an inherent structural unity, a transcendent self, or soul by any other name. The Personalists, however, have generally been regarded more as heretics than schismatics.

Just how the Tibetans fit into this ancient debate, and precisely what they consider to be reborn, would of course provide the substance for at least one, and quite possibly a whole series of books. However, as far as most ordinary Tibetans are concerned, the situation is a good deal simpler. In their eyes, the great religious leaders – reincarnate lamas, otherwise known as rinpoches or tulkus – have triumphed over the powers of death, and in migrating from life to life are clearly endowed with a very superior kind of occult power. They have inherited the mantle of the shamans and magicians of Tibetan prehistory, and are seen as beings partly of this world and partly of the world beyond.

Of course, such oversimplification is not the special prerogative of Tibetan Buddhists. Most Christian lay believers would be less than entirely reassured by the suggestion that the word 'God' merely refers to something which, by definition infinite, is otherwise inexpressible. The bearded patriarch of the Sistine ceiling, or Blake's cosmic geometrician, are bound to have more popular appeal than the more nebulous propositions of theology.

It was from the fifteenth century onward, with the reforms of Tsongkhapa and the rise of the Gelugpa sect, that the idea of the reincarnate lama began to be adapted in Tibet to the needs of social organisation. The rinpoche of the local monastery gradually became the primary structural component in a steadily evolving theocracy. Buddhism and society were now welded together so as to be almost indistinguishable, and before long the practitioners of an ascetic and contemplative religion found themselves in exclusive possession of the reins of worldly power. An ostensibly feudal system of great monastic estates worked by a landless peasantry was bound together by the religious faith of the laity, so that paradoxically the old Tibet – regarded as pernicious exploitation by the Chinese communists – was actually an idiosyncratic form of government by consent. At the epicentre of this system, the nexus of both worldly power and religious devotion, was the most important reincarnate lama of all: the Dalai Lama himself.

We had been waiting in the small, austere antechamber for only a few minutes, when Tenzin Tethong, the Dalai Lama's Private Secretary, appeared in the doorway and beckoned. A solitary Khampa bodyguard, looking rather uncomfortable in a tweed jacket and tie, gave us a cursory glance, before nodding respectfully to a scholarly-looking man, who passed us on his way out.

'That's the brother who's the academic in America,' Tenzin whispered.

The familiar figure of the Dalai Lama, bespectacled, burly in his red and yellow robes, was standing in the doorway of his Audience Chamber, looking out thoughtfully over a well-tended, well-watered garden. He turned to greet us. Tenzin, who was wearing a formal Tibetan *chuba* for the occasion, presented him with a white *khata* and bowed.

Beaming as though he'd never seen one before and couldn't imagine a nicer present, the Dalai Lama accepted the gift, reached out for my hand, shook it vigorously, and invited us to follow him inside. It was a comfortably furnished room, not at all grand, in which the only two noteworthy features were a fairly sizeable throne and a large relief map of Tibet attached to the right-hand wall. The boundaries marked there, I noticed, bore little resemblance to those in a modern atlas. Settling himself in an easy chair, the Dalai Lama slapped the arm of the sofa next to it. I sat down.

Although I had met him on two previous (and unrelated) occasions and was therefore prepared for this informality, I still found his evident wish to communicate with his visitors – rather than to stand on sterile ceremony – extremely touching and impressive. His whole manner spoke of a complete absence of worldly pride. Here was a man, idolised by 6,000,000 Tibetans, who patently had no wish to play the Great Leader, or the Oriental Sage.

Tenzin, his voice a decibel or two lower than usual, began to explain what we had been doing and why we had come. The Dalai Lama gruffly cut him short. He had heard about our travels, he said. He hoped that all the

Tibetan officials had been helpful. I replied that I had been extremely impressed by the selflessness and sense of public duty we had everywhere encountered. The Dalai Lama looked slightly doubtful, but said that he was pleased to hear it.

'Yesterday afternoon we went to see the reincarnation of Ling Rinpoche.' The Dalai Lama's face lit up. Here clearly was a subject after his own heart. How, I asked, had he become convinced of the correctness of the identification?

'Oh, as a result of different procedures; some quite mysterious experiments,' he replied, showing little inclination to be more specific. 'But for me the most important thing is the way, without being introduced, he clearly recognises people who were closely acquainted with the previous Ling Rinpoche. Even Westerners. He seems able to make a clear distinction between those he has met before and those he has not. You see, the younger the children – particularly before they learn to talk properly – the stronger the memories of their previous life.'

'Did you experience this yourself?'

'Yes. Once upon a time, I think. . . . Oh I don't know really. I can't remember.' He laughed and shook his head. 'It's a long time ago now.' This apparent lapse of memory seemed to cause him remarkably little anxiety. Might this ability have been sustained, perhaps further developed, had he not been obliged to live the demanding life of a politician?

'Definitely. Some kinds of religious practice need long periods of complete isolation. For me this is not possible. But involvement in politics – having to argue and to fight for Tibetan freedom – these are opportunities to test the validity of spiritual experience. Anyway . . .', he continued, having briefly looked rather glum, '. . . good or bad, that's the way it is.'

'Is it possible . . .', I enquired tentatively, not at all sure what reaction to expect, '. . . that reincarnate lamas are ever wrongly identified? When I spoke to Samdong Rinpoche in Banaras, he didn't seem entirely convinced about his own spiritual lineage. Perhaps this was just modesty.'

'I think there have been such mistakes. In Tibet I am sure there were. But as far as Ling Rinpoche is concerned, this is a very clear case.' He smiled, as if fondly remembering the child. There was a pause while I hesitated to change the subject.

'Have you ever decided whether the slaughter of the Tibetans, and the subsequent material destruction, was directly ordered by the Chinese leadership? You met Mao many times: would he have ordered such a massacre? Or was it a case of local army commanders getting out of political control? We are often told nowadays that the people in Peking have no idea what is being perpetrated in their name fifteen hundred miles away in Lhasa.'

The Dalai Lama sighed and stared out of the window. A heavy silence descended on the room, relieved only by the sound of a clock ticking. 'I'm convinced . . .', he said at last, heavily, almost regretfully, '. . . that the order for the suppression came from the highest level. But the question is "Did the Chinese commanders in Tibet report the real situation?" I think in communist countries people become quite expert at cheating their own leaders in order to be patted on the back. On the other hand, there is a story about a Chinese general. He is supposed to have told Chairman Mao that the Tibetans disliked the Chinese so much that if he had to arrest all the troublemakers there would not be enough space in the gaols. Mao is said to have replied: "Don't worry. If we have to imprison the entire Tibetan population, we'll still manage somehow.'

'A true story?'

'I don't know. Perhaps. Between 1954 and 1955, I spent ten months in China, of which four months were in Peking. I met Mao many times. On one occasion we both attended a meeting with the two Chinese generals who had been posted to Tibet. Mao said to me: "We are sending these two generals to help you; to serve you. If they create problems, or do not carry out your wishes, then let me know and I will recall them." On another occasion, he said to me: "At present, Tibet is a very backward country, so we are sending Han Chinese to help you develop it. After twenty years you will have reached a certain stage. Then we will withdraw the Han Chinese and it will be your turn to help us." So I returned to Lhasa in 1955 with a positive enthusiasm for working with the Chinese. At that time I even wanted to join the Chinese Communist Party. But then in 1956 the first news reached Lhasa of the uprising in Kham: of beating and killing and really merciless repression. So I started to write to Chairman Mao in my own handwriting. Some letters I sent through official channels; some I arranged to be delivered by individuals. Either way there was no reply. I began to realise that although when we had met the atmosphere had seemed very friendly, very genuine, there had actually been a big difference between the appearance of things and his real intention. Mao's attitude to religion was the same. When we first met and he did not know me, he praised Buddhism. Then at our last meeting, when I was about to leave Peking, he remarked to me at one point: "Religion is poison." I did not understand why he had said this, so I asked my Chinese friends and they explained that Mao had gained the impression that I was scientifically-minded, open to new ideas, and that therefore I might be receptive to his true opinion. You see again there was a difference between the official statement and the real feeling or intention. Chairman Mao's manner seemed very gentle, very honest, very straightforward. Nonetheless I have been forced to conclude that in reality he was not that kind of man at all. So, to answer your question, yes, I believe that the cruel and ruthless policy in Tibet came directly from Chairman Mao.'

'So what, finally, is the dominant impression of Mao that remains with you?'

'He had a kind of inborn presence. I was afraid of him. He looked like an old Chinese peasant, but at the same time he seemed very powerful. If you compare Mao to Pandit Nehru, then Nehru seemed more clever, more sophisticated. But Mao had much more natural dignity.'

Despite the catastrophic effects of Chinese rule in Tibet, I wondered whether it was still possible for him to feel residual respect for the founders of the Chinese revolution.

'Do you think that they had the right intentions, but employed the wrong methods? Were they evil men, or merely misguided?'

'Misguided I think. In the initial stage – up to '56, maybe even '57, '58 – you could have meaningful discussions with the Chinese: not just the senior leaders in Peking, but with ordinary party members. If you started a conversation, they were very straightforward, and expressed great enthusiasm for developing their country. You see at that time, one of my favourite subjects was internationalism. I was convinced there should be no national boundaries; that all working-class people on the planet were the same. This made me sympathetic to certain Chinese ideas. Even in '56 when the fighting broke out in the Chamdo area, I heard stories of ordinary Chinese soldiers being moved to tears. They said to the Tibetan people there: "We came to help, not to cause you all this suffering." At the beginning their motivation was genuine. But then came a lack of self-discipline and self-awareness. You can't blame them: they had no faith. If you have a faith, then things are different. For example,

Buddhists believe in karma. It doesn't matter if you are very powerful and nobody dares to criticise you, because if you are doing wrong you will still have to face the consequences. This life is very short, but the effects of our behaviour can continue for an infinite number of lives, Similarly, if you believe in God, then there is some check on your actions. The Chinese were under no such restraint.'

'In March '59, do you suppose that if you *had* attended the theatrical performance to which you had been invited, you should indeed have been kidnapped and taken to Peking, just as the people of Lhasa feared?'

The Dalai Lama looked thoughtful, as though this were the first time he had been invited to speculate about the incident which had led directly to the Lhasa Uprising and to his own abrupt flight into exile.

'I don't think I've been asked that question before.' He looked across to Tenzin Tethong as if for confirmation. 'Actually, you know, I myself had no particular suspicion. But as soon as the news reached the masses. . . . But then at that time, the Chinese authorities *were* starting to impose unusual restrictions on me. Before I used to go to see the Chinese accompanied by my bodyguards. Suddenly they would not allow it. This was strange. And of course in Kham and Amdo there had been many occasions on which high Lamas and local officials had been invited to banquets and never came back. This had happened on numerous occasions, so I suppose it could have happened to me.'

'When you made this decision to flee to India did you expect so many Tibetans to follow you?'

'No,' the Dalai Lama said shortly.

'Was it an unpleasant shock?'

'Yes. Very. At that time there was not even a word in the Tibetan vocabulary for "refugee". I first become aware of the problem in Bomdila, after I'd been in India for two or three weeks. I was told that some soldiers, and also some monks, had decided to follow me. The situation didn't sound too complicated. It was not until I reached Mussoorie that I received clear information that seven thousand people had already crossed the border and many were on their way. It was April. The summer heat was coming up. It was the very worst time of year. And the initial transit camp at Misamari was especially hot. It was a most unsuitable place. The next two or three years were a *very* difficult period. The only thing we could do was to save as many lives as possible. There was no alternative to sending them up high to work on the roads . . .' He stopped as if he wanted me to be aware that this decision still caused him considerable anguish. 'No alternative, but of course it was also very dangerous and many, many Tibetans lost their lives. It was a terrible period.'

'Did you ever feel during those first three years that you simply couldn't cope?'

'Well, we were very fortunate at that time. There were many international organisations, as well as the Government of India, which helped a great deal. Because of their tremendous support, all we had to do at first was to show them precisely what needed to be done. So this lessened our anxiety and we were able to begin thinking about a long-term plan. The priorities, we decided, were as far as possible to keep the Tibetans separate from the Indians, and to provide a good standard of education for our children. It was in '61, I think, when we first approached the Indian government and asked them to help us start Tibetan settlements and Tibetan schools. Of course, all the money had to come from Delhi. We had just a little gold and silver and because of some mistakes a large portion of that had been lost.'

'Was your own relationship with Nehru very important in gaining this support?'

'Well, my friendship with Nehru was, I think, really genuine. I had first met him in 1956 at the time of the Buddha Jayanti celebrations in Bodh Gaya. We had talked for about ten hours. Finally I asked him whether or not I should return to Tibet. I thought perhaps I should stay in India and try to win international support. Nehru strongly advised me to return. So after the unfortunate events of 1959, I think he felt a kind of special moral responsibility. Later he used to tell me that the best way of keeping the Tibetan question alive was to give a good education to the young Tibetans in India. He advised me that the primary medium of instruction should be English, despite the opinion of his own Minister for Education, who wanted the Tibetans to be taught in Hindi. I think Nehru was fond of me . . .'

'Like a father?' I suggested.

'Perhaps. I was the right age to be treated as a son. And then I think, leaving aside political complications, among Indians there is a natural affection for Tibet. For Indians, Tibet is the land of God and Mount Kailas is the palace of Shiva. Whether they are Westernised like Nehru, or more orthodox, there is instinctive feeling for Tibetans.'

'On our travels around India, we've spoken to many people who are uncertain and concerned for the future. Do you think that over the past thirty years you have been successful in educating young Tibetans in exile?'

The Dalai Lama sat forward in his chair abruptly. 'This is perhaps the most important single issue. There is no doubt that standards nowadays are declining. We are extremely anxious about this and we are doing everything we can to tackle the problem. Basically it boils down to the people involved. We must have young teachers who have both a modern outlook and a thorough knowledge of our own cultural background. It's the *people* who matter. Take the school here in Dharamsala: the TCV. It has the same curriculum as elsewhere, but the teaching staff are better, so the quality of results is much higher.'

'Some people say the longer they stay in exile, the more Indianised the Tibetans will become. They think the process of assimilation is inevitable and that it is an extremely bad thing.'

'We can't blame the Indians for our problems. The standard of our own teachers is not so high. Besides there are many good Indian traditions. It is true, however, that there are also bad Indian habits: carelessness about work and a lack of ambition to excel.'

I mentioned that the rector of Mussoorie Central School thought that the Indian film industry had a lot to answer for.

'He is right. It is a bad influence.'

'Whereas the headmaster at Choglamsar in Ladakh went so far as to advocate a completely separate education system, in which Tibetan would be the main language of instruction.'

'That would create other problems. If the Tibetans are to live in this country, then they must speak a foreign language. Otherwise day-to-day life would be impossible. Also, in ten or fifteen years, if they are able to return to Tibet, being able to speak English will be a great advantage.'

'Despite such problems with secular education, are you reasonably happy with the standard of learning in the monasteries? Is it as high as it was in Tibet?'

'No. As far as Buddhist philosophy is concerned, the general standard cannot be compared with that which existed in Tibet. On the other hand, there are some positive factors. Today the monks have access to a wider variety of knowledge. They have contact both with other religions, and also with modern scientific explanations of reality. I feel very strongly we must make every effort to promote dialogue between all the major religions, as well as with other disciplines and forms of knowledge. I would like to see close communication between the monasteries in South India and other academic institutions throughout the world. I want these monasteries to become centres of education; centres of higher learning. Therefore we will have to put additional subjects on the monastic curriculum.'

'Samdong Rinpoche in Banaras doubted the viability of traditional Tibetan learning within the context of a modern university syllabus. He felt that traditional Buddhist studies took too long to be confined within the limits of a degree course.'

'Of course in one sense he is right, but my idea is that within areas – Sera monastery, say – there should be the facilities available for many different kinds of subject. Students studying Buddhist philosophy may well take much longer than the normal four or five years, but still the institution itself would be more complete. It would be more like a university, in contact with many different kinds of people, not just a religious centre with a few hundred monks. Still, under the present unfortunate circumstances, I suppose the level of study and of organisation in the major monasteries is really quite commendable.'

'One of the most difficult decisions of these past years must have been ordering the Tibetan guerrillas in Mustang to lay down their arms and to surrender to the Nepalese. Was there no alternative? After all, it led to the death of a great Tibetan patriot, General Wangdu.'

'There was no alternative. Of course the Khampas wanted to carry on fighting. They could have stopped the Nepalese for a few months, perhaps even a year, but eventually they would have been defeated. So what was the point? They were there to fight the Chinese not the Nepalese. And then there were the other settlers in Nepal to consider. If some Tibetans are openly at war with the

Nepalese government, then what would have been the position of the rest?'

'So were you quite relieved when Mustang was over? After all, it severely compromised your commitment to non-violence.'

'Yes, definitely. I was very relieved. But I was also very sad because one man took his own life, and because later the Nepalese put so many Tibetans in prison.'

'I suppose Mustang is a good illustration of the difficulty of combining the tasks of religious and secular authority. Do you think that while you are alive, it will be possible for the Tibetans to find a purely political leader? to elect a Prime Minister?'

'I think they should do. It is what I am always telling them! There is really no other choice. Sooner or later there will come a time when they will have to manage without a Dalai Lama. That is for sure. I am already fifty-six. So I have left twenty, thirty, a maximum of forty years. No more. Despite the fact that I may be the reincarnation of Chenrezig, I have to die. I want to see created the habit of genuine democracy. If I am to remain as a leader, it must not be as an authoritarian one. I should hold my position only because of the people's respect. The trouble at the moment is that whatever I say, generally speaking, the Tibetans agree to. This is not good. This attitude is a hindrance to free expression. I have said on several occasions that if a kind father bears all the responsibility, then this provides no experience or training for his children. Also, in the case of the Tibetans, it is a dangerous attitude. Although 99 per cent of the time there is no danger, the 1 per cent remains. Some unfortunate event might occur.'

'You mean you could be assassinated?'

'It could happen. It is possible.'

'But in general do you feel that the political landscape is improving? Could recent events in China – the Tiananmen Square massacre – perversely have positive consequences for the Tibetan cause?'

'This is a very complicated matter. In the short term, such events undoubtedly make things worse. If the Chinese hardliners do not hesitate to kill their own people, they will certainly not hesitate to kill Tibetans. However, Westerners now have a far more realistic attitude about the Chinese. They are beginning to understand what kind of people we have been fighting all these years. I also think this recent repression will only increase the growth of liberal opinions among the younger Chinese. Not long ago I was in America where I met some Chinese students who had recently escaped from Peking. They openly said to me that before this tragedy happened they knew very little about Tibet and cared very little about what happened there. But now, they said, they had much greater sympathy and understanding. And it is not only the young. I believe that before Tiananmen Square, if you had taken one hundred ordinary Chinese people, out of that one hundred, fifty would have believed strongly in the advantages of the communist system. Nowadays, take the same one hundred people and the majority would be in favour of change. I believe that this repression has actually shortened the life of Chinese communism. Before I would have said that the lifespan of the Chinese Communist Party would be about another thirty years. Now I would say less than half that. Maybe the communist system has less than another fifteen years to live.'

'So perhaps you will see Tibet again.'

'Perhaps. Who knows?'

What, I wondered, did he miss most about Tibet? What made him feel his own exile most keenly?

'Right now I am perfectly comfortable, thank you. I don't miss anything.'

'But when you go up to Ladakh . . .', I insisted, '. . . and see the white *gompas* by the Indus and that brilliant blue sky, don't you feel nostalgic for the landscape and architecture of Tibet?'

'Not really, to be honest. Here in Dharamsala in the monsoon, when it's humid and raining, I sometimes remember the Lhasa climate: dry; not too hot; not too cold. And then sometimes I think of Tibetan food: good *tsampa*; good meat. These you cannot get in India. But as regards Tibetan architecture, it may look all right, but it's not very comfortable or convenient. Especially the Potala, which is dark, cold, and full of rats. I do recall my happy childhood days at the Norbulingka. But these things are gone. Of course, the older Tibetans living down in South India still find exile very painful to bear. For me, however, it's different. I'm a monk, and once you become a monk, you are always isolated from your family, from your native place. And then there is the Buddhist doctrine of non-attachment to worldly things. The nature of being a Buddhist monk makes exile easier to accept. It's more difficult for the ordinary Tibetan people.'

'So after thirty years, what achievements of the Tibetans in exile personally give you most satisfaction? What have been the positive aspects of this time of trial?'

'The preservation of Tibetan identity. The preservation of Tibetan culture. Politically, of course, our main strength comes from Tibet itself. In the last three or four years we have had much more international attention due to events in Lhasa and the great courage of the Tibetan people there. But the pure form of Tibetan culture is now found *outside*, not inside Tibet. Which is why many people still come to join us here. In exile we have both preserved our culture and introduced it to the world. I think these have been our main contributions to the Tibetan cause. These are certainly the ones in which we can take most pride.'